P9-DMM-016

stick your picture here and become one of my students

Other stuff written by me

The Naked Chef
The Naked Chef Takes Off
Happy Days with the Naked Chef
Jamie's Kitchen
Jamie's Dinners
Jamie's Italy

COOK
withJAMIE

MY GUIDE TO MAKING YOU A BETTER COOK

JAMIE OLIVER

Photography
David Loftus and Chris Terry

HYPERION
NEW YORK

Published by arrangement with Michael Joseph / The Penguin Group

Copyright © 2007 Jamie Trevor Oliver

Photographs copyright © David Loftus and Chris Terry, 2007
Illustrations copyright © Alice Tait, 2007
Color reproduction by Dot Gradations Ltd
Set in Helvetica
Printed in Italy

All rights reserved. No part of this book may be used or
reproduced in any manner whatsoever without the written
permission of the Publisher. For information address Hyperion,
77 West 66th Street, New York, New York 10023-6298.

ISBN-13: 978-1-4013-2233-5

Hyperion books are available for special promotions,
premiums, or corporate training. For details contact
Michael Rentas, Proprietary Markets, Hyperion,
77 West 66th Street, 12th floor, New York, New York 10023,
or call 212-456-0133.

FIRST U.S. EDITION

10 9 8 7 6 5 4 3 2 1

CONTENTS

introduction 6

salads 16

pasta, gnocchi and risotto 56

meat 138

fish 200

vegetables 292

desserts 370

some bits and bobs 424

thanks 436

index 438

Dear possibly great cook! Welcome to my seventh book, *Cook with Jamie*. In a funny sort of way I feel this should have been my first cookbook, where I take you on a journey through the basics of food, shopping and cooking with great ingredients, a bit like the Fifteen students when they start on day one of their course.

As I've been writing this book, we've taken on more students at our Fifteen restaurants in London and Amsterdam, opened a restaurant in Cornwall and are about to open another one in Melbourne. Over the last five years we've concentrated on breaking down cheffy procedures into something that the students – most of whom have never, ever cooked before they turn up on their first day – can get stuck into: butchery, fishmongery, making fresh pasta. Whether you've cooked before, or you're cooking for the first time, I wanted to give you a smidgeon of our Fifteen cookery course.

Over the years, I've been amazed to hear of all the different types of people who have started to cook for the first time – you'd think it would mostly be twenty-year-olds at university, but that's absolutely not the case. It's kids, teenagers, middle-aged people, men, women, singles, marrieds, working-class and posh people – all sorts, who come across cooking for whatever reason. And the one thing that I hear over and over again when it comes to those who've discovered cooking after, say, the age of thirty, is that they wish they'd started earlier. Well, here's your chance!

I N T R O D

In this book I'm going to be brutally frank at times and tell you how I think it is – and I do have some pretty strong opinions about how we should buy and cook food! I've included recipes that are going to be easy to buy ingredients for, and you'll notice that in every chapter I've given you some really nice and simple recipes to show you the importance of getting the basic cooking bit right and to show you how just one or two ingredients can make a dish work. For instance, if you take a beautiful brisket of beef and cook it slowly in a pot with a lid on for seven or eight hours, or overnight, in the morning the meat will be a little crisp on top and beautifully soft underneath, rich in intense flavor, really gorgeous. That's simply the quality of the meat speaking and the benefit of patient, slow cooking – and that's before you've even added any other ingredients.

Things were so different fifty-odd years ago, when the general public had a good knowledge of cooking. In actual fact, I wouldn't need to be writing this book if we were all as well informed as people were back then, but our priorities about food have changed. It always amazes me how these days people can be totally up-to-speed and knowledgeable about so many different things – computers, music, fashion – but they don't give a toss about what they put in their mouths every day. If it's meat, they don't care where the animal has come from, how it's been reared or what it's been fed on. If you walk round your average supermarket, even though big efforts have been made, there are still lots of products riddled with additives, hydrogenated fats and a whole catalogue of fillers – fake food. What I want to try and do in this book is make cooking and eating real food, natural food, healthy food, normal again. And as much as it sounds like I'm ranting, or putting too much importance on cooking, I do think we've reached a crucial point in history now – the way we produce and cook our food is going to radically affect what the next generation grows up on. Either we change back to the natural methods of food production or things will get ever more "sci-fi" and mass-produced. I often wonder what everything will be like in, say, three hundred years' time. Will things be better or worse? Will people look back at our generation and think that the things we do now are crazy? Will we drink our dinner through straws or eat little capsules? Will our meals simply be different-flavored jelly beans?

Now, you must think I've completely lost the plot! The thing is, the more I learn about the history of food, the more I realize that one thing we should agree on with our ancestors is that good food is important; that it has always been essential. Festivals are identified by it, families are pulled together by it, it represents good times or bad times. I suppose what I'm trying to say is that, historically, food has always had one of the most important places in the home, in the town, in our different cultures. For thousands of years we farmed reasonably respectfully and in harmony with nature, and this was followed up with cooking good stuff. But now, with our clever technology, computers and busier lives, we have moved further away from the importance of home-cooked food. Who would have thought, all those decades ago, that we would be able to buy pre-packed portions of dinner, complete with a steam valve and disposable packaging, that can be microwaved in a few minutes? Things like this would have been considered science fiction, an impossibility, yet now it's everyday life. Of course, this has all resulted from a demand from generations who haven't learned how to cook. Imagine our great-grandparents' amazement at the choice of ingredients we now have, from places like India, the Mediterranean, China even. Yet at the same time they would have wondered what the world had come to if they read the adverts in farming magazines explaining how to make animals gain more weight by making them retain more water . . . And imagine what farmers in the old days would have thought of today's battery farming practices. They'd have told you it wouldn't be allowed to happen, that it would never happen. Why would birds be housed all together with no room to move when the big man upstairs gave them legs to run around on?

Cooking should be as normal to you and me as it was to our moms and grandmas, and the only way this is going to happen is if it becomes compulsory to teach kids how to cook at school again. It's important to learn about the integrity of homemade food before this knowledge is lost for ever. In the future will there be more choice or less? Will it be healthier food? Somehow, I don't think so. And I also don't think we can possibly imagine what scientists and mass food manufacturers might come up with next.

I've written this book, then, to give you some of the basics of modern-day cooking. I want to encourage you to try something new, to come to grips with a handful of simple techniques, to make informed choices. I want you to shop well and recognize when you're being ripped off by a market seller or a supermarket, when you're being sold rubbish or average stuff. But more than that, I want you to have fun, not just from cooking and eating but also from sharing your food with others. I'm going to give you helpful hints and some brilliant recipe combinations, from basic salads to fantastic family meat dishes. I want to take the opportunity to show you, for instance, how a whole animal breaks down into the different cuts. And I want you to understand a bit more about cooking methods – slow, fast, how and why.

So in this book I'm going to treat you just as I would one of my students and give you some inspiration for good, rock-solid cooking. I hope this book will get you thinking about shopping and cooking in ways that you might not have considered before. Remember, cooking isn't hard or elitist. It's just about learning little bits of information and trying something different once in a while. Just think, if you're lucky you're going to live for about seventy-five years and you're going to be eating three times a day, every single day for the rest of your life – you might as well learn how to cook properly and enjoy it!

A little chat about Fifteen

Many people still talk about Fifteen as though it was just part of the *Jamie's Kitchen* television series from a few years ago. But Fifteen is going from strength to strength! So let me tell you what's been going on since the TV cameras left. We are on our fifth intake of students in London, our third intake of students in Amsterdam and, as I write this, we've just opened a restaurant in Cornwall and are about to open one in Melbourne. So pretty soon there will be four amazing restaurants offering thousands of customers a great experience and offering hundreds of young people the chance of a lifetime.

The idea behind Fifteen is pretty simple – every year we give a unique opportunity to a group of young people to become professional chefs. The kids we take on have had a bit of a hard time and could do with a break. Many of them are homeless, have been raised in difficult circumstances, have spent time in prison or gone off the rails and got into drink and drugs. But at Fifteen we believe that we can inspire them to break habits and believe in themselves to become incredibly passionate chefs.

All our students attend catering college before working in the restaurant kitchen, where they learn what it takes to cook in a high-pressure environment. They're taken on regular sourcing trips to see some of the amazing things that our suppliers are up to, and to give them first-hand experience of where the incredible fresh ingredients used in the Fifteen kitchens come from. To me, making that connection between the food they cook and the inspirational people that produce it is a real part of the magic of Fifteen.

But that's not all. It may sound a bit corny but I see Fifteen as a family – a place for students to feel safe and appreciated. Students get all the support they need when it comes to their housing issues, debt and other personal problems. So when they're in the kitchen, cooking for the guests or learning from the professionals, they can focus on that 100 percent.

The students do work experience at some of the best restaurants in the world alongside exceptional chefs. When they graduate and go on to work in the industry, we are always there to offer them help when they need it. This is why we have recently set up Fifteen Ventures, to provide help with the financial and business side of things for graduates who want to run their own restaurants. I believe that pretty soon our students' presence in the restaurant industry will make a real difference and there will be more professional kitchens that are run like a family, not a military boot camp.

I want to finish by thanking you for buying this book. Every penny of my profit from it is going back to Fifteen and will without a doubt benefit the students for years and years to come. The proceeds will get more disadvantaged young people, in more cities all over the world, out of their rut and into cooking. So thanks, guys, for buying this book and making that happen. If you want to find out more about what we do, are interested in being a student, would like to come to any of our restaurants or even feel inspired to trust us with a donation, go to www.fifteenrestaurant.com.

Love – Jamie O xxx

A few words about food and wine

Matt Skinner is our sommelier at Fifteen and a great mate of mine. I've learned more about wine from him than from anyone else because he makes the whole subject so accessible. That's why I asked him to make wine recommendations for some of the recipes in this book. Now, don't worry, he hasn't listed a lot of fancy expensive wines you'll never find, he's kept it simple and listed countries and grape varieties, so no matter where you shop for wine, you should be able to find something along the right lines.

One or two of the recipes actually go best with beer ... and we all like a beer now and again, don't we? So anyway, over to Matt:

- Matching food and wine is not supposed to be tricky or expensive. Some of the best matches are the simplest, and often bring together affordable wine and ingredients.

- For food and wine pairings to work you'll need to know a bit about what you're eating, how it feels in your mouth once it's cooked or prepared and what the key flavors are. Remember, you're not only matching flavors, but textures too.

- A good retailer should be your first stop – this is your link to drinking better. Get to know the people that work there, describe what you like drinking, give them a budget and let them pick something new for you.

- Don't be afraid to experiment with different wines. The best way to learn about wine is to step outside your comfort zone and try new things.

- Keep an open mind. Try to leave behind any preconceived ideas you might have about particular grape varieties, styles or regions. Try them all!

- Love them or hate them, screw caps ensure that your wine will reach you in perfect condition – just as the winemaker intended. They're definitely not an indication of cheap wine.

- Don't fall for the packaging – it's never going to tell you how good or bad a wine is.

- Organic wine might be fashionable but it won't save you from a hangover!

If you're interested in learning a bit more about wine, check out Matt's books, *Thirsty Work* and *The Juice.*

Top gear that makes a difference in the kitchen

Here's a list of some of the things that, for me, make a real difference in the kitchen. They're bits of equipment that I use every day and help me make better, tastier food. I promise they won't end up gathering dust in the back of the cupboard!

Before everything else, I want to talk to you about your stove. Most people forget that it's one of the most essential things in a kitchen! Great cooking starts with the best heat source – and gas is where it's at. It gives off a more predictable heat than ceramic or electric stoves, it's easier to control and you can see exactly what's going on. So if you're a proper cook, get yourself a gas stove.

Speed peeler A good-quality U-shaped speed peeler is a godsend in the kitchen, whether you're peeling veg, shaving Parmesan or finely slicing fennel or asparagus. Quick and precise, it's a genius piece of kit.

Tongs Tongs give better control when grilling or turning meat on the barbecue and are great for picking up hot things and for serving food.

Flavor Shaker and pestle and mortar A pestle and mortar is my ultimate kitchen gadget, but sometimes its size and weight can be off-putting. A Flavor Shaker is a modern, downsized version of a pestle and mortar and is really user-friendly. Both will help you bash and bruise and get the flavor out of loads of ingredients.

Knives At home I have three knives that I use all the time when cooking: an 8-inch chef's knife, a small vegetable paring knife and a serrated carving knife. You should also invest in a trusty steel to keep them sharp. Don't use a steel on serrated knives though, it'll ruin the blade.

Food processor I love mine! Food processors help you chop, mix and purée ingredients, saving you loads of time – cooking becomes a doddle.

A big pot A very large, thick-bottomed cooking pot is really useful for dinner parties, curries, stews and cooking big batches. Every house should have one. And I'm not talking about big, but double big.

Non-stick frying pans Great ones have a good non-stick coating, a nice thick bottom and an ovenproof handle. I think it's worth investing in a few different sizes as they can be used for so many things. Remember to use wooden spoons – they're much kinder on the non-stick surface. Hang them, don't stack them, and they'll stay in great shape.

Good-quality grater There are some fantastic high-tech graters out there these days. They're perfect for zesting fruit and grating all sorts of things from chocolate to cheese to nutmeg. Be careful with your fingers though, they can be extremely sharp.

Salad spinner Many people don't quite get it, but salad spinners are incredibly important for making wicked salads. After washing your salad leaves, you don't want any water clinging to the leaves, otherwise they'll be tasteless and the dressing won't stick. So get spinning!

Nest of mixing bowls I want you to really go for it with these and get a whole selection – either cheap metal ones or porcelain ones. You'll use them all the time for mixing, marinating and storing stuff in the fridge. Look out for ones with handy measurements on the inside surface.

Chopping board Try and get your hands on a thick wooden chopping board. They're quite expensive (maybe you can ask for one for your birthday!), but you'll be using it for the rest of your life and it will age beautifully along with you. Slightly less glamorous but still essential is a plastic chopping board for fish and meat that fits in your dishwasher.

salads

THE WORLD OF SALADS

I don't believe we've even halfway explored the world of salads yet – that would be like asking the Beatles in the 1960s if they'd run out of songs! There's so much out there to experiment with and get excited about; anything is possible, and yet, let's be honest, how many of us get much further than lettuce, tomatoes, maybe a bit of chopped pepper and spring onions? We have this idea that a salad is just a salad, something that isn't all that important, maybe just a bit of garnish on the side of a plate. Well, I hope that by the end of this chapter you'll really have a grasp of the wonderful world of salads. There are so many exciting things that can go into one – it's not just about a piece of boring iceberg with some wedges of tomato.

I held a big salad seminar for a new intake of students at Fifteen this year and the first thing I did was to prepare the most boring salad I could think of, making it look as if I was really into it, and pass it around the room for everyone to have a taste. "What do you think of that?" I asked them. At first they were a bit quiet, then the comments started coming: "Rustic", "Lots of primary colors", "A bit cheap", "Basic, but nice at the same time . . ." Now, at Fifteen we try to get everyone to be really honest about what they think – their reaction to the flavors and textures of ingredients, what they like and don't like – at the same time as being totally open to new ideas. But this was early days, and you could tell the guys and girls weren't quite sure whether I wanted them to say it tasted brilliant or rubbish. Eventually someone just said, "Well, it's boring. Nothing, really . . ." Finally! This was spot on. Suddenly everyone had the courage to agree. Because, you know what, salads made without any love and care are guilty as charged: boring.

I'd like to say the lettuce, cucumber and tomato salad, perhaps with a bit of chopped pepper or grated carrot, is just a memory from twenty years ago, but shockingly, it is probably still the most common salad today; the token gesture on the edge of your plate when you order fish and fries or a steak in the majority of places which haven't yet been allowed to insert the word "gastro" in front of "pub". Yet look around you: there are so many fantastic ingredients out there – Italian, Thai, you name it. There's absolutely no reason why a salad can't be as exciting a dish as anything else you make.

Chances are your old-school salad had no dressing to speak of either, except maybe a dollop of salad dressing on the side. When I started filming the *Jamie's School Dinners* TV series, the kids weren't eating salads at all because the stuff they were used to had no dressing. How can you blame these kids for not liking salads when they don't mean anything? If they're not dressed it's just a load of chopped-up stuff. And, yes, you can turn a carrot into a beautiful carrot salad, but not using massive chunks. It needs to be sliced delicately and thinly so it has a good crunch. After introducing some nice salads, with dressings, my heart nearly broke at the amount of times I heard them say, "Oh, I liked that! I've never eaten salad before," as they asked for second helpings. I then got them on to making their own and this really did bring salads to life for them. You could have a salad in the middle of the table every day and it wouldn't be out of place. And the great thing is that you can get the kids involved by asking them to tear or spin the leaves, or shake a dressing up in a jar. If you delegate these jobs to them, they'll love the responsibility and eat them of their own accord.

Like any other dish, a great salad is only as good as the quality of its ingredients. Buy whatever is fresh and colorful and in season and then think about working all the flavor sensations together: salty, sweet, sour, bitter. Hundreds of years ago all our food was much more bitter than it is now, but we've lost our taste for it because our palates have got used to so much sugar and salt from processed foods. The truth is, not only do bitter leaves like dandelion, treviso or radicchio add an extra dimension of flavor to a dish, especially when you offset it with sweetness from something like balsamic vinegar, but they are incredibly good for you as well – especially for cleansing the liver, and when your liver is happy, the rest of your body is happy! Think peppery, too. Not so long ago, no one had heard of arugula. Yet these days you can find it in all the supermarkets. And what about playing with different textures: a contrast between soft and crunchy, rough and smooth ingredients? Now you're talking ...

Understanding flavors

I want to get you really thinking about and understanding flavors, and about all the things that can go into a salad, from cheese (not a handful of grated Cheddar on top, but a salty cheese, or something creamy to add to a dressing, or a cool, fresh mozzarella) to nuts, toasted seeds, pickled vegetables, beans and pulses. You can use fish – raw, cooked, smoked or even canned, like tuna – or barbecued or grilled shellfish; meat, from cold, shredded duck confit and chunks of grilled chicken breast to crispy bacon and cured meats like prosciutto, bresaola and salami. Or use fruit like clementines in a salad with smoked meat, and blackberries and pomegranates with game, smoked venison or duck.

But I especially want to get you tuned in to the links that take you from one idea to the next, and to recognize that some ingredients are best friends with others, like smoked salmon and lemon, chilli and mint, walnuts and cheese, orange and duck, figs, prosciutto and mozzarella. I don't care what anyone in the world says about salads – as long as they are dressed intelligently and have a contrast of salty and sweet, crunchy and soft, bitter and smoky, you're probably going to be in for a treat.

What makes up a salad?

Leaves

Most people associate salads with lettuce. Everyone knows the basic round lettuce, with a small crunchy core and floppy leaves on the outside, and we've got used to red-leaf lettuce, with its red-fringed leaves, frilly escarole and iceberg, with its crunch but not much flavor – all honest ingredients, but pretty unexceptional. Have a look around and you'll find there are plenty more interesting leaves out there that can give you color, crispiness, sweetness, bitterness or peppery heat.

Romaine lettuce with its tightly packed long crunchy leaves, and its cheeky younger brother, the little Boston or butter, are the next step up in the lettuce world. Romaine is the star of the famous Caesar salad and little Boston makes a fantastic shrimp cocktail.

Leaves with a slightly bitter, refreshing flavor work especially well with salty, rich or creamy ingredients, and they tend to give you more than just flavor. The yellow white inner leaves of the curly endive have a great springy texture, chicory has a brilliant crunch, while dandelion has an amazing long curly shape and Italian radicchio has a brilliant ruby-red color and bitterness.

Arugula has a fiery, peppery flavor that can be a bit much on its own, but mix a little of it into a salad and it will give it a kick. The same goes for watercress, with its beautiful dark green leaves that can make any salad look elegant. Peppery leaves like these are great with sharp or sweet dressings, and can stand up well to pungent flavors like mustard or horseradish.

Baby spinach and tiny red-veined chard leaves have a great earthy flavor. Mustard leaf is long and green with purply edges and tastes slightly pungent, and then there is sorrel, an old-fashioned salad leaf that we've almost forgotten about, which has an incredibly fresh lemon flavor.

There is a huge amount of choice out there, so have a go at using something different to what you normally go for – no excuses! Oh, and by the way, don't forget that just about any inner leaf or new bud on most vegetables is amazing in salads. Savoy cabbage is great, or any of the little baby shoots from the cabbage family. The small shooting leaves of Swiss chard or beetroot are brilliant. And then there are edible flowers or the curly little shoots you get on the pea plant. Parsley, fennel, mint, dill, even thyme or marjoram tips are also delicious. (Just avoid potato flowers, as they aren't very good for you – they're part of the deadly nightshade family, though they won't actually kill you.) If you've had boring salads for the last twenty years, for crying out loud don't die eating them!

Preparing and washing salad leaves

It's wise to wash your leaves, as you can never be sure what's been sprayed on them, who's touched them or what might have wriggled around on them! These days it's also wise to wash any bagged salad bought from the supermarket, even if it says "prewashed" on it. I've been told by both nutritionists and people who work in supermarkets that most of these salads have been washed with chlorine-like chemicals which do the job and get rid of the bacteria, but at the same time also get rid of vital nutrients. So it's not all that healthy to eat them anyway. Whatever you buy, from here on you're going to have to wash your own – sorry for the bad news, but I've got to be honest!

First of all, make sure your sink is clean and then fill it with cold water. Salad leaves are quite delicate and they can bruise easily if handled roughly. Let the pieces fall into the water. Roll up your sleeves and turn the leaves gently with your hands, then put a colander over a bowl and gently lift the leaves into it to drain. Have a look at the bottom of the sink. If there is a lot of dirt there, you'll need to wash the leaves again until the water is clean, just to make sure you've got it all off. Once the leaves are clean and drained they need to be dried well or they will turn your dressing watery and make your salad soggy.

Salad spinners will spin your leaves dry in seconds, but if you don't have one, put a handful of leaves in a dish towel then go outside and spin it round your head. Keep your prepared leaves in the fridge or in a bowl under a damp cloth until you're ready to use them. Once or twice a week I get a load of different lettuces and herbs and wash and spin them. I then take the plastic drawer out of the bottom of the fridge, line it with dish towels and put my lovely clean leaves in there. They'll keep as fresh as a daisy for two to four days if you look after them. I really like having a good mixture of clean salad leaves
on tap all the time.

Vegetables

"I've never had a salad made from just raw vegetables before," piped up a student when my good mate Pete Begg showed off one of his favorite salads (the recipe is on page 43). But raw veggies are great in salads. The thing to remember is that they can be quite hard, so slice them very thinly, or shave them with a speed peeler. Deseed peppers, and especially chillies, so you don't suddenly get a blast of heat.

Cooked vegetables can be fantastic in salads too. Peas, beans, asparagus and corn, cooked very briefly, add crunch and color. Instead of raw zucchini, you could grill the slices, or tear up chunks of sticky, sweet roast squash – fantastic with a balsamic vinegar dressing.

Herbs

I absolutely love herbs. So much so that I've devoted a couple of pages to them at the back of this book (see pages 432-3). Soft, aromatic herbs are great in salads – you just tear them in at the last minute. The woodier, sturdier herbs like bay, rosemary and thyme are best left for cooking, though you can use rosemary or thyme tips, very finely chopped, in a salad (especially if you have a crumbly, salty cheese to go with them).

Dressings

What is a dressing? For me it is the link that pulls everything together in a salad and makes things work. It brings the flavor out, and at the same time puts flavor in. I was making a fricassee with chicken one day, a nice little classic stew that was chugging away in the oven, waiting for me to add grapes and tarragon towards the end. For some reason, I absentmindedly dressed the grapes and tarragon in lemon and oil with some salt and pepper as if they were a salad. I threw them on top of the chicken before I realized my mistake but ate it and thought it was just incredible. Using the tarragon like a salad leaf with complete conviction made it taste different to when it's used as an herb. The fricassee was absolute heaven and within a week was on the menu at the restaurant!

The interesting thing was that I'd never thought about tarragon as having that "wow" factor before. What it needed was a bit of richness, so I tried a little Parmesan with the grapes. It was good, but it needed something more, so I tried some salted ricotta, and it was just right. I even gave a plate to some food critics to try and they agreed. Just four ingredients (mind you, they have to be brilliant quality), ricotta, grapes, tarragon and a lemon oil dressing, make a great salad. So simple, but it's the dressing that brings the flavors together and makes everything happen.

There are thousands of ready-made bottled dressings out there, most of which reek of dried garlic, stale herbs and cheap vinegar, and are full of strange gums and starches to keep them emulsified. For half the price of any one of them, you can buy the basic ingredients to make your own dressing and it'll be miles better than anything from a bottle, no matter whose name is on the label. All you need is a jam jar to shake it up in.

Oil

When I was a kid, olive oil was something that was dripped in my ears before the nurse syringed them! So the dressing I grew up with, until I was about fourteen, was 4 parts sunflower oil to 1 part malt vinegar and a big, big spoon of wholegrain mustard mixed in. Pretty aggressive stuff; whereas now there are so many fantastic oils and vinegars out there, you can go as delicate or as peppery or as fruity as you like.

Olive oil has a rich green or gold color and can vary from gentle and aromatic to fruity and peppery, depending on which country or region it comes from, what variety of olives it is made from, and what grade it is. Use extra virgin if possible, as it has the best flavor. Or try bright green, sweet, quite nutty, avocado oil.

Sunflower, vegetable and peanut oils are all perfectly good for a basic vinaigrette. They don't have strong flavors and work well with just about any other ingredient.

Nut oils like walnut or hazelnut give an amazing aroma and flavor to salads, but they are strong and quite expensive, so it's best to combine them with a lighter vegetable oil: 1 part nut oil to 3 parts vegetable oil.

Sesame oil is made from crushed, roasted sesame seeds and is used in a lot in Asian dishes – again, because it is pretty strong, dilute it with some vegetable oil before dressing your salad.

Vinegar

As well as red and white wine vinegars and cider vinegar, which generally speaking are as good as the wine or cider they are made from, think about rice vinegar, which is used in salads and pickles all over eastern Asia.

Balsamic vinegar, which can be produced only in Modena in northern Italy, is made from pressed grape juice fermented in wooden barrels for years until it is rich, sweet and thick but still with a vinegary twang. But you don't have to use vinegar at all; instead you could go for citrus juice. Lemon is the best as it's about the same sourness as vinegar, and lime works well too.

A basic dressing

Always start with a ratio of 1 part vinegar to 3 parts oil, with a few twists of salt and pepper. Put the ingredients in a clean jam jar and give it a good shake – or whisk them in a bowl. The more you shake or whisk, the more emulsified your dressing will be and the longer it'll take to separate back into oil and vinegar again. Unless you have added dairy products, fresh herbs or raw garlic, homemade dressings will keep for ages in the fridge; just remember that they will divide again, so always give them a good shake or whisk before using.

Balance

Try dressing a few leaves and taste for balance. Does it need more vinegar? Is it too sharp? (In which case, add a little more oil.) Keep tasting and balancing, balancing, balancing. You are looking for the right blend of oiliness and refreshing acidity that will lift and cut through anything that is rich in your salad. Then, might it need something else: a little chopped chilli, onion or crushed garlic? These can make your dressing more butch, and work well if you have root vegetables or meat in your salad. How about a pinch of chopped herbs or ground spice? Cilantro and cumin are great for Middle Eastern-style dressings. You'll need to break them down first, though. Just toast whole spices briefly in a dry pan to release their aroma (taking care not to burn them!), then pop them in a pestle and mortar or a Flavor Shaker and give them a bit of a bash.

Maybe you just fancy the old classic: mustard, which can be mild like Dijon, sweet and grainy, or fiery English – only add a little, though, unless you want your dressing to taste really mustardy. If you want a creamy, thicker dressing, just add a spoonful or so of cream, crème fraîche or yogurt.

What I find exciting is to be able to take an ingredient that might taste way too bitter or salty or sweet on its own, and bring it back to something palatable by balancing it with a different flavor. With the students I grilled some treviso, which is a bitter leaf and part of the radicchio family. This introduced a bit of charry smokiness (it would be even better if done on the barbecue) to offset the bitterness. I passed it around naked like that, for the students to taste, and frankly, their faces said it all! They thought it was far too bitter and had nothing to offer. Then we made a hot, peppery, pungent dressing for it – using rosemary tips, garlic, sweet balsamic vinegar and some very fruity olive oil – and something magical happened. What a transformation! Suddenly, everyone was very happy to sit and munch the dressed treviso! If you'd like to check out the recipe, have a look in my book *Jamie's Italy*.

Dressing your salad, or finding your "fairy fingers"!

First of all, only dress your salad just before serving, or you'll end up with an unappetizing mush. If you don't dress your salad properly it will taste miserable, and by properly, I mean coat every leaf and ingredient without swamping them. The chef's way of doing this is to put the dressing into a big bowl first, before you add your salad, but if you're not sure how much dressing to use, you can put the salad in the bowl first and then add enough dressing to coat everything. Then get your (clean!) fingers in there, turning the salad over and over gently so you can feel what you are doing. Rotate your hands round each other, then twinkle your fingers as if you're a bit nervous. I don't care who you are – big, small, tough or gentle – I really want you to find your fairy fingers, so you can dress a salad without bruising the leaves. Go on, try doing it now – even if you're reading this in bed! And before your partner thinks you're a raving nutcase, give them a wink and tell them you've found your fairy fingers!

Lemon oil dressing

A classic, delicate all-round dressing that's especially lovely on herby or smoked salmon salads. Use the dressing within 24 hours for the best flavor.

3½ tablespoons fresh lemon juice (the juice of approximately 1 lemon)
10 tablespoons best-quality extra virgin olive oil
sea salt and freshly ground black pepper

Put the lemon juice and oil into a jam jar and season. Tighten the lid and shake. Try out your dressing on a salad leaf and adjust the seasoning to taste.

Balsamic vinegar dressing

Brilliant for Italian salads, green salads and antipasti.

3½ tablespoons good aged balsamic vinegar
10 tablespoons best-quality extra virgin olive oil
sea salt and freshly ground black pepper

Put the balsamic and oil into a jam jar, season and shake. Taste on a salad leaf and adjust if needed.

Sicilian dressing

Wonderful in a warm grilled tuna salad or with shellfish. And don't cheat – make sure you squeeze your oranges!

1½ tablespoons fresh lemon juice
1½ tablespoons fresh orange or blood orange juice
10 tablespoons best-quality extra virgin olive oil
a few pinches of dried oregano
sea salt and ground black pepper

Put all your ingredients into a jam jar and shake, mixing everything together. Taste the dressing and adjust the seasoning accordingly.

Creamy French dressing

Great with green salads and bitter leaves like endive or radicchio.

5 tablespoons white wine vinegar
4 tablespoons walnut oil
½ cup crème fraîche
1 teaspoon Dijon mustard
sea salt and freshly ground black pepper
a handful of chopped parsley leaves
8 tablespoons best-quality extra virgin olive oil

Put all your ingredients into a jam jar. Shake, taste and season again if needed until your dressing is perfect. You may need to add a little more vinegar or oil to balance it.

Spiced vinegar dressing

Lovely with cheesy salads or cold roast beef.

8 tablespoons white wine vinegar
2 cloves
1 star anise
10 tablespoons best-quality extra virgin olive oil
sea salt and freshly ground black pepper

Pour the vinegar into a pan and add the cloves, star anise and a splash of water. Bring to the boil and reduce the liquid by half. Allow the spiced vinegar to cool, then pour into a jam jar. Add the oil and some salt and pepper. Tighten the lid and shake your jar. Taste and add more oil or vinegar if needed.

Japanese dressing

Great with cold noodles or a warm squid salad.

2½oz onion, peeled and finely chopped
3 tablespoons soy sauce
2 tablespoons rice vinegar
½ teaspoon granulated sugar
¼ teaspoon English mustard powder
1 tablespoon grapeseed oil
1 tablespoon sesame oil
sea salt and freshly ground black pepper

Shake all the ingredients together in a jam jar. Once the salt has dissolved, add and shake in 2 tablespoons of water and season again if needed.

Grilled chilli dressing

Fantastic with crunchy root vegetable salads and strong-flavored herbs.

3 fresh red chillies
10 tablespoons extra virgin olive oil
3½ tablespoons fresh lemon juice
a small bunch of fresh mint, leaves picked and
  finely chopped
sea salt and freshly ground black pepper

Prick the chillies with the tip of a sharp knife – this stops them popping or exploding when they are cooked. Hold your chillies, one at a time, with a pair of metal tongs in a gas flame until they're blackened and blistered all over. If you don't have a gas stove, pop them under a hot broiler instead. Place the chillies in a small bowl, cover with plastic wrap and leave for 15 minutes. This way they will steam in their own heat and the skins will peel off very easily.

Peel the chillies, open them up and scrape out all the white seeds. Discard these, then finely chop the flesh of the chillies. Put in a mixing bowl, add the oil, lemon juice and mint, and mix well. Season to taste.

Mayonnaise

Mayonnaise is not really a dressing – it's much more versatile than that – but I thought I'd put the basic recipe here as it comes in handy, both in this chapter and the rest of the book. Mayonnaise is great for dressing coleslaw (see page 38) and robust salads, but it's also lovely dolloped on top of a fish stew (see page 208) or a beautiful crab crostini (see page 273). The best thing about mayonnaise is that you take it in any direction you like by adding stuff like herbs, spices or garlic. It can be tricky to get the hang of making mayonnaise but if you keep trying, you'll crack it!

The first couple of times you make mayonnaise, I would recommend replacing half the olive oil with vegetable or sunflower oil. Start off by adding the vegetable or sunflower oil drop by drop, switching to olive oil when the mixture begins to come together. This means that if things go wrong and your mayo splits, you haven't lost all that lovely (and expensive!) olive oil. When you get a bit more confident, you can start upping the amount of olive oil to 15 oz, and use 5 oz vegetable or sunflower oil. Once you feel you've cracked it, go for 100 percent olive oil. You can even upgrade to extra virgin olive oil – this will give your mayo a stronger flavor, too.

PS Mayo from a jar is OK – I use it now and then when I'm in a hurry – but for a special occasion you can't beat the real McCoy!

Put the egg yolk and mustard into a bowl and whisk together – you can use a food processor or a hand-held whisk. While you're whisking, very slowly start to add the olive oil drop by drop, making sure each drop is whisked in thoroughly before adding the next. Once you've blended in about 3 tablespoons of the oil and the mixture begins to thicken, you can pour in the rest of the oil in a thin, continuous trickle. If you have someone around to hold the bowl for you while you pour and whisk, that's really helpful.

If your mayo splits, then a little hot water will sometimes bring it back together again, but I find the best thing to do is to start a new batch of mayo and, once it starts to thicken, you gradually whisk in your split mayo. This way your ingredients don't go to waste!

When you've used up all your oil, add a good squeeze of lemon juice and season to taste. Once you've made your mayo, get it straight into the fridge until you're ready to use it.

1 large free-range or
   organic egg yolk
1 teaspoon Dijon mustard
about 1 pint olive oil
1 lemon
sea salt and freshly ground
   black pepper

Simple crunchy side salad

Trim the tops of your green beans, leaving the tails on. Blanch the beans in boiling, salted water for 3 to 4 minutes, then drain and leave them to one side to cool down. Meanwhile tear, wash and dry the leaves of your little Boston and romaine lettuce. Peel your cucumber and carrot. Cut the cucumber in half lengthways, and remove and discard the inner core. Finely slice the cucumber and carrot. Finely slice the celery heart lengthways.

To serve, mix all the ingredients together, add enough of your chosen dressing to coat and toss together, making sure that everything is dressed nicely.

serves 2

a handful of slender green beans
sea salt and freshly ground black pepper
1 little Boston lettuce
1 romaine lettuce
½ a cucumber
1 firm carrot
1 celery heart, yellow leaves reserved
1 handful of fresh flat-leaf parsley, leaves picked
1 x balsamic vinegar, lemon oil or creamy French
   dressing recipe (see page 24)

Simple green side salad

Trim the fennel bulb, reserving the herby tops, and finely slice it. Wash and dry your arugula, dandelion, watercress and baby chard leaves. Snap the woody ends off the asparagus spears (they will break naturally at exactly the right point) and discard them. Holding the base of the asparagus, finely slice each spear with a speed peeler into thin slivers.

Put the asparagus shavings in a bowl with the sliced fennel, the reserved fennel tops and all the salad leaves and herbs. Add some of your chosen dressing and toss together well so everything gets coated – that's it; fancy but easy!

serves 2

½ a fennel bulb
a handful of arugula
a handful of dandelion leaves
a handful of watercress
a handful of baby chard
4 spears of asparagus
a handful of fresh chervil or parsley leaves
1 x lemon oil or creamy French dressing recipe (see page 24)

Amazing potato and horseradish salad
with fine herbs and bresaola

I love this salad. It can be a delicate starter for a dinner party or, even better, a quick Saturday lunch-time snack. If you ever get the chance to buy fresh horseradish at a farmers' market you must give it a try – the heat is fantastic and goes right up your nose. Cured beef or bresaola is available in just about all good supermarkets now, so you should be able to find it, and it's pretty lean so it's not too indulgent . . .

Boil the new potatoes in a pot of salted water until nicely cooked. Drain them and allow to cool for 5 minutes while you get the rest of the plate together.

Pour most of the lemon juice into a large bowl and add a good pinch of salt, some pepper, the celery, parsley and horseradish. Mix in the crème fraîche or sour cream. While they're still hot, cut the potatoes in half or into quarters and add to the bowl. Season carefully with more salt and pepper and toss everything together. Have a taste and add some more lemon juice if needed – you're after a good balance of lemon and horseradish. The flavors will improve as the salad sits in the dressing.

In the meantime, overlap 6 slices of the bresaola or cold roast beef in a circle on each plate, pile the salad in the middle and then draw up the edges of the meat as I did in the picture. Sprinkle over the tarragon and celery leaves, drizzle with a little olive oil and eat up.

serves 4

1½lb new potatoes,
  scrubbed
sea salt and freshly ground
  black pepper
juice of 2 lemons
½ a celery heart, yellow
  leaves only reserved and
  the rest finely sliced
a bunch of fresh flat-leaf
  parsley, leaves picked
  and chopped
2–3 heaped teaspoons
  grated horseradish
3 heaped tablespoons
  crème fraîche or
  sour cream
24 slices of bresaola or
  cold roast beef
a bunch of fresh tarragon,
  leaves picked
extra virgin olive oil

Proper tomato salad

What makes a good tomato salad? Well, obviously the tomatoes. We are lucky to have so many more varieties, sizes and flavors available to use these days – red, yellow, large, small, fat, thin, long, round – so a tomato salad can never be called boring! Next time you're in the supermarket, have a second look and you might be surprised at how many different types are on offer. I always use a selection of shapes and sizes in my salad, so I might cut some into quarters, some into thick slices, some into erratic pieces. I might leave very small cherry tomatoes whole, or quarter the slightly bigger ones. A good tip: salting tomatoes brings the water out and intensifies their flavor, so it is always worth salting them and leaving them for 20 minutes before you start making your salad. Try it, you'll really notice the difference.

I love the use of basil in this salad. It is one of tomato's best mates and works so well. Keep back some small leaves for sprinkling on top before serving and use nice big ones torn in half in the salad itself. For me, chillies should always go in a tomato salad, along with a few leaves of marjoram and a tiny amount of finely chopped garlic – not too much, as raw garlic is pretty potent. Oil and vinegar (balsamic if you like), and that's it.

Chop up the tomatoes in an irregular fashion, from the size of a cherry tomato to the size of a ping pong ball – be brave and bold! Season from a height with sea salt, using slightly more than you usually would. I'm not asking you to eat this amount of salt, it's just there to draw out all the intense tomato flavors. Put the tomatoes in a colander over a bowl and leave for 20 minutes to let any excess water and salt drip out of them. Then pour the liquid away, dry the bowl and put the tomatoes in it. Dress them with a generous glug of peppery extra virgin olive oil and a splash of herb or balsamic vinegar. Add some pepper, the chilli, marjoram, garlic and the large basil leaves, torn up. Toss together and correct the seasoning if necessary. Tumble the tomatoes on to a large platter, drizzle with a little extra virgin olive oil and sprinkle over the baby basil leaves.

PS Any leftovers are great tossed with hot spaghetti – delicious!

serves 4

4 big handfuls of mixed tomatoes
sea salt and freshly ground black pepper
peppery extra virgin olive oil
herb or balsamic vinegar
1 fresh red chilli, halved, deseeded and finely sliced
1 tablespoon freshly chopped marjoram
½ a clove of garlic, peeled and finely chopped
a big handful of fresh basil, leaves picked and divided into large and small ones

Return of the egg salad

serves 4

To be honest, throughout my youth, egg salads and egg sandwiches evoked nothing in me other than disgust and revulsion! Overcooked eggs mixed with a bit of old mayo and little else – not something to really get me going. However, I think it's worth revisiting the humble egg salad and showing how it can be put together in ways that make it a bit more exciting and delicious. Common sense means you've got to start with the freshest, most beautiful free-range or organic eggs, otherwise don't bother. And don't think you have to draw the line at hens' eggs – try duck, quail or goose eggs too, as they can all be found easily these days. Go on, spice things up a bit and break the monotony! I like this salad when served as a little pre-dinner snack, or as a small salad in its own right, with some good-quality grilled or toasted bread.

Cook a couple of eggs per person in boiling, very lightly salted water until they're a tiny bit soft in the middle. The salt in the water helps prevent the shells from cracking. A large hen's egg will need 8 minutes, a normal-sized goose egg 12 minutes, a duck egg 9 minutes and a quail egg just 2 minutes. Once you've cooked the eggs, place them in cold water to stop the cooking right away. Drain them and peel them, then carefully cut each one in half and lay them yolk-side up on a serving plate. Whether using homemade mayonnaise (see page 26), or a jar of ready-made, to add a bit of life to it I like to mix 6 tablespoons of mayo with the fragrant zest of a lemon and enough lemon juice to give it a delicate twang. Season with salt and freshly ground black pepper. At this stage the mayo will be a little thinner than usual because of the lemon juice but this is fine. Carefully spoon some flavored mayo over each egg, with a twist of black pepper on top.

To accompany this salad there are a few things that I like to do. The first is to get myself two big packages of cress. Cut the cress out of the containers, then wash it, drain it and spin it in a salad spinner. Simply serve on the side of the plate next to the eggs. Anchovies are also a great addition – just get hold of some good-quality Spanish or Italian anchovies in oil and marinate them for an hour in a little white wine and some chopped fresh parsley. Take them out of the marinade and serve a couple per person with the cress next to the egg salad. A great alternative is to cook a couple of thin slices of bacon until incredibly crisp then stack them on the side of the plate. Serve the lot with rounds of hot toast.

Crunchy raw beetroot salad with feta and pear

When most people think about beetroot in salads, they think of big vinegary crinkle-cut chunks from a jar and immediately say no! But remember, beetroots are only vinegary when they're pickled. When simply boiled or roasted they are juicy and sweet as you like. Raw beetroot is amazing in salads, giving you a deep, earthy, minerally flavor, lots of crunch and, of course, incredible colors! Did you know you can get golden and stripy beetroot as well as purple? Have a look next time you're at a farmers' market or buy some seeds and grow a few yourself.

Remember to wear an apron when chopping beetroot, and wash your board and hands afterwards or you'll get red fingerprints everywhere. If your knife skills aren't up to speed yet, buy one of those matchstick peelers or matchstick mandolins in good cookware shops. Then you'll be really quick at it.

Dress the beetroot and pear matchsticks in a little of the lemon oil dressing and season with some salt and pepper. Taste to check that the flavors are balanced and lovely, and add a little more lemon juice to check the sweetness of the pears and beetroots if you need to.

Divide the salad between four plates or put it on a big platter, crumble over the creamy white feta, and sprinkle over the baby mint leaves and the sunflower seeds if you're using them. Simple, but it's a treat and a half.

serves 4

4 good-sized beetroots, lovely different colors if possible, scrubbed, peeled and cut into fine matchsticks (see page 431)
3 ripe pears (or you could use apples), peeled, cored and cut into matchsticks
1 x lemon oil dressing recipe (see page 24)
sea salt and freshly ground black pepper
7oz feta cheese
a small bunch of fresh mint, smallest leaves picked
optional: a large handful of sunflower seeds

My favorite coleslaw

Coleslaw is quite a cool little retro salad, provided you get the balance right between the thinly sliced cabbage, carrot and onion, and you don't just use plain mayonnaise – the flavor should be balanced with some lemon juice, chopped parsley and maybe even some apple or pear to make it special. Good store-bought mayo is fine to use, because once you've cut it with the lemon juice and run the parsley through it, you'll lift it out of the ordinary.

The thing that's unusual about coleslaw, in terms of it being classed as a "salad", is that it is a composed salad, not a dressed one. And instead of it being light and delicate, it's much more filling. Yet it can be amazing when made well. So many people choose to buy it ready-made from the supermarket, which is just not the same thing. Bought coleslaw has a shininess to it that comes from all the additives – like a can of paint with bits in it – and the cabbage is usually grated, which tends to make it soft, instead of being finely sliced to give it crunch. So next time you consider buying it ready-made, buy the ingredients instead and have a go at making your own.

When it comes to the mayonnaise, you can add a little or you can go a bit heavier, depending on what you prefer. I know that this recipe will knock your socks off. It's a great one to serve with lamb, or with a steak and a baked potato or homemade fries. Give this coleslaw a bash and you'll wish you'd never wasted time buying those terrible little pots in the first place!

As cabbage is quite a uniform vegetable, it's pretty easy to slice, but you want to do this as finely as possible, using a sharp knife or the thin setting on a mandolin (it's definitely worth getting hold of one). Remember to mind your fingers and use the guard. Or, if you have a food processor (I love to do it in my Magimix!), you can put the slicing attachment on to it and do it in seconds. When sliced, put the cabbage into a bowl and slice up the onion in the same way, adding it to the cabbage when done.

With the carrots and apples you can either skim their sides to get a flat edge, then slice along and across into matchsticks, or put the julienne attachment on to your mandolin or food processor. Add to the bowl of cabbage and onion, with the chopped parsley, lemon juice, mayonnaise and mustard. Have a taste and add seasoning if needed.

PS I've made a very delicious coleslaw in the past using one of those frilly Chinese cabbages. Shredded red cabbage looks good too. And it's lovely to sprinkle over some sunflower seeds or toasted walnuts.

serves 6

½ a white cabbage, core removed, outer leaves discarded and cut into quarters
1 small red onion, peeled
3 carrots, washed and peeled
2 red apples, washed and cored
a small bunch of fresh flat-leaf parsley, leaves picked and roughly chopped
juice of 1–2 lemons
a couple of dollops of mayonnaise (see page 26)
1 heaped teaspoon English mustard
sea salt and freshly ground black pepper

Greek salad

This is a good old classic that has been on menus for years. If you can make a special effort to use ripe tomatoes, and to buy olives with their pits in and pit them yourself, you'll end up with a fantastic-tasting salad.

PS I'm not sure it's totally authentic, but I like to put avocado in mine – it just works.

Cut your tomatoes erratically into roughly ½ inch shapes. Mix them in a bowl with the olives, avocado, shallot, most of the oregano, a few small splashes of the vinegar, a glug of olive oil, salt and pepper and set to one side for 5 minutes.

Tear your larger lettuce leaves into pieces and leave the smaller leaves whole, add them to the bowl, then dress everything with some of the lemon oil dressing. Move your dressed salad to a large plate or platter, leaving the wedges of avocado in the bowl. Place these around the outside of the plate – not for any particular reason, I just think that it's nice for everyone to be able to get some avocado! Crumble large chunks of feta over the salad or arrange pieces around the outside of the plate with the avocado. Drizzle the salad once more with extra virgin olive oil and sprinkle with the rest of the oregano.

serves 4

6 ripe plum tomatoes
a handful of black olives
2 avocados, peeled, halved and pitted, then cut into wedges and tossed in lemon juice
1 large shallot, peeled and finely diced
1 heaped teaspoon dried oregano
herb or red wine vinegar
extra virgin olive oil
sea salt and freshly ground black pepper
1 romaine lettuce, outer leaves discarded, inner leaves washed and dried
1 x lemon oil dressing recipe (see page 24)
12oz feta cheese

Unbelievable root vegetable salad

This salad is a favorite of my good mate Pete Begg. He was inspired to make it when he lived in Italy, where each stall at the local market would offer its own seasonal salad mix. His favorite was an autumnal selection of peppery radishes, which are just made for salads; lovely earthy-sweet beetroots in different shades of orange and red, even some with stripes; the aromatic heart of a celery; sweet carrots; and some beautiful, crunchy, aniseedy-sweet fennel. Come spring and summer, a beautiful veggie salad can be made with baby asparagus, fava beans or small, sweet zucchini (which you can treat just like cucumbers: slice them thinly or cut them into long strips with a speed peeler).

All these vibrant flavors need a powerful dressing to bring them together, so Pete decided to flavor his with chilli and mint as they are very good friends – brilliant!

Very finely slice or shave the beetroots and carrots, using good knife skills, a mandolin on a fine setting or, most easily, a speed peeler, until you have a pile of thin, wavy, crunchy slices. Place in a big mixing bowl. With a sharp knife, slice the celery heart and leaves, the radicchio, the radishes and the fennel as finely as you can and add to the bowl of root veg slices.

Toss the root vegetables in the grilled chilli dressing, season carefully to taste, and serve sprinkled with the reserved fennel tops.

serves 4

3 fresh beetroots (all
    different colors if
    possible), peeled
3 carrots, peeled
1 celery heart, with leaves
½ a small radicchio,
    washed and dried
a bunch of radishes,
    topped and tailed
1 fennel bulb, herby
    tops reserved
1 x grilled chilli dressing
    recipe (see page 25)
sea salt and freshly ground
    black pepper

Fifteen Christmas salad

This is a classic salad that has become part of the family at Fifteen – we usually serve it in December, when the clementines are at their sweetest and most fragrant, but at other times of the year blood oranges or peaches, pears or figs work really well. If you look at all the elements you can understand why it is such a brilliant combo: sweet, cold clementines from the fridge, sliced at the last minute so they are shiny and juicy; salty, smoky speck; creamy mozzarella (at the restaurant we are lucky enough to use burrata mozzarella, which is killer stuff, the best!); salty, rich Parmesan; fragrant mint; peppery, crunchy arugula; bitter treviso (or radicchio), which also gives a bit of color; and balsamic vinegar. As a salad goes, it really has got everything – sweetness, bitterness, crunch and softness. It's probably my favorite salad ever!

Get four individual serving plates out and tear a ball of mozzarella into rough chunks on to each plate. Sprinkle with salt and pepper and grate over the lemon zest. Arrange the clementine slices over the mozzarella – one clementine per plate.

In a bowl, dress the arugula, treviso or radicchio and mint leaves in a little dressing, reserving a few small picked mint leaves for serving.

On a chopping board, lay out a slice of speck and use this to pick up and wrap about a quarter of the dressed leaves.

Place the little package on one of the plates, on top of the clementine slices. Repeat this for the other plates. Serve with a shaving of Parmesan, a sprinkling of mint leaves and a drizzle of aged balsamic vinegar. Eat immediately! Absolutely delicious.

serves 4

4 4½oz balls of buffalo mozzarella
sea salt and freshly ground black pepper
1 lemon
4 clementines, peeled and sliced into ¼ inch thick discs
2 handfuls of arugula, washed and dried
1 treviso or radicchio, roughly torn, washed and dried
a small bunch of fresh mint, leaves picked
1 x lemon oil dressing recipe (see page 24)
4 slices of speck (smoked prosciutto)
a small handful of freshly shaved Parmesan cheese
aged balsamic vinegar

Warm salads

The only rule I know about warm salads is that there has to be a warm element to them! After that you can get as inventive as you like. Think about all those Asian salads, with crunchy vegetables, possibly noodles, and grilled or crispy deep-fried squid, duck, or maybe some rare beef, with ginger, soy, lime, chilli . . .

When I was about eleven, my dad used to serve a warm salad in the pub, which was probably quite brave for those days. He would take some interesting leaves like red-leaf lettuce, endive and frisée, make a sherry vinaigrette with some shallots through it, get a pan on, put in some clarified butter, then quickly sauté some chicken livers, flame them in port, and they would go straight from the pan on top of the salad. It was really tasty.

When I was a bit older, skint and living in a studio flat in London, I'd make a salad of smoked bacon (which every good British bloke should have in the fridge at all times) or pancetta if I had any. I would fry it in a pan until it was lovely and crispy, then I'd toss in a few pinenuts to get them golden. I'd have a bowl of mixed leaves ready, which I'd washed and spun in a salad spinner, then I'd dress them with some good oil and vinegar. I'd tip in the contents of the pan, lovely tasty fat and all, and toss it all together. It's nothing profound, but it's a great little salad, with so many flavors and textures going on: sweet, salty, bitter, crispy, soft . . . Serve some in a big bowl with roasted chicken – happy days!

- Think about what might go well with the main ingredient of your salad before you make your dressing. Lemon juice is great with fish, orange juice with duck, balsamic vinegar with smoked bacon, sherry vinegar with chicken livers.

- Make sure you have all the ingredients prepped and to hand before your meat or fish is ready; if you're scrabbling around at the last minute everything will go cold and your salad won't be a warm one any more!

- Tear or slice your meat or fish into bite-sized pieces before you toss them in your salad so the lettuce doesn't get weighed down and squashed by big heavy chunks.

- Don't put too much meat in! 1¾–3½oz of meat per person is all you need for a starter, and 5½oz is fine for a main course.

- If you're making a warm salad with meat, don't forget to add any resting juices to the dressing.

Warm salad of crispy smoked bacon and Jerusalem artichokes

This is a brilliant salad that always makes me smile when I eat it. The smokiness of the bacon goes so well with the potatoey-mushroomy-garlicky flavor of the Jerusalem artichokes (which you can find in good supermarkets and markets). If you can't get hold of any then use some good new potatoes instead.

Remember, the trick to a warm salad is to get everything ready to go. Ask your family or guests to make their way to the table while you finish it off, and don't let them talk until they've cleared their plates, so they get the salad while it's good (I'm only joking about the talking!).

First of all, scrub your Jerusalem artichokes or potatoes and boil them in salted water until tender. Once cool, cut them in half and set aside. Meanwhile, carefully remove the core of the radicchio or treviso, then halve, break apart and finely slice. Wash and dry in a salad spinner. Put the butter lettuce leaves in a large bowl with the radicchio or treviso and the parsley or chervil.

Cut your bacon into ½ inch slices. Pour a small amount of olive oil into a non-stick frying pan and fry the bacon. When it's lightly golden, add the sliced onion and your cooked and drained Jerusalem artichokes or potatoes. Fry on a medium heat until the bacon is golden and crisp, the onion is sticky and soft and the Jerusalem artichokes have sucked up all the flavors and turned crispy. The important thing to remember here is that you need enough color, but not so much that you're on the edge of burning everything.

Now is the time to get everyone round the table, holding their knives and forks ready to tuck in! Divide half the contents of your pan between four plates, then add 5 tablespoons of olive oil and the balsamic vinegar to the pan, with a little pinch of salt and pepper. Mix everything together so the flavors improve and then pour immediately over the salad leaves waiting in the bowl. Toss lightly and quickly (using your fairy fingers!) so each leaf is coated in the tasty balsamic dressing. Put a nice handful of the salad leaf mixture on top of the hot bits and pieces that are already on each plate. Eat at once as it is, or quickly shave over a little Parmesan – nice both ways.

PS This is my favorite warm salad – but have a go at finding your own versions. Instead of bacon, try opening out some good-quality sausages and frying the meat until crisp. Or some nice crispy roasted meat like chicken, duck, quail or even game birds, torn up, with some sautéed mushrooms and roasted tomatoes, would go really well in a salad like this.

serves 4

2 handfuls of large
  Jerusalem artichokes
  or new potatoes
sea salt and freshly ground
  black pepper
1 radicchio or treviso,
  outer leaves discarded
3 little butter lettuces,
  leaves washed, dried and
  stalks removed
a small handful of fresh
  flat-leaf parsley or chervil,
  leaves picked and finely
  sliced
extra virgin olive oil
8 slices thickly sliced
  bacon or pancetta
1 small red onion, peeled
  and finely sliced
3 tablespoons balsamic
  vinegar

Warm grilled peach and frisée salad
with goat's cheese dressing

I love this salad – it's so simple. It's based on one that was cooked for me by the brilliant Jean-Georges Vongerichten at his New York restaurant, Perry Street. The flavor and juicy sweetness you get from a grilled ripe peach, or pear for that matter, served bravely and simply next to a crunchy single leaf salad of frisée or curly endive, are perfection. Especially with the creamy dressing. You might feel as if you're being a little bit wasteful when you're preparing this lettuce because the key to making it successfully is to remove and discard all the dark green, ridiculously bitter outer leaves of the lettuces, as you only want to use the sweet, white, crunchy inner leaves.

To make your dressing, put the goat's cheese in a pestle and mortar with a little salt and pepper. (Goat's cheese is salty anyway, so go easy on the salt.) Add the olive oil and lemon juice and mix up. Add the walnut oil and the Parmesan and mix again, but not for too long or it will split.

Put your peaches, cut-side down, on to a white-hot griddle pan and char them nicely on both sides. Remove and put on a large platter or divide between four plates. Drizzle the peaches with a little olive oil and sprinkle with salt and pepper. Put your frisée or endive leaves into a bowl with enough of your goat's cheese dressing to coat the leaves, and toss together gently and beautifully. Grate a little Parmesan over the dressed salad and put a pile of it on each plate, next to the peach halves. Scatter over some baby mint leaves. A genius, simple combo!

PS Some warmed, crumbly walnuts would be delicious sprinkled over the top. Also a plate of Parma ham, Spanish serrano ham or speck would be great to serve next to this salad.

serves 4

for the goat's cheese dressing
2½oz crumbly goat's cheese
sea salt and freshly ground black pepper
5 tablespoons extra virgin olive oil
juice of 1 lemon
1 tablespoon walnut oil
1oz Parmesan cheese, freshly grated

2 large ripe peaches, halved and pits removed
extra virgin olive oil
sea salt and freshly ground black pepper
2 frisée or endive lettuces, dark outer leaves discarded, inner leaves washed and dried
freshly grated Parmesan cheese
a small bunch of fresh mint, smallest leaves picked

All day breakfast salad

I made this recipe up while I was sitting in the car the other day, thinking about warm salads. I'm not sure if the name does it any favors, but it's a winning combination all the same. It is the sort of thing you'd expect to eat in a gastropub with a pint of beer or at home for a lovely brunch.

Cut the endive into bite-sized pieces, wash them in plenty of cold water and spin-dry in a salad spinner. Mix them in a bowl with the snipped cress and place to one side.

To make a dressing, whisk the extra virgin olive oil, vinegar and mustard together and season lightly with salt and pepper. Bring a small saucepan of water to a simmer, ready to poach your eggs when you need to.

Heat a splash of oil in a large non-stick frying pan and fry the bacon and blood sausage for a couple of minutes. Add the bread chunks and fry until everything is crispy, then remove from the heat.

Poach your eggs in the simmering water for about 2 minutes. Now get your plates ready. Drop your hot and crispy bacon, blood sausage and bread chunks into the salad, mix quickly with enough dressing to coat everything, and divide on to your plates. With a slotted spoon, lift out the eggs one at a time and gently prod the yolk with the tip of your finger. It should be slightly soft to the touch – this means it will still be runny in the middle. Carefully place a poached egg on top of each plateful of salad and gently nick the egg yolk with a knife so the yolk seeps down into the leaves. Drizzle with a little extra olive oil, sprinkle with the chives and serve.

serves 2

1 small curly endive lettuce, outer green leaves discarded, yellowy white leaves washed and dried
2 packages of cress, snipped
8 tablespoons extra virgin olive oil
3 tablespoons white wine vinegar
1 teaspoon English mustard
sea salt and freshly ground black pepper
olive oil
4 slices of bacon, sliced into strips
a few slices of good-quality stale bread, torn up
3½oz good-quality blood sausage, sliced up
2 large free-range or organic eggs (the freshest you can get!)
a small bunch of fresh chives, chopped

Middle Eastern duck salad

Duck is quite a rich meat, and a full-on roast with all the trimmings can be a bit heavy. Here I've torn up a crispy slow-cooked duck with some arugula, herbs, fruit and nuts, Middle Eastern style, and suddenly it becomes light enough for a lazy summer lunch!

Preheat your oven to 350°F. Wash the duck and wipe it dry, inside and out, with paper towels. Mix a teaspoon of salt and a teaspoon of pepper with the cinnamon and season the duck with it, both on the inside and outside. Stuff the duck with the rosemary and the tangerine or orange halves – they will hold everything inside. Place the duck in a roasting pan, breast-side down, and roast in the preheated oven for an hour.

Take the pan out of the oven and spoon all the fat out of the roasting pan. (Don't forget to save it for your roast potatoes!) Turn the duck breast-side up and roast for another hour. Turn the oven up to 400°F for the last 15 minutes if the skin needs some extra crisping up.

Near the end of the cooking time for the duck, halve the pomegranates. Scoop the insides out of the preserved lemons and reserve. Chop the lemon skins roughly. Pick the parsley and mint leaves.

Remove the duck from the oven and leave it to cool down a little. When it's cool enough to handle, take the tangerine halves out with a spoon and set aside. Rest the duck on a clean serving dish while you prepare the rest of the salad.

Hold a pomegranate half, cut side down, over a bowl in the palm of your hand. Smack the skin side with a wooden spoon. The seeds should tumble out from the fruit and fall between your fingers into the bowl below. Do the same with the other 3 halves. Once you have all the pomegranate seeds, put two-thirds to one side and pulse the rest in a food processor with the juice from the tangerine halves and the insides of the preserved lemons. Pour through a sieve and mix in an equal amount of olive oil to make a dressing. Season it lightly with salt and pepper, and put to one side.

In a large mixing bowl, combine most of the parsley and mint leaves with the toasted almonds, the pistachios, the sour cherries, the skins of the preserved lemons, the whole pomegranate seeds and the lamb's lettuce. Toss in some of the dressing. Pull the duck meat off the bone, including the crispy skin (you can wear a pair of clean rubber gloves to do this if it's still a bit hot) and tear it up into chunks. Arrange the warm duck on a large serving plate, top with the dressed salad and the rest of the parsley and mint leaves, and drizzle with a little more dressing before serving.

serves 4

1 duck
sea salt and freshly ground black pepper
1 level tablespoon ground cinnamon
a sprig of fresh rosemary
1 tangerine or 1 small orange, halved
2 large pomegranates
6 small preserved lemons
a large bunch of fresh flat-leaf parsley
a large bunch of fresh mint
extra virgin olive oil
1¾oz flaked almonds, lightly toasted
1¾oz shelled pistachios, chopped
a handful of dried sour cherries or cranberries
2 large handfuls of lamb's lettuce, washed and dried

pasta
gnocchi and risotto

THE MAGIC OF PASTA

When I see someone discover the magic of making real pasta for the first time, it's the best feeling in the world. Take Lloyd, for example, a Fifteen student. He doesn't mind me telling you that when he first started at Fifteen he was a bit up and down, not turning up in the kitchen: 'It's too much like hard work; what are you trying to do to me?!' he used to say. Then one day he discovered how to make fresh pasta and risotto, and suddenly he was turning up at work early every morning to make his own. And then there's Aaron, another student, who makes beautiful pasta, and who even won *Restaurant* magazine's award for best pasta dish in the UK last year for his oxtail gnocchi. Working with the family of pasta, gnocchi and risotto is like being given a bunch of keys to unlock the door to a whole new world of recipes.

What is pasta made of?

If you're new to pasta you might be surprised to learn that all you need to make it are flour and liquid, and the kind of flour and liquid you choose will determine the color, texture, richness and flavor of your pasta.

Flour

There are two basic types of wheat flour available. One is made from grains with a high protein content – 'hard' wheat – and one from lower protein grains, or 'soft' wheat. The protein content of flour is important because, when mixed with water and kneaded, it's this protein that turns into gluten, which is what makes a dough elastic and springy. Hard-wheat flour, or 'strong' flour (also known as *farina di grano duro* in Italy), is mainly used to make bread, and soft-wheat flour (*farina di grano tenero*) is an all-purpose flour used for cooking and baking. When soft-wheat flour is ground and sieved extra fine, it is called pasta flour or tipo 00 (type double 0) and is used to make fresh pasta.

Semolina flour is creamy yellow in color, and is made from a different kind of hard wheat, called durum wheat. When it's ground finely it can be used to make fresh and dried pasta, and when ground more coarsely, it is used to make bread – especially in the Puglia region of southern Italy.

There are a couple of other flours you can use to make pasta: chestnut flour and polenta flour, which is fine ground dried corn. These don't produce as much gluten as wheat flours, though, so if you want to use them for pasta it's best to mix them with a good proportion of wheat flour to make sure it works.

Liquid

The simplest liquid to use is water, giving you a very basic plain pasta. Some people like to substitute some or all of the water with egg, as this gives pasta its richness and color (especially if you substitute some of the eggs with egg yolks). Finely puréed vegetables like spinach, red peppers or even herbs can be added to your pasta dough too as part of the liquid content. By doing this you can add lovely color and flavor.

Thoughts on flavors

One thing I've found when it comes to pasta is that you can never stop learning about it, and all the different things you can do with it. The more I travel in Italy, the more I realize that although there are guidelines, that's all they are. Nothing is really right or wrong, and everywhere you go people will tell you completely different things about how to make the dough, what ingredients to use, and how to shape it. And each person will tell you that their way is 'the only way'! So, what works best and what doesn't? Well, like everything in cooking, it's all to do with balancing flavors and textures. And sometimes, even when you think something shouldn't work, it will surprise you and work beautifully. Take the dish that Aaron dreamed up in the kitchen one night: tagliatelle with chicken livers and apricots soaked in vin santo. To be honest, I wasn't sure about it, but it was actually very clever, because, if you think about it, the French have that whole foie gras thing going on with sweet things: figs, wine, grapes . . . so Aaron was playing with combinations that he knew could work, and it was fantastic.

When I was deciding which recipes to put into this chapter, I got together with three graduates from the Fifteen course, Lloyd, Aaron and Anna – and, of course, my old mate Gennaro, who can't resist getting in on the act – and we had a big session preparing as many different shapes and styles of pasta as we could think of. Picture the scene (and the mayhem!): Gennaro was making a rabbit ragù for ravioli, the boys were playing around with pears, walnuts, taleggio and gorgonzola cheese, and Anna was stuck into crab and chilli, fennel and lemons . . . I love it when the students talk about what flavors they think will work. Aaron says he sees a kind of flavor map in his head now to help him out with what goes with what. There are some that are just meant to be, like peas and mint, cheese and fruit, pork and fennel, balsamic vinegar and rosemary.

Having talked a bit about flavors and fillings, the next thing we considered on our pasta day was how best to shape our filled pastas. I was trying to show Gennaro a little shape I'd come across in Italy called *cuscino* (cushion), which I wanted to fill with a creamy mixture of pears and taleggio, but Aaron reckoned that having a meltingly soft cheese filling inside a soft, silky pasta wouldn't work because when you cut into it the cheese would ooze out, and the whole thing would lose its character. His point was that if you have a shape like agnolotti or cappelletti, which forms a little cup of filling, it stands up strongly when you put it in your mouth. What could I say? He was right! So we decided to keep back the cuscino idea for a meaty ragù instead.

The way I look at it, all these balancing acts with flavors and textures are a bit like dressing according to the season: on a sunny day you want a thin jacket, and lighter, delicate seafood or zucchini-lemony things inside; on a cold day you go for a thicker jacket, and heavier, more robust fillings. I guess what I'm trying to say is that both dried and fresh pasta dishes are simple to get the hang of, but at the same time they demand the same concentration and focus as any other dish. There are some rules you should stick to, but then again there are others that can be broken. The only thing that matters is that the balance and the taste feel right, and that you enjoy what you are eating.

DRIED PASTA

Dried pasta is one of the most essential modern-day cupboard staples. I've lost count of the hundreds and hundreds of shapes that are offered these days, but don't be misled into thinking that dried pasta is any less credible or luxurious than fresh pasta. That's absolutely not true. The attention to detail in the making and shaping of dried pasta, and the quality of the wheat and even the local water with which the dough is made, all work towards making a superior and tastier product. Here are some things to think about next time you're cooking pasta. Even though you can't generalize, dried pasta is usually associated with oily or tomato sauce and is incredibly friendly with the world of fish.

- Look for good brands like De Cecco, Barilla or a supermarket's specialist selection. You get what you pay for, and you'll find the cheaper pastas not tasting as good and becoming flabby in texture when you cook them.

- Always, always salt your cooking water, otherwise it will affect not only the taste of your pasta but also the taste of the sauce.

- Cook your pasta in plenty of water (about 4½ quarts for every pound or so of pasta) and never add your pasta until the water is boiling fast.

- Immediately after dropping your pasta in the boiling water, mix it round with a spoon, and place a lid on the pan until the water comes back to the boil.

- There's no need to add olive oil to your cooking water – I've never met a good pasta chef who does this unless they're cooking a large quantity of filled pasta. Personally I never bother and think it's a bit of a cowboy trick. If you give the pasta the attention it deserves, it won't ever stick.

- You want to cook your pasta *al dente*. To do this, cook your pasta according to the package instructions and when it's nearly done, try a piece. When it's soft enough to eat but still has a little bite, drain in a colander.

- Try to avoid dried pasta with a really smooth, glossy finish. Try and get pasta with a matt, powdery finish, because it's slightly rougher and your sauce will stick to it better.

Real quick mussels spaghetti in a white wine and basil oil broth

For me this dish is about simplicity, something clean and fresh and not too complicated. Cooking mussels this way gives you an honest flavor and adding a little basil-flavored oil works very well. Real, fast cooking; feel-good food.

First, pick all the leaves off your bunches of basil and put the small inner leaves into a cup of cold water. Put the rest of the leaves into a pestle and mortar with the anchovy fillets and a good pinch of salt, and pound into a green paste. Add the juice of 1 lemon and about 8 tablespoons of extra virgin olive oil. You will end up with a lovely intense basil-flavored oil.

Pick through your mussels, and if you find any that are open, put them on a hard work surface and tap them sharply. If they don't close up immediately, chuck them away. Cook the spaghetti according to the package instructions in a large pan of salted boiling water. When cooked al dente, drain the pasta in a colander.

While your spaghetti is cooking, heat a large saucepan. When it's screaming hot, throw in your mussels and white wine and cover with a lid. Give a good shake and cook for a couple of minutes until all the mussels have opened (discard any that remain closed). You will have some lovely mussel juices in the pan. Toss in your cooked spaghetti, along with the basil oil. Stir around, adding extra lemon juice and seasoning to taste, then serve immediately, pouring over all the lovely green juices. Sprinkle over the chopped chilli and the drained small basil leaves.

Matt's wine suggestion: New Zealand white – Sauvignon Blanc

serves 4

2 large bunches of fresh basil
4 good-quality anchovy fillets in oil, drained
sea salt and freshly ground black pepper
juice of 2 lemons
extra virgin olive oil
1lb 2oz good-quality dried spaghetti
3½lb mussels, cleaned and debearded
a large wineglass of white wine
2–3 fresh red chillies, deseeded and finely chopped

Jools' favorite Saturday afternoon pasta

This is Jools' favorite quick Saturday afternoon pasta. Every time I make it, even though it only uses a tiny fraction of my brain and takes a few minutes in the pan, she seems to be really impressed with it, so on that basis I decided to put it in this book.

PS If you're going to make this, treat yourself and buy some good-quality tuna – it makes all the difference. And if you can find any fennel tops, they're great stirred in with the tomatoes.

Heat a splash of olive oil in a heavy-bottomed pan and cook the onion, chilli, cinnamon and basil stalks on a medium to low heat for 5 minutes until the onion has softened and is slightly sweet. Turn up the heat and add your tomatoes, tuna and a good pinch of salt. Break the tomatoes up using the back of a spoon, then bring to the boil and simmer for about 20 minutes. Taste for seasoning.

Meanwhile, cook the rigatoni in a pan of salted boiling water according to the package instructions. When al dente, drain the pasta in a colander, reserving some of the cooking water. Toss the pasta into the tuna and tomato sauce with the roughly torn basil leaves, a glug of olive oil, the lemon zest and juice and Parmesan and mix together well. Loosen the pasta with a little of the reserved cooking water if needed. Check the seasoning and serve immediately.

Matt's wine suggestion: Italian red – Dolcetto

serves 4

olive oil
1 red onion, peeled and
   finely chopped
1–2 fresh red chillies,
   deseeded and finely
   chopped
1 level teaspoon ground
   cinnamon
a bunch of fresh basil,
   leaves picked, stalks
   chopped
2 x 14oz cans good-quality
   plum tomatoes
2 x 10oz cans good-quality
   tuna in olive oil, drained
   and flaked
sea salt and freshly ground
   black pepper
1lb 2oz good-quality
   rigatoni or penne
zest and juice of 1–2
   lemons
a small handful of freshly
   grated Parmesan cheese

Macaroni cheese

This is my twist on the old-school frumpy dish of macaroni cheese. Using these four different cheeses together, each one with its own characteristics, works really well. For the classic finish, it has to be popped under the broiler to crisp up and go brown on top – lovely. Once you see how quick it is, you won't be making any bechamels or claggy old sauces for a long time.

Preheat your oven to 400°F. Cook the macaroni in a pan of salted boiling water 2 minutes short of the timing on the package instructions, then drain in a colander and reserve a little of the cooking water. Heat the butter in a large heavy-based frying pan. When it starts to foam, add the marjoram or oregano and fry for a minute until it starts to crisp up, then turn off the heat. Add your cooked pasta to the marjoram or oregano butter, along with a couple of spoonfuls of the reserved cooking water and the Parmesan, fontina or taleggio and mascarpone. Return to a medium heat and toss and stir around until most of the cheese has melted and you have a lovely gooey sauce – you may need to add a little more of the reserved cooking water. Season to taste, then tip it all into an earthenware dish. Grate over the nutmeg, tear over the mozzarella and sprinkle over the extra Parmesan. Bake the macaroni cheese in the preheated oven for about 10 minutes, finishing up with a quick whack under the broiler, until golden brown and crispy on top.

Matt's wine suggestion: Italian white – Verdicchio

serves 4–6

1lb 2oz good-quality
   macaroni
sea salt and freshly ground
   black pepper
a knob of butter
a small bunch of fresh
   marjoram or oregano,
   leaves picked
3½oz Parmesan cheese,
   freshly grated, plus extra
   for grating
3½oz fontina
   or taleggio cheese,
   roughly torn
3½oz mascarpone cheese
¼ of a nutmeg
a small ball of buffalo
   mozzarella cheese

Summertime tagliarini

When I worked at the River Café we used to make a similar dish to this using basil, oil, Parmesan and lemon juice. When I was in Italy last year I came across this recipe, which seems to be an older version and uses parsley instead of basil, and pinenuts to give the sauce a creaminess – almost like a blond pesto. It's incredibly quick to make, a great one for the summertime, and most people love it. Everyone should make this at least once.

Smash up half of the pinenuts to a paste, then put it into a big heatproof bowl with the rest of the whole pinenuts, the lemon juice and zest, the finely chopped parsley and the extra virgin olive oil. Stir and add the Parmesan and pecorino. What you should have now is a reasonably thick sauce, which you should think of more as a dressing, so taste it and think about how the different flavors are coming through. I want you to balance the flavors so you end up with something quite zingy because, as the sauce heats up and the cheese melts, the flavor of the lemon will calm down a lot. Season with some freshly ground black pepper. Taste it and if you think you haven't got the balance right, simply add a little more oil and Parmesan.

Put a large pot of salted water on to boil for your pasta. Sit the sauce bowl on top of the pan while the water's heating up – this will take the chill out of the sauce and warm it through slightly. When the water starts to boil, remove the bowl and add your pasta to the water. Cook it according to the package instructions then drain in a colander, reserving a little of the cooking water. Toss the pasta with the sauce and a little of the reserved cooking water to help loosen it up a bit. The heat from the pasta will melt the cheese, allowing all the lovely sauce to coat it. If you find the sauce is too thick then add a little more water. It's not supposed to be claggy, thick and miserable, but incredibly silky, fresh and fragrant. Have one last taste to balance the flavors, and serve with a little extra Parmesan shaved over the top and a sprinkle of parsley leaves. Eat immediately.

Matt's wine suggestion: Australian white – Semillon

serves 4

4oz pinenuts
juice and zest of 2 lemons
a large bunch of fresh flat-leaf parsley, leaves picked, half finely chopped and half left whole
1 cup minus 1 tablespoon extra virgin olive oil
5½oz Parmesan cheese, freshly grated, plus extra for shaving
1¾oz pecorino cheese, freshly grated
sea salt and freshly ground black pepper
1lb 2oz good-quality tagliarini or tagliatelle

Super squid linguine

This is a great one to eat outside in the summer with a large glass of Spanish white wine. If you're lucky enough to have a good local fishmonger, ask him to open the squid out for you, score it in a criss-cross pattern and slice it into fine strips. Then when you get home you can quickly marinate the squid, put the pasta on right away and get your frying pan on for the squid. As soon as the pasta has cooked, the sauce will be done too – so quick and absolutely delicious.

In a bowl, mix the squid with the garlic, most of the lemon zest and chilli, half the lemon juice, the parsley stalks and leaves and a splash of extra virgin olive oil, and leave to gently marinate for 15 minutes at room temperature while you bring a large pan of salted water to the boil. Cook your linguine according to the package instructions. Meanwhile, put a large frying pan on a high heat. Once the pan is hot, add the squid and the marinade, and toss around vigorously. After a minute the squid will begin to curl up and you will start to smell it cooking. This is the time to add your peas and wine. Give it a stir and cook for another 3 to 4 minutes to allow the sauce to reduce slightly and the flavors to come out.

Once it's cooked al dente, drain your linguine in a colander, reserving a little of the cooking water, and immediately toss it in the pan with the squid along with a few spoonfuls of the reserved cooking water, a couple of generous glugs of extra virgin olive oil, another squeeze of lemon juice, the reserved lemon zest, some salt and pepper and the chopped mint. Serve! Eat!

Matt's wine suggestion: Spanish white – Verdejo

serves 4

14oz squid, cleaned, opened out, scored and finely sliced (see page 286) into ¼ inch strips
2 cloves of garlic, peeled and finely sliced
zest of 2 lemons, plus juice of 1 lemon
1–2 fresh red chillies, deseeded and sliced very finely into long strips
a handful of fresh flat-leaf parsley, stalks and leaves finely chopped
extra virgin olive oil
sea salt and freshly ground black pepper
1lb 2oz good-quality linguine
3 handfuls of frozen peas
a large wineglass of white wine
a small handful of fresh mint leaves, chopped

Proper blokes' sausage fusilli

This is a real blokey, gutsy yet simple pasta dish – but saying that, girls tend to like it as well! It hasn't really got a sauce of any description because all the flavor that comes out of the ingredients will stick to the pasta and that's enough. I will even go so far as to say that this is one of my top ten pasta dishes! Remember to buy the best sausages you can afford – if you get cheap sausages it just won't work.

Bash up the fennel seeds and chillies in a pestle and mortar or Flavor Shaker until coarsely crushed, then put to one side. Heat a splash of olive oil in a heavy-bottomed frying pan. Squeeze the meat out of the sausage skins and put into the pan, really breaking it up using the back of a spoon. Fry for a few minutes until the meat starts to color and the fat has rendered slightly, then crush it once more so it resembles coarse mince. Add the bashed-up fennel seeds and chillies and cook on a medium heat for around 10 minutes until the meat becomes crisp, golden brown and slightly caramelized.

Stir in your oregano, then pour in the white wine and allow it to reduce by half. Add the lemon zest and juice. Turn the heat down to low while you cook your pasta in a large pan of salted boiling water according to the package instructions. When the pasta has cooked al dente, drain it in a colander, reserving some of the cooking water, and toss it in the pan with your sausagemeat. Coat the pasta in all the lovely flavors then add the butter, Parmesan, chopped parsley and a few spoonfuls of the reserved cooking water. This will give you a lovely loose, shiny sauce. Taste and check for seasoning, then serve immediately with a little extra grated Parmesan sprinkled over the top.

Matt's wine suggestion: Italian red – Valpolicella Classico

serves 4

2 heaped teaspoons fennel
  seeds
2 dried red chillies,
  crumbled
olive oil
1lb 6oz good-quality
  coarse Italian or other
  high-quality sausages
1 tablespoon dried oregano
a wineglass of white wine
zest and juice of 1 lemon
1lb 2oz good-quality fusilli
  or penne
sea salt and freshly ground
  black pepper
a couple of knobs of butter
a handful of freshly grated
  Parmesan cheese, plus
  extra for serving
a small bunch of fresh
  flat-leaf parsley, leaves
  picked and chopped

Lovely crab linguine

Crab linguine is a bit of a classic on the menu at Fifteen – it's hard to take it off because people want to order it all the time! Crab has a delicate flavor, so what you do with it in a dish has to be well considered. However, flavors like fennel, chilli, a delicate extra virgin olive oil and lemon juice really help to make this dish an absolute winner. Try and get hold of freshly picked crabmeat from your fishmonger as opposed to those packets of pre-picked crab, as the meat will have lost most of its sweetness and will be much drier. Or, if you want to, try cooking and picking your own crab, which isn't hard at all (see page 268).

In a pestle and mortar smash up your fennel seeds, then put them into a big heatproof bowl. Add most of your chopped chilli, the lemon zest and juice, your finely shaved fennel and the extra virgin olive oil. Mix the white and brown crabmeat together and fold into the mixture. Taste and season with salt and pepper if need be. Drizzle with a little more extra virgin olive oil, then fill your pasta pan with cold, salted water, put the bowl on top and bring to the boil over a high heat. Give the crab mixture a little stir every now and then – it will start to warm up as the water comes to the boil. Now's a good time to prepare your asparagus. Shave each spear lengthways with a speed peeler and put in a little bowl.

Carefully put the crab mixture to one side (the bowl will be hot!) and add the linguine or spaghetti to the pan of boiling water. Cook the pasta according to the package instructions, then drain it in a colander, reserving a little of the cooking water. It's important to work quickly at this point, otherwise it won't be hot enough when you come to eat it, so don't hang about! Toss the hot steaming pasta and crab mixture together, adding a little of the reserved cooking water to lighten the sauce if needed – you don't want it to be too stiff. Have a final taste – you might need to add a little more lemon juice or seasoning.

Serve the pasta either on one large platter or divide it between plates, then finish it off by flicking over the reserved, chopped chilli and the fennel tops. Dress your shaved asparagus with a little squeeze of lemon juice, a tiny glug of extra virgin olive oil and a pinch of salt, then sprawl it all over the top. Serve immediately.

Matt's wine suggestion: Italian white – Vernaccia di San Gimignano

serves 4

1 heaped teaspoon fennel seeds
2–3 fresh red chillies, deseeded and very finely chopped
zest and juice of 1 lemon, plus a little extra juice
1 fennel bulb, outer leaves trimmed, halved and very finely shaved with a speed peeler, herby tops reserved
½ cup plus 2 tablespoons extra virgin olive oil, plus extra for drizzling
14oz freshly picked white crabmeat
5½oz freshly picked brown crabmeat
sea salt and freshly ground black pepper
a bunch of medium-sized asparagus, trimmed
1lb 2oz good-quality linguine or spaghetti

Honeycomb cannelloni

This is a fantastic cannelloni recipe with a little twist in the tail. Rather than laying the cannelloni tubes on their sides, as is traditional, I've decided to stack them facing up in a snug-fitting pan so they look a bit like a honeycomb pattern. All topped off with a white sauce and cheese, baked in the oven. Absolutely delicious and something a bit different!

PS The shin stew on page 151 would be a great alternative to your vegetable sauce for this cannelloni.

The first thing to do is find yourself a casserole pan or earthenware dish that will snugly hold all of your cannelloni standing upright, as shown in the picture opposite. I used one that's 8 inches in diameter and 5 inches deep, if you want to be precise – and in this recipe, being precise helps!

Preheat the oven to 375ºF. To make your ragù, put your dried porcini in a bowl and just cover them with boiling water. Leave to soak for 5 minutes. Meanwhile, put a large heavy-based saucepan on a medium heat and add the olive oil, carrots, celery, onion and leek. Cook gently for 8 to 10 minutes, then add the garlic and Portobello mushrooms. Remove the porcini from the bowl, add them to the pan and cook for a further 5 minutes until the veg has softened. Strain the porcini liquor through a sieve and add this to the pan with a large wineglass of water. Allow the liquid to reduce slightly, then tip in your tomatoes and add your chopped basil stalks. Season with salt and pepper, and bring to the boil. Simmer for up to 45 minutes, until you have a thick, rich vegetable ragù. Tear in the basil leaves.

In a saucepan, heat a splash of oil and add the spinach, stir, then leave to wilt down. Season with salt, pepper and a grating of nutmeg and put aside.

To make your quick white sauce, all you have to do is mix the cream, crème fraîche, anchovies and grated Parmesan. Then check the seasoning and that's it! Now get out that dish or pan you located at the beginning of the recipe and spoon in ½ inch of the cheese sauce. Sprinkle with grated Parmesan and top with the spinach. Carefully ladle over half your vegetable ragù and stand your cannelloni tubes in it. Press the tubes down into the sauce with the palm of your hand – the sauce will come up and half fill the tubes. Spoon over the rest of the ragù, smoothing it down into the holes. Pour over the remaining cheese sauce, sprinkle over some more grated Parmesan, drizzle with olive oil and bake in the preheated oven for 45 minutes until golden and bubbly. Bloomin' tasty.

Matt's wine suggestion: Italian white – Pinot Bianco

serves 6–8

sea salt and freshly ground
  black pepper
Parmesan cheese, for grating
1lb 2oz good-quality cannelloni
  tubes
olive oil

for the vegetable ragù
a small handful of dried porcini
½ cup plus 3 tablespoons olive
  oil
3 carrots, peeled and diced
4 sticks of celery, trimmed and
  finely diced
1 large red onion, peeled and
  finely diced
1 leek, trimmed and outer
  leaves discarded, finely diced
2 cloves of garlic, peeled and
  sliced
5 Portobello mushrooms, finely
  chopped
5 x 14oz cans good-quality
  plum tomatoes
a large bunch of fresh basil,
  leaves picked, stalks finely
  chopped

for the spinach
1½lb fresh spinach
nutmeg, for grating

for a quick white sauce
1 cup light cream
17½fl oz crème fraîche
4 good-quality anchovy fillets in
  oil, drained and finely
  chopped
a handful of grated Parmesan
  cheese

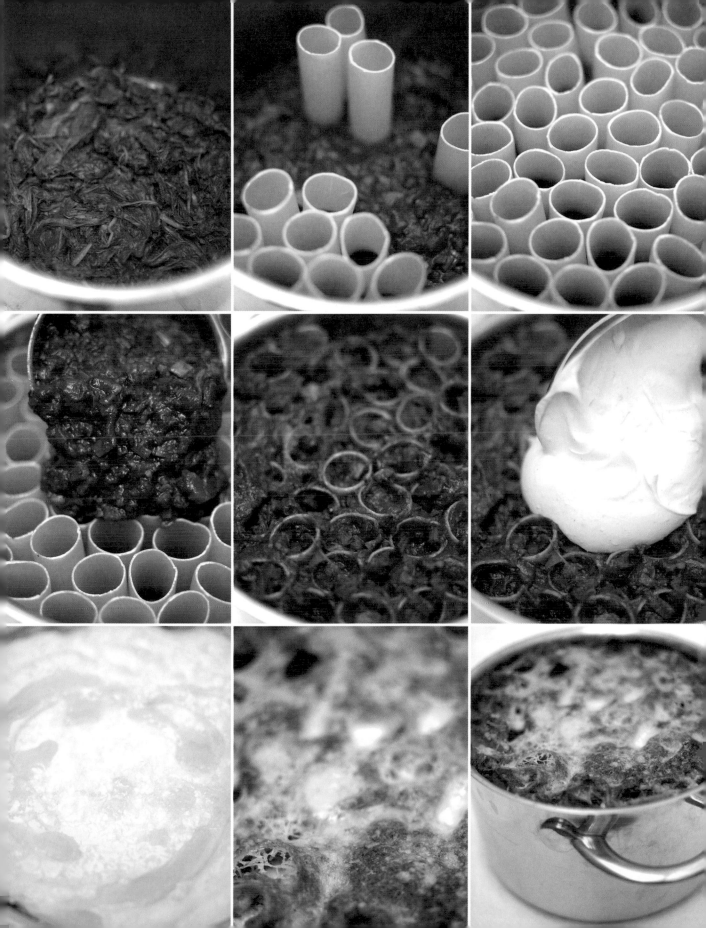

Fantastic fish lasagne

This is a Venetian-style baked fish dish that is really special. It's like an Italian version of fish pie, using pasta instead of potatoes. The Italians are usually very strict about not using fish and cheese together, but when it comes to this they do let a little bit of Parmesan slip in to make it fully work (but they often won't admit to this as deep down they feel it's a bit naughty!).

Preheat your oven to 350°F. Melt a quarter of the butter in a large, deep saucepan over a medium heat. Add the onion, carrots, celery and fennel and sweat slowly with a lid on for 10 minutes. Stack the parsley stalks and bay sprig together, wrap them in the pancetta and tie with a piece of string. Add to the pot of vegetables with the shrimp heads and cook for about 15 minutes until the vegetables are soft but not colored, and the shrimp heads have turned pink. Add the wine and boil for a few minutes until reduced. Pour in the milk and bring slowly back to the boil. As soon as the milk boils, turn off the heat and cover with a lid to let all the flavors infuse.

Heat the rest of the butter in another deep saucepan and when melted and bubbling, add the flour and stir together until smooth. With a pair of tongs, fish the shrimp heads and herb bundle out of the hot milk, squeezing any liquid that's left in them back into the milk before throwing them away. Add a ladleful of hot milk and vegetables to the butter/flour mix and stir until absorbed. Add another ladleful, stir as before, then add another, until all the milk and vegetables have been added and you have a thick white sauce. Bring to the boil gently, stirring all the time, and simmer gently for a few seconds to cook out the flour. Take off the heat and season with salt, pepper and the nutmeg. If you see any whiskers that have come off the shrimp, fish them out now. Check the instructions on your pasta package in case you need to blanch the sheets for a minute in boiling salted water.

Ladle a quarter of the sauce into a large lasagne dish and smooth out evenly, making sure it goes right into the corners. Scatter with a third of the fish, a third of the tomatoes, a third of the chopped parsley and about a quarter of the Parmesan, and cover with a layer of lasagne sheets. Build two more layers of filling and pasta, spread the last of your sauce over the top sheets of pasta and sprinkle with the last of the Parmesan. Whiz the breadcrumbs, parsley leaves and lemon zest in the food processor and sprinkle over the top.

Cover the lasagne with aluminum foil and bake in the preheated oven for 45 minutes, removing the foil after half an hour. Make sure the lasagne is piping hot all the way through before serving with a little dressed arugula.

Matt's wine suggestion: Italian white – Soave

serves 4–6

8 tablespoons butter
1 white onion, peeled and
  finely chopped
2 medium carrots, peeled and
  finely chopped
3 sticks of celery, trimmed
  and finely chopped
1 small fennel bulb, trimmed
  and finely chopped
a small bunch of fresh
  parsley, leaves picked and
  chopped, stalks reserved
a sprig of fresh bay leaves
a rasher of pancetta or bacon
12 whole fresh shrimp, heads
  removed and reserved
½ cup white wine
3 cups milk
½ cup all purpose flour
sea salt and freshly ground
  black pepper
½ a nutmeg, grated
1lb 6oz fish fillets (try cod,
  red mullet, sea bass, bream,
  salmon), skinned and cut
  into small chunks
10½oz cherry tomatoes, cut
  in half
2½oz freshly grated
  Parmesan cheese
9oz lasagne sheets, dried or
  fresh
a bunch of arugula, washed
  and dried

for the breadcrumbs
scant cup breadcrumbs
a small bunch of fresh flat-
  leaf parsley, leaves picked
zest of 1 lemon

Gorgeous slow-cooked duck pasta

The sweet and sour nature of this dish is achieved by using flavors like orange, tomatoes, sultanas and red wine together – not pineapples and cheap vinegar like you might get in your local Chinese restaurant. At Fifteen we love to serve this dish with pappardelle, tagliatelle or, as in the picture here, little rings of pasta called *occhi di lupo*, which literally translates as 'wolf's eyes'. The meat sauce is equally delicious and comforting served as a stew with polenta or even mashed potatoes, so do have a go at making it.

Preheat your oven to 350°F. Rub your duck all over with olive oil, season generously with salt and pepper and push the orange quarters inside the cavity. Place the duck breast-side down in a roasting pan in the oven for 2 hours, turning it in the juices every 30 minutes until the skin goes thin and crispy and the meat is tender and delicious with a slight fragrance of orange. Remove the duck from the tray and put it to one side to cool down for 15 minutes. During cooking, a lot of fat will come out of the duck so pour it into a jar (making sure it's just the fat and no meat juices) and save it for roasting your potatoes another day.

To make your sweet and sour sauce, pour a little glug of olive oil into a large pot and fry the diced pancetta in it until lightly golden, then add the onion, carrots, celery, rosemary, cinnamon and garlic and fry slowly for 10 minutes until the veg have softened. Add the tomatoes to the pan and pour in the red wine. Simmer slowly, allowing the sauce to blip away nicely, for another 25 minutes, then pull all the duck meat from the bone, shred it and add it to the tomato sauce. Simmer for another half an hour, adjusting the consistency if need be by adding a little chicken stock or water. Remove the cinnamon stick, taste the sauce, correct the seasoning and throw in your sultanas and pinenuts.

Put your pasta in a pot of salted boiling water and cook it according to the package instructions, then drain in a colander, reserving some of the cooking water. Toss the pasta into the sauce, mix well, then remove from the heat and stir in the butter, Parmesan, parsley, orange zest and juice and a good splash of vinegar. Loosen the sauce with some reserved cooking water if you need to. Check once more for seasoning, then serve immediately, either on one large platter or on individual plates, with another grating of Parmesan.

Matt's wine suggestion: Italian red – Barbera

serves 4–6

1 duck
olive oil
sea salt and freshly ground black
  pepper
1 orange, quartered
1lb 6oz occhi di lupo
  or rigatoni
2 knobs of butter
a large handful of freshly grated
  Parmesan cheese, plus extra
  for serving
a small bunch of fresh flat-leaf
  parsley, finely chopped
zest and juice of 1 orange
red wine vinegar

for the agro dolce sauce
olive oil
6 slices of pancetta, finely diced
1 red onion, peeled and fincly diced
2 carrots, peeled and finely
  chopped
2 sticks of celery, trimmed and
  finely diced
6 sprigs of fresh rosemary, leaves
  picked and finely chopped
1 stick of cinnamon
4 cloves of garlic, peeled and finely
  sliced
2 x 14oz cans good-quality plum
  tomatoes
½ a 750ml bottle of fruity red wine
  like Valpolicella or Barbera
optional: chicken stock
a handful of sultanas
a large handful of pinenuts

FRESH PASTA

You have to have a go at making fresh pasta – think of it as a bit of fun. Just follow the simple but strict guidelines, and you'll see that it's incredibly quick to make, even for four or more people.

Although most areas of Italy make fresh pasta, it's more common in the north and even though you can't generalize too much, fresh pasta is usually associated with creamy,

buttery sauces; meaty, stewy sauces; filled pastas like ravioli and baked pastas like lasagne.

Fresh pasta is just as stylish, as luxurious and as flexible as dried pasta, but instead of buying into pre-made shapes, this time you're in the driving seat, for better or for worse. Good luck!

● Once you've mastered fresh pasta, try adding finely chopped herbs, puréed cooked spinach, beetroot etc to your dough to flavor and color your pasta.

● Get yourself a little water spritzer from your local garden centre and use it to stick your pasta together when you're making ravioli. It's far easier and more effective than using

a brush, which is what I was always told to use.

- You can keep it covered on a tray, either at room temperature or in the fridge, for a maximum of four hours. Make sure you dust the tray with ground semolina flour though; this way the pasta won't get stuck in the tray, breaking the pasta and ruining your hard work.

- Once you've made your fresh pasta, it can be dried to preserve it. However, I would be more inclined to freeze it. Many good restaurants make fresh pasta once a week, freeze it, and then literally cook from frozen in boiling salted water – it cooks a treat.

- Just as with dried pasta, cook your fresh pasta in plenty of

salted boiling water and give it a good stir as soon as you've dropped your pasta in.

- There's no need to add olive oil to the cooking water. Pasta cooked with some attention will never stick.

A basic recipe for fresh egg pasta dough

Try to get hold of tipo 00 flour – this is a very finely sieved flour which is normally used for making egg pasta or cakes. In Italy it's called *farina di grano tenero*, which means 'tender' or 'soft' flour.

Place the flour on a board or in a bowl. Make a well in the center and crack the eggs into it. Beat the eggs with a fork until smooth. Using the tips of your fingers, mix the eggs with the flour, incorporating a little at a time, until everything is combined. Knead the pieces of dough together – with a bit of work and some love and attention they'll all bind together to give you one big, smooth lump of dough!

You can also make your dough in a food processor if you've got one. Just bung everything in, whiz until the flour looks like breadcrumbs, then tip the mixture on to your work surface and bring the dough together into one lump, using your hands.

Once you've made your dough you need to knead and work it with your hands to develop the gluten in the flour, otherwise your pasta will be flabby and soft when you cook it, instead of springy and al dente.

There's no secret to kneading. You just have to bash the dough about a bit with your hands, squashing it into the table, reshaping it, pulling it, stretching it, squashing it again. It's quite hard work, and after a few minutes it's easy to see why the average Italian grandmother has arms like Frank Bruno! You'll know when to stop – it's when your pasta starts to feel smooth and silky instead of rough and floury. Then all you need to do is wrap it in plastic wrap and put it in the fridge to rest for at least half an hour before you use it. Make sure the plastic wrap covers it well or it will dry out and go crusty round the edges (this will give you crusty lumps through your pasta when you roll it out, and nobody likes crusty lumps!).

serves 4

5 cups (1lb 6oz) tipo 00 or
  pasta flour
6 large free-range or organic
  eggs or 12 yolks

How to roll your pasta

First of all, if you haven't got a pasta machine it's not the end of the world! All the mammas I met while travelling round Italy rolled pasta with their trusty rolling pins and they wouldn't even consider having a pasta machine in the house! When it comes to rolling, the main problem you'll have is getting the pasta thin enough to work with. It's quite difficult to get a big lump of dough rolled out in one piece, and you need a very long rolling pin to do the job properly. The way around this is to roll lots of small pieces of pasta rather than a few big ones. You'll be rolling your pasta into a more circular shape than the long rectangular shapes you'll get from a machine, and they won't look like the step-by-step pics on the next few pages, but use your head and you'll be all right!

If using a machine to roll your pasta, make sure it's clamped firmly to a clean work surface before you start (use the longest available work surface you have). If your surface is cluttered with bits of paper, the kettle, the bread box, the kids' homework and stuff like that, shift all this out of the way for the time being. It won't take a minute, and starting with a clear space to work in will make things much easier, I promise.

- Dust your work surface with some pasta flour, take a lump of pasta dough the size of a large orange and press it out flat with your fingertips. Set the pasta machine at its widest setting – and roll the lump of pasta dough through it. Lightly dust the pasta with flour if it sticks at all. Click the machine down a setting and roll the pasta dough through again. Fold the pasta in half, click the pasta machine back up to the widest setting and roll the dough through again. Repeat this process five or six times. It might seem like you're getting nowhere, but in fact you're working the dough, and once you've folded it and fed it through the rollers a few times, you'll feel the difference. It'll be smooth as silk and this means you're making wicked pasta!

- Now it's time to roll the dough out properly, working it through all the settings on the machine, from the widest down to around the narrowest. Lightly dust both sides of the pasta with a little flour every time you run it through. When you've got down to the narrowest setting, to give yourself a tidy sheet of pasta, fold the pasta in half lengthways, then in half again, then in half again once more you've got a square-ish piece of dough. Turn it 90 degrees and feed it through the machine at the widest setting. As you roll it down through the settings for the last time, you should end up with a lovely rectangular silky sheet of dough with straight sides – just like a real pro! If your dough is a little cracked at the edges, fold it in half just once, click the machine back two settings and feed it through again. That should sort things out.Whether you're rolling by hand or by machine you'll need to know when to stop. If you're making pasta like tagliatelle, lasagne or stracchi you'll need to roll the pasta down to between the thickness of a beer mat and a playing card; if you're making a stuffed pasta like ravioli or tortellini, you'll need to roll it down slightly thinner or to the point where you can clearly see your hand or lines of newsprint through it.

Once you've rolled your pasta the way you want it, you need to shape or cut it right away. Pasta dries much quicker than you think, so whatever recipe you're doing, don't leave it more than a minute or two before cutting or shaping it. You can lay over a damp clean tea towel which will stop it from drying.

Pappardelle, tagliatelle and tagliarini

- Cut your sheet of pasta into 8 inch lengths. Dust well with flour.
- Fold in half, fold in half again and then once more, dusting with flour each time.
- Cut into ¾ inch for pappardelle, ½ inch for tagliatelle, ¼ inch for tagliarini.
- Make a cage with your fingers and shake until the pasta separates out.

Caramelle

- Cut the pasta into 4 x 2½ inch rectangles.
- Place a teaspoon of filling in the middle and brush lightly with water.
- Roll up and pinch hard to secure at each end.
- Keep on a flour-dusted tray in the fridge until you need them, and try to cook them as fresh as possible.

Cushions

- Cut the pasta into equal-sized 4 inch squares.
- Place 2 teaspoons of filling along one half of each square, making sure you leave a ½ inch gap around the edges. Brush the edges with water.
- Fold the shape in half, covering the filling.
- Use your fingers to push any air out and to seal the edges. Your cushions should look like little pillows.

Ravioli and raviolini

- Cut the pasta into a 6x12 inch strip.
- On one half of the pasta strip place 4 teaspoons of filling for ravioli, or 9 half-teaspoons for raviolini, in a grid.
- Lightly brush the pasta with water.
- Fold the other half of the pasta over and mould it carefully around the filling on the bottom sheet, pushing out any air bubbles.
- Cut into squares with a knife or crinkle cutter, or into circles with a pastry cutter.

Tortellini

- Cut the pasta sheet into 4 inch squares.
- Place a teaspoon of filling in the center of each one.
- Brush the pasta lightly with water.
- Fold the square in half, corner to corner, enclosing the filling.
- Mold carefully around the filling, pushing out any air bubbles.
- With the flat edge of the tortellini facing you, roll once towards the tip.
- Fold the two side flaps around the filling and squeeze together.

Stained-glass lasagne

- Sprinkle half of your pasta sheet with a large handful of herbs (fennel tops, flat-leaf parsley and sage leaves are great).
- Fold the sheet over, sandwiching the herbs between the pasta, and run through your pasta machine.
- Cut into 8 lasagne-sized pieces.

Pappardelle with a ragù of tiny meatballs

This is a fantastic, classic, easy-pleaser of a dish. Make this for a dinner party or for your family and you'll be incredibly popular! The brilliant thing about it is that you can make the meatballs, the pasta and the sauce in advance, so when it comes to putting it all together it can be quite quick. If you're making fresh pasta, try cutting it out using a crinkly cutter as I've done in this picture – I think it just takes it into another league. Of course you can use dried pappardelle or tagliatelle instead.

When it comes to the meatballs, I would suggest that you ask your butcher to grind the beef in front of you; that way you know exactly what you're getting and that it's nice and fresh. The reason I mention this is because very often (and I'm not for a minute suggesting your butcher is a con-man) ground meat gets treated a little bit like a dustbin for random cuts of meat. So if you can be specific about what you want, you might as well be. Or you can buy the cuts of meat yourself and pulse them up in your food processor when you get home.

If you're making fresh pappardelle do this first (see page 88) and lay it out on a floured pan while you get on with the meatballs and tomato sauce. To make your meatballs, mix and scrunch together all the meatball ingredients in your hands and shape into marble-sized balls. When rolling the meatballs, run your hands under cold water every now and then – it will help to make the meatballs dense and hold their shape better. Place them in a pan and put in the fridge while you make your tomato sauce.

Get a pan on the heat and add a glug of olive oil to it. Gently fry the garlic, basil stalks and the whole chilli, then add the tomatoes and red wine vinegar. Season with salt and pepper then gently simmer for half an hour.

Heat up a little olive oil in a frying pan and throw in your meatballs. Cook until they've got a really good color on them, then add them to your tomato sauce. Remove the chilli from the sauce and check for seasoning. Continue to simmer for 10 to 15 minutes. Meanwhile, if you're using dried pasta, bring a large pan of salted water to the boil and cook according to the package instructions. Otherwise, when your meatballs are almost done, cook your fresh pasta for 2 to 3 minutes until al dente. Drain the pappardelle in a colander, reserving a little of the cooking water, then toss it in the meatball sauce. Add the knob of butter, the Parmesan and tear over half the basil leaves. Now, toss around to coat the pasta. Add a little bit of cooking water to loosen the sauce if needed. When it's superb, serve on a big platter or divide up between individual plates, scatter with the rest of the basil leaves, grate over some Parmesan and serve as soon as possible.

Matt's wine suggestion: Italian red – Sangiovese

serves 4–6

1 x basic pasta dough recipe (see page 84) or use 1lb 6oz good-quality dried pappardelle
a knob of butter
a handful of freshly grated Parmesan cheese

for the meatballs
1lb good-quality coarse ground beef (chuck, skirt or brisket)
1–2 dried red chillies, crumbled
a pinch of ground cinnamon
½ a nutmeg, grated
3 cloves of garlic, peeled and finely chopped
sea salt and freshly ground black pepper
1 large free-range or organic egg
a handful of freshly grated Parmesan cheese, plus extra for serving
zest of 1 lemon

for the tomato sauce
olive oil
2–3 cloves of garlic, peeled and chopped
a bunch of fresh basil, leaves picked, stalks chopped
1 fresh red chilli, pierced with the tip of a knife
2 x 14oz cans good-quality plum tomatoes
a little swig of red wine vinegar
sea salt and freshly ground black pepper

Black angel tagliarini

This is called 'black angel tagliarini' because the scallops are supposed to look like angels in the black pasta . . . ah, you know what the Italians are like – they're romantic! It's one of the simplest pastas you can make and it looks amazing. Black pasta is made using squid ink and it doesn't really taste any different from normal pasta. You can have a go at making your own by using squid ink from your fishmonger's or an Italian deli. Or you can buy dried black pasta ready-made from good specialty shops or supermarkets. The sauce pretty much comes together in 3 or 4 minutes so there's no excuse for not trying it! The one thing to remember, though, is that you only want to make it with lovely fresh scallops and not the piddly little things you sometimes see sitting around in salted water, as these taste like rubber. You need to buy freshly shelled scallops, or ones that are still in their shells.

To make your own fresh black tagliarini follow the instructions on page 88, adding the squid ink with your eggs. Lay the dough out on a floured pan and put it to one side. Bring a large pan of salted water to the boil and leave the water on the boil, ready for the fresh pasta to be chucked in as the scallops are cooking. If you're using dried pasta, put it on now as it'll take a bit longer to cook.

To make the sauce, put a large casserole-type pan or frying pan on a high heat and put 2 or 3 glugs of delicate extra virgin olive oil into it. Season your scallops, then, when the oil is nice and hot, add them to the pan in one flat layer so that each slice takes on a nice bit of color. Shake the pan around and add the chillies, garlic and half of your chopped parsley. Now is the moment to cook your fresh pasta for 2 to 3 minutes until al dente. Once the scallops have had a good couple of minutes, and have a little color on them, add the white wine and allow to reduce a little. Add the butter and reduce for another minute, then just turn the heat down to low while your pasta finishes off. Drain the pasta in a colander, reserving a little of the cooking water, then toss it into the pan with the scallops and a squeeze of lemon juice so every piece gets coated in the lovely white wine sauce and juices.

Now get everyone around the table. If the pasta looks a little dry then add some of the reserved cooking water to loosen it slightly. Toss the pasta with the rest of the parsley, then serve immediately on a large platter in the middle of the table or on individual plates.

Matt's wine suggestion: French white – Chablis

serves 4

1 x basic pasta dough recipe (see page 84) and 2 packets of squid ink or 1lb 2oz good-quality dried black spaghetti
sea salt and freshly ground black pepper
delicate extra virgin olive oil
8 large fresh scallops, sliced in half lengthways and scored
1–2 fresh red chillies, deseeded and finely chopped
3 cloves of garlic, peeled and finely sliced
a large bunch of fresh flat-leaf parsley, leaves and stalks very finely chopped
2 wineglasses of white wine
3 large knobs of butter
½ a lemon

Pappardelle with wild rabbit, olives and marjoram

This is a beautiful way to cook rabbit – whether as a stew or as a pasta sauce. Once you've made the sauce you could even serve it with gnocchi or stir it into a risotto towards the end of cooking. I love it because it's so flexible and utterly delicious. Try and get hold of wild rabbit if you can, as they have a better flavor. And it's best to marinate the meat overnight if you have the time.

Preferably the night before, but at least 4 hours before you start cooking, mix the marinade ingredients together and rub them over your rabbit pieces, then leave to marinate in the fridge (you can even leave the meat in the marinade for up to 2 days in the fridge if you want a stronger flavor).

On the day, preheat your oven to 350°F. In an appropriately sized heavy-bottomed ovenproof saucepan, heat a splash of olive oil with a knob of butter. Season your rabbit with salt and pepper, then add to the pan and gently brown the pieces for a couple of minutes on each side until golden. Add the thyme, rosemary and garlic cloves, give everything a quick stir and pour in the wine – you want the meat to be almost covered. Put a lid on the pan and place it in the preheated oven for 2 hours or until the meat pulls easily away from the bone. When cooked, remove from the oven and put to one side to allow the meat to cool.

While the rabbit is cooking, make your pappardelle (see page 88), lay it out on floured pans and set to one side.

Once the meat has cooled, take it out of the pan. Use your hands to shred all the meat away from the bones into roughly 1 inch pieces and discard the bones. Remove the thyme, rosemary and garlic cloves from the pan, then put it on the heat to reduce the cooking liquor until slightly thickened. Turning the heat down to low, stir your shredded rabbit, olives and marjoram into the sauce and season to taste.

Bring a large pan of salted water to a boil and cook your fresh pappardelle for 2 to 3 minutes until al dente (or, if using dried, according to the package instructions), then drain in a colander, reserving a little of the cooking water. Turn up the heat under the meat sauce and toss the cooked pappardelle in it. Taste one last time for salt and pepper, turn the heat off and add the Parmesan and remaining knob of butter. Sometimes I like to add a tiny bit of orange or lemon zest at this point to lift the flavor of the stew, but don't hang about too long – do it quickly! You may also need to stir in a few spoonfuls of the reserved cooking water to loosen the sauce. Serve as soon as you can with the reserved thyme leaves scattered over the top, either on a large platter in the middle of the table or on individual plates.

Matt's wine suggestion: Italian red – Nebbiolo

serves 6

for the marinade
a small bunch of fresh
   thyme, leaves picked
6 cloves of garlic, unpeeled
   and squashed
a glug of olive oil
zest of 1 lemon

1 x wild rabbit, jointed
olive oil
2 knobs of butter
sea salt and freshly ground
   black pepper
a few sprigs of fresh thyme,
   a few leaves picked and
   reserved for serving
2 sprigs of fresh rosemary
4 cloves of garlic, unpeeled
3 wineglasses of white wine
1 x basic pasta dough
   recipe (see page 84) or
   1lb 6oz good-quality dried
   pappardelle
a small handful of good-
   quality green olives,
   pitted and very
   roughly chopped
a bunch of fresh marjoram,
   leaves picked
a handful of freshly grated
   Parmesan cheese
optional: zest of ½ an
   orange or lemon

Open stained-glass lasagne with roasted squash

I made up this dish when I was rolling out some pasta sheets the other day and had a bunch of really nice herbs going spare. It's Italian in the combination of flavors, but it doesn't really fit into a category as it's not a baked pasta or one with a sauce. Instead it has a bit more of a – dare I say it – camp French twist because it looks so beautiful! Not only is it unusual and stunning but it tastes amazing. Great on a big platter served in the middle of the table and probably unlike anything you've ever seen before.

Preheat the oven to 400°F, then make your fresh pasta dough and get it in the fridge to rest. In a pestle and mortar or Flavor Shaker bash up the coriander seeds, chillies and fennel seeds then mix in the cinnamon. Toss your chunks of butternut squash in olive oil and coat well with a sprinkle of salt and pepper and your smashed-up spices. Put the squash in a snug-fitting roasting tray, cover it with aluminum foil and roast in the preheated oven for 40 minutes until soft and golden.

Meanwhile you can roll out your pasta into a sheet and shape it into stained-glass lasagne (see page 90). Place the sheets on a floured pan, with flour between each layer, in the fridge until you're ready to cook them.

When your squash is cooked, leave the skin on as it will be soft and sweet, and smash it all up in a large bowl. You want it to look like chunky baby food, so if you need to loosen it slightly then do so with a little water or vegetable stock. Season to taste with salt and pepper and either put it in the fridge until you're ready to start cooking, or get yourself a big pot of salted water on to boil and get cracking! Cook the herby lasagne sheets for around 2 to 3 minutes, then get your squash nice and hot by reheating it in a pan with good glug of olive oil.

To serve, simply smear half the squash across the bottom of your warmed serving plates. Remove the cooked sheets to a bowl with a couple of splashes of the cooking water and carefully toss with the butter and Parmesan. Take half the sheets out of the bowl and divide between your plates. Divide the rest of the squash on top and finish with the rest of the pasta. Sprinkle the rest of your herbs and a little finely chopped fresh chilli (if using) over the top, drizzle with a good glug of extra virgin olive oil and serve immediately with a block of Parmesan and a grater on the table.

Matt's wine suggestion: South African white – Viognier

serves 4

1 x basic pasta dough recipe (see page 84)
1 teaspoon coriander seeds
1–2 small dried red chillies
1 teaspoon fennel seeds
½ teaspoon ground cinnamon
1 medium butternut squash, halved, deseeded and cut into large chunks
olive oil
sea salt and freshly ground black pepper
a large handful of fresh herbs (fennel tops, flat-leaf parsley and sage leaves)
optional: vegetable stock
a good knob of butter
a handful of freshly grated Parmesan cheese, plus a block for grating
optional: 1 fresh red chilli, deseeded and finely chopped
extra virgin olive oil

Lovely easy caramelle with ricotta, basil and black olives

Caramella means 'sweetie' in Italian, and this lovely sweetie-shaped pasta is really simple to make. The combination of the ingredients is one of classic friends – cheese, tomatoes, olives and basil. Such a great pasta to make for summertime eating. And if you can get hold of some great tomatoes and basil, this dish will be absolutely amazing.

PS Caramelle are great to serve at a dinner party because you can make them in advance and leave them on a generously floured pan in the fridge. You can also have the sauce made up in advance so it's just a case of cooking the caramelle and reheating the sauce. Simple!

The first thing you need to do is make your pasta dough and put it in the fridge to rest while you make your filling.

From your pile of picked basil leaves, separate out the smaller delicate inner leaves and put them in a little cup of cold water. Put this to one side. Finely chop the larger basil leaves and the upper parts of the stalks, discarding the bottom half. Put half of this chopped basil into a bowl with your ricotta, grated nutmeg, olives and half the Parmesan. Season with salt and pepper and add a splash of extra virgin olive oil. Put to one side until you are ready to fill your caramelle.

To roll out your pasta and fill your caramelle, see page 88 and follow the instructions, then come back to this page . . .

To make the sauce, gently heat a knob of butter with a splash of olive oil in a saucepan. When the butter starts to foam, add your sliced garlic and the rest of your chopped basil. A minute later add your tomatoes. Allow them to almost come to the boil, then simmer for up to 5 minutes until they have softened. You will be left with a lovely, fresh, rustic sauce. Taste and season with salt and pepper and a tiny swig of balsamic vinegar.

Bring a large pot of salted water to the boil and add your caramelle. Cook for 2 to 3 minutes, until they begin to float, then carefully remove them to a colander using a spider or slotted spoon and reserve some of the cooking water. Add the caramelle to the simmering tomato sauce and gently toss around. Sprinkle in a handful of Parmesan, then gently shake around and place a lid on the pan for 30 seconds while you get the plates out. Divide your caramelle between the plates, sprinkle with the drained basil leaves and eat immediately.

Matt's wine suggestion: Italian white – Pinot Grigio

serves 4–6

1 x basic pasta dough
  recipe (see page 84)
a large bunch of fresh
  basil, leaves picked,
  stalks reserved
9oz buffalo ricotta cheese
¼ of a nutmeg, grated
a small handful of
  good-quality black olives,
  pitted and chopped
2 handfuls of grated
  Parmesan cheese
sea salt and freshly ground
  black pepper
extra virgin olive oil
2 knobs of butter
olive oil
2 cloves of garlic, peeled
  and finely sliced
14oz of the ripest
  tomatoes, halved,
  deseeded and roughly
  chopped
balsamic vinegar

Ravioli of pecorino, potato and mint

Pecorino, potato and mint is a classic combination that works really well, whether in a salad or a soup, or as a filling for ravioli, as here. Try and see if you can get hold of aged pecorino, as it has a slightly stronger flavor and is really nice. However, most supermarkets will have mild pecorino in stock, or Parmesan will do.

First, make your pasta dough. Then preheat the oven to 400°F. Prick your potatoes with a fork, then roll them in a little salt and bake them in the oven for about an hour. When cool, cut them in half and scoop the potato out into a bowl, discarding the skins. Pick your mint leaves and finely chop half of them. Add the butter, grated pecorino, nutmeg, lemon zest and the chopped mint and mash well with the potato. Have a taste and correct the seasoning. You want the intensity of this filling to be quite punchy, with the mint and cheese really coming through when you eat the ravioli. Once you've got the flavors balanced, go to page 90 to make your ravioli (or try out other shapes if you fancy). Once you've made them, put a pot of salted water on, bring to the boil and cook your ravioli for 3½ minutes.

While the ravioli is cooking, put the couple of knobs of butter into a frying pan and heat gently. Remove and drain the ravioli with a spider or slotted spoon, or carefully drain them in a colander, reserving a little of the cooking water. Add the ravioli to the butter with a little of the cooking water and lightly simmer until the butter and water have turned into a little sauce that just coats the ravioli. Serve on a large platter in the middle of the table, or divide between individual plates. Sprinkle with the whole mint leaves and a little pepper and, using a speed peeler, shave over some extra pecorino.

Matt's wine suggestion: Italian white – Arneis

serves 4–6

1 x basic pasta dough recipe (see page 84)
1lb 2oz floury potatoes
sea salt and freshly grated black pepper
7 tablespoons butter, plus 2 knobs
1–2 handfuls of grated pecorino cheese, plus extra for serving
¼ of a nutmeg, grated
zest of 1 lemon
a bunch of fresh mint

The best stew with potato and arugula pasta cushions

When I made this it reminded me of tucking into a big plate of stew and mashed potatoes as a kid. So instead of serving it with a pasta like pappardelle, I realized that potato ravioli would be the perfect match. Even though it's an Italian dish, there is something very English about it which makes me smile. I know you'll love it.

Get yourself a casserole-type pan and put it on a medium heat. Pat the veal cheeks with a little olive oil and sprinkle them with salt and pepper. Fry on all sides until golden, then add the carrots, onions, celery, garlic, thyme and rosemary to the pan. Allow to sweat slowly for about 10 minutes until all the veg has softened. Stir in the flour then add the wine and tomatoes. Stir gently then lightly season the sauce and put a lid on the pan. Simmer slowly for 2 to 3 hours, or until the meat falls apart – it should be so tender that you can pull it apart using two forks. If the sauce seems to be cooking a little dry, make sure that the heat isn't turned up too high and just top it up with a little water.

While the sauce is simmering, make your pasta dough. To make the filling, preheat the oven to 400°F. Prick your potatoes with a fork, then roll them in a little salt and bake them in the oven for about an hour, or cook them for 25 minutes in a pressure cooker. When cool, cut them in half and scoop the potato out into a bowl, discarding the skins. Add the grated nutmeg, Parmesan, arugula, butter and lemon zest and juice. Mix this all together well, then season to taste.

To make the cushion ravioli, go to page 88 – you've got plenty of time to put them together while the stew is simmering. Once they're done, put them to one side in a floured pan.

As soon as the meat is good and ready and falling apart, break it up using a fork. Give it a mix, taste it and adjust the seasoning if you need to. The sauce should be like a stew, but if it looks too thick then simply add a little water to loosen it and keep it simmering for a short while longer.

Put a pan of salted water on to boil, and get your family or guests round the table. When the pan of water is boiling fast, add your pasta parcels and cook for 3 minutes. Remove them from the water using a spider or slotted spoon, or drain them very carefully in a colander. At this point you can stir the cushions through the stew, but I prefer to drizzle them with extra virgin olive oil in the colander then give them a very light shake and just pour them on top of the stew. Sprinkle with the chopped parsley, put a spoon in the pan and take the whole thing to the table so that everyone can help themselves. A bloody good dinner!

Matt's wine suggestion: Italian red – Primitivo

serves 4–6

for the stew
1¾lb veal cheeks or another stewing cut
olive oil
sea salt and freshly ground black pepper
4 carrots, finely chopped
2 red onions, finely chopped
3 sticks of celery, trimmed and finely chopped
4 cloves of garlic, peeled and finely chopped
a bunch of fresh thyme, leaves picked and chopped
6 sprigs of fresh rosemary, leaves picked
1 heaped teaspoon flour
½ a 750ml bottle of white wine
2 x 14oz cans good-quality plum tomatoes
1 x basic pasta dough recipe (see page 84)
extra virgin olive oil
a small bunch of fresh flat-leaf parsley, leaves picked

for the filling
1lb 2oz floury potatoes
½ a nutmeg, grated
3 large handfuls of freshly grated Parmesan cheese
a big bunch of arugula, chopped
a large knob of butter
zest and juice of 1 lemon

Oozy egg ravioli

I ate a variation of this dish in Piedmont, Italy, about seven years ago where they used mashed potato instead of ricotta. The inspiration to put this ricotta-filled version in the book came from Fifteen Amsterdam, where it was cooked for me the other week. It was equally amazing! You always get loads of oohs and aahs when you serve this dish to people because the egg yolks are still runny when you cut into the ravioli – it looks the business.

First, make your basic pasta dough.

Crumble your ricotta into a mixing bowl, sprinkle with the nutmeg, a little salt and the chopped truffle, if using. Mix everything together, have a taste and correct the seasoning of your filling if you feel you need to.

Once you've got the flavors balanced, go to page 90 for instructions on how to make your ravioli. But instead of rolling a large sheet to make 4 ravioli, roll a 3x6 inch sheet and make them one at a time, as these ravioli are very delicate.

Use 1 tablespoon of filling for each ravioli and press the filling down lightly on to the pasta with the back of a wet teaspoon to create a little hollow in it. Very carefully separate an egg, saving or freezing the egg white to make a lovely meringue later, then place the egg yolk on top of the mound of ricotta filling so it sits in the hollow. Complete the ravioli as normal, being extra careful not to burst the egg yolk as you seal it. Repeat so you end up with 12 ravioli.

Bring a pot of salted water to the boil and cook your ravioli for a couple of minutes. Fish one out with a slotted spoon and press it lightly with your fingertips. If the egg yolk feels very soft and squidgy, it's not quite there yet. If the yolk feels like it's just starting to firm up, spoon the ravioli out on to a plate. Reserve a bit of the cooking water.

Drop the butter into a large frying pan and heat gently. Add the ravioli and a little of the cooking water and lightly simmer until the butter and water have turned into a sauce that just coats the ravioli. Serve on a large platter in the middle of the table, or divide over individual plates. Sprinkle with grated Parmesan and serve.

Matt's wine suggestion: Italian white – Orvieto

makes 12

1 x basic pasta dough recipe (see page 84)
9oz good-quality ricotta cheese
a pinch of ground nutmeg
sea salt and freshly ground black pepper
optional: 1 teaspoon chopped fresh black truffle
12 large free-range or organic eggs
a couple of knobs of butter
freshly grated Parmesan cheese, to serve

Tortellini of chicken and gorgonzola
in a fragrant thyme broth

If you're ever feeling ill or just a bit under the weather, this is the kind of proper therapeutic food that will make you feel better. There's very little fat or anything heavy in this dish – just pure goodness. And there's nothing better than slurping a tasty wholesome broth! The chicken is the hero ingredient in this dish, so buy the best one you can afford.

Put your chicken, celery, carrots, leeks, fennel, thyme and bay leaves into an appropriately sized pot, then fill the pot with enough water to cover the chicken. You can place a small heatproof plate, or pan lid that fits inside the pot, on top of the chicken to keep it submerged. Then put a lid on the pot and bring the water to the boil. Simmer for 1¼ hours and skim the fat off the top from time to time using a spoon.

While the chicken is cooking you can make your fresh pasta dough and put it in the fridge until you're ready to shape and fill it. When the chicken is cooked remove it to a plate. Taste the broth – if it's a bit on the weak side, then season it with salt and pepper and leave the pot on the heat for a bit longer, with the lid off, to reduce the liquid a little more and intensify the flavor. When you're happy, take the broth off the heat. Strain into a large bowl, then pour back into the pot, discarding the veg. You should be left with a nice clear-ish liquid (to make it even clearer you can pass it through cheesecloth but I think it's okay to have a few bits in it!). Once the chicken has cooled, strip all the breast meat off the bone into little pieces and put back into the broth.

To make your filling for the tortellini, pick off the leg and thigh meat from the chicken and chop up finely. Place into a bowl and stir in the gorgonzola, chopped parsley stalks, lemon juice and Parmesan. Season and put to one side while you make your tortellini.

Roll out your pasta dough on a floured surface and make your tortellini (see page 90), filling each one with a teaspoon of the chicken and gorgonzola filling. Cook the tortellini in salted, boiling water for 2 minutes then remove them using a spider or slotted spoon, or drain them carefully in a colander.

Put your slightly undercooked tortellini back into the pot with the broth and the chicken strips and bring back to the boil for another 1½ minutes. Taste the broth one more time for salt and pepper, then sprinkle with the roughly chopped parsley leaves and celery leaves and drizzle with a good glug of extra virgin olive oil. Serve at the table in one big bowl or divide into individual bowls.

Matt's wine suggestion: French white – Pinot Gris

serves 4–6

1 x 3½lb chicken,
  preferably free-range
  or organic
5 sticks of celery, trimmed
  and roughly chopped,
  yellow leaves reserved
4 carrots, peeled and
  roughly chopped
2 leeks, outer leaves
  discarded, roughly
  chopped
1 fennel bulb, roughly
  chopped, herby tops
  reserved
a small bunch of fresh
  thyme, leaves picked
3 bay leaves
1 x basic pasta dough
  recipe (see page 84)
sea salt and freshly ground
  black pepper
2¾oz gorgonzola cheese
a bunch of fresh flat-leaf
  parsley, leaves picked and
  roughly chopped, stalks
  finely chopped
juice of 1 lemon
a handful of freshly grated
  Parmesan cheese
good-quality peppery extra
  virgin olive oil

Raviolini of celeriac and thyme

I had a similar dish to this cooked for me at the famous Spago restaurant in LA. The head chef, Lee, gave us a seriously good meal, including a raviolini of smashed celeriac – it was really light and tasty and I've never forgotten it. If you ever come across fresh truffles, buy them and shave them over, or pick up some truffle oil from the supermarket to drizzle over at the end of the cooking. Don't worry if you can't get either – it will taste great just as it is.

Make your pasta dough according to the instructions on page 84, adding in the spinach with the eggs, then leave it in the fridge wrapped in clingfilm while you get on with making your filling and thyme butter.

Get a saucepan nice and hot, then add a tablespoon of olive oil, the celeriac, half the thyme leaves and a good pinch of salt and pepper. Cook until the celeriac has a little color on it then turn the heat down to medium. Throw in the garlic and chopped chilli and continue to cook for another 3 or 4 minutes. Then add 2 ladles of boiling water and cover the pan with a lid. Continue cooking on a low heat for 20 to 25 minutes, or until the celeriac is soft. Once done, and all the water has evaporated, roughly smash the celeriac up with a potato masher, giving you some chunky bits and some smooth bits. Season to taste and put to one side to cool. (As it is now, this could be used as a side dish or as a base for soup.)

Remove the pasta dough from the fridge, roll it out and shape into raviolini (see page 90). Drop them into a large pot of salted boiling water and cook for 3½ minutes. While these are cooking, get a frying pan on the heat and put in the butter and the rest of the thyme leaves. Once the pasta is done, remove it carefully using a spider or slotted spoon and toss gently in the pan with the thyme butter. Add a splash of cooking water – this will give you a shiny, delicate sauce which will be just enough to coat the pasta. Season with a little salt and pepper and sprinkle with the Parmesan. Toss around in the pan and serve immediately on a big platter or on individual plates. Before tucking in, shave a little truffle over the top if you are lucky enough to have some.

Matt's wine suggestion: Italian white – Gavi

serves 4–6

1lb 6oz tipo 00 or pasta flour
¼ cup puréed cooked spinach
5 large free-range or organic eggs
olive oil
1 large celeriac, peeled and diced into ½ inch cubes
1 tablespoon freshly picked thyme leaves
sea salt and freshly ground black pepper
2 cloves of garlic, peeled and finely chopped
½ a fresh red chilli, deseeded and chopped
4 knobs of butter
a small handful of grated Parmesan cheese
optional: a fresh black or white truffle

GNOCCHI

Gnocchi literally means 'lumps' in Italian, and there are a few different ways of making them. In Tuscany, gnocchi are made out of ricotta and seasoning; in Rome *gnocchi alla romana* are made from stamping out pieces of semolina pasta that are then covered with cheese and grilled or roasted. But the most widely known and loved gnocchi are the plain old potato ones, and the chefs at Fifteen make some of the best you'll ever taste! Take Aaron's award-winning oxtail gnocchi, which you can find on page 117. The sauce is based on the old butcher's style dishes (known as *alla macellaio*) that Aaron discovered in the north of Italy when he was on a trip to learn about matching food and wine with Fifteen's wine wizard, Matt Skinner. He found out that years ago, if no one had bought his oxtail, the butcher would take it home and cook it up in a big pot with tomatoes and herbs from the garden, and feed it to his family. When Aaron got back to the restaurant he played around with the idea, added some cinnamon and sage, and made it into a ragù for serving with gnocchi. And it is just beautiful!

Proper potato gnocchi are made from mashed potato, flour, egg and seasoning – nothing else. The secret to making good gnocchi is to get the potato as dry as possible – this means that less flour is needed to bind the mixture together and this in turn gives you a lighter end product.

If you boil your potatoes they'll absorb too much water and end up too wet. The best way to cook your potatoes to ensure they're dry and fluffy inside is to bake or steam them with their skins on. It can take a while, so what I sometimes do is get the old pressure cooker out, put the potatoes in the basket with an inch of water in the bottom of the pan, clamp the lid on and steam them on the meat setting for 25 minutes – sorted!

A basic recipe for the lightest potato gnocchi

Preheat the oven to 425°F. Rub your potatoes with olive oil, prick them with a fork and lay them in a roasting tray. Put in the preheated oven and bake for an hour until the potatoes are fluffy on the inside and crispy on the outside. Allow them to cool for a couple of minutes and then, when they are still nice and hot, use a dish towel to pick up your potatoes one at a time, cut them in half and carefully scoop the flesh out of the skins into a mouli or ricer. When you have lovely and smooth mashed potato, put it into a bowl. Add the nutmeg, a tablespoon of salt, a pinch of pepper, the egg yolk and enough of the flour to bind your mixture – you may not need it all. Mix together and then knead with your hands until you have a dry, doughy consistency. Add a little water if you feel it's too dry, or a little more flour if it's too wet. To get the hang of perfect gnocchi dough, you'll have to practice a few times. If you're unsure, try testing one by chucking it in some boiling water – if it falls apart, add a bit more flour to the dough.

Once you have your gnocchi dough, divide it into 3 pieces and roll each piece out on a floured surface into long tubes the thickness of a sausage. Cut each of the tubes into 1 inch pieces. Place them on a bed of semolina flour on a tray and put in the fridge for 10 to 20 minutes to set.

serves 6

6 medium potatoes
olive oil
½ a nutmeg, grated
sea salt and freshly ground
  black pepper
1 large free-range or organic
  egg yolk
1–2 handfuls of all-purpose or
  tipo 00 flour
semolina flour

Gnocchi with gorgonzola dolce

First of all, make your basic potato gnocchi recipe and put in the fridge to set. Put a pan of salted water on to boil, then get yourself a frying pan and put it on a very low heat. Add your gorgonzola, butter and heavy cream with a pinch of black pepper. Mix together using the back of a wooden spoon – the back of the spoon is particularly good for breaking down little lumps in your sauce – until you have a lovely melted cheese sauce. Cook your gnocchi in the boiling water for 4 minutes or until they float, then drain them carefully in a colander – carefully, as cooked gnocchi are very delicate – and toss in the gorgonzola sauce. Serve with a scattering of marjoram leaves and a good grating of Parmesan.

Matt's wine suggestion: Italian white – Grecanico

serves 6

1 x basic gnocchi recipe (see page 112)
sea salt and freshly ground black pepper
2 tablespoons gorgonzola dolce cheese
3 tablespoons butter
6 tablespoons heavy cream
a small bunch of fresh marjoram,
  leaves picked
Parmesan cheese, for grating

Gnocchi with mushrooms and sage

First of all, make your basic gnocchi recipe and put in the fridge to set. Then get a frying pan hot and put in a splash of olive oil. Add your mushrooms and toss for 2 to 3 minutes, then add the chopped chilli, garlic, salt and pepper and butter. When the garlic is slightly golden, add your stock or water and continue to cook on a medium heat for 5 minutes. Meanwhile, cook your gnocchi in a pan of salted boiling water for 4 minutes or until they float. Once cooked, the gnocchi are very delicate, so carefully drain them in a colander. (If you're too heavy-handed, they'll just turn into mashed potato.) Add them to the mushroom mixture with the chopped parsley and mix well. Serve with the crispy sage leaves, some grated Parmesan and the remaining chilli sprinkled over.

Matt's wine suggestion: Chilean white – Chardonnay

serves 6

1 x basic gnocchi recipe (see page 112)
olive oil
5½oz mixed wild mushrooms,
  cleaned and torn
1 fresh red chilli, deseeded and
  finely chopped
1 clove of garlic, peeled and finely sliced
sea salt and freshly ground black pepper
2 knobs of butter
a ladleful of vegetable stock or water
24 sage leaves
a small handful of fresh flat-leaf parsley
  leaves, roughly chopped
Parmesan cheese, for grating

Herby gnocchi with arugula and butter sauce

Wash the arugula leaves and spin dry, then finely chop most of them, keeping a few leaves whole for serving. Make your basic gnocchi recipe, adding the finely chopped arugula to the doughy mixture before you start kneading. Put them in the fridge to set. Bring a pan of salted water to the boil and cook your gnocchi for 4 minutes or until they float. Get yourself a frying pan and put this on the heat. Melt the butter in the pan with a pinch of salt and pepper. Once it's melted, add the stock or water and shake the pan in a circular motion until your sauce looks like a loose custard. Take off the heat and add the lemon zest and a handful of Parmesan. Drain your gnocchi carefully in a colander, tip them into the pan with the butter sauce and gently toss. Scatter the whole arugula leaves over the top.

Matt's wine suggestion: Italian white – Soave

serves 6

a bunch of arugula
1 x basic gnocchi recipe
  (see page 112)
sea salt and freshly ground
  black pepper
9 tablespoons butter
a ladleful of vegetable
  stock or water
zest of 1 lemon
a handful of freshly grated
  Parmesan cheese

Gnocchi with braised oxtail

Preheat the oven to 300°F. Make your basic gnocchi recipe and put in the fridge to set. Get a large ovenproof saucepan hot and add a splash of olive oil. Sear the oxtail until brown on all sides, then add the celery, onion, carrot and leek. Cook gently until golden brown and add the wine and your crushed spices, cinnamon, chilli, tomato purée and tins of tomatoes. Top up with a little water – you just need enough to make sure all the meat is covered – and put a lid on. Put the pan in the oven for 4 to 4½ hours, until the meat is falling off the bone. Remove from the oven and lift the meat out of the stew. When cool enough to handle, shred all the meat off the bones. Pick through the meat with your fingers to make sure that no bony bits remain, then put the meat back in the pot. Add the oregano, simmer for 15 minutes and season to taste. Meanwhile, put a pan of salted water on to boil and cook your gnocchi for 4 minutes, or until they float. While your gnocchi are cooking, fry the sage leaves in the butter until crispy and dark green, then drain them on paper towels. Carefully drain your gnocchi, toss in the oxtail stew with some fried sage leaves and serve with some freshly shaved Parmesan if you like.

Matt's wine suggestion: Argentinan red – Malbec

serves 6

1 x basic gnocchi recipe (see page 112)
olive oil
1 oxtail, cut into 4 inch chunks
1 stick of celery, finely chopped
1 onion, peeled and finely chopped
1 carrot, peeled and finely chopped
1 leek, trimmed and finely chopped
½ a 750ml bottle of white wine
1 tablespoon fennel seeds, crushed
1 tablespoon juniper berries, crushed
½ a cinnamon stick
1 dried red chilli, crushed
sea salt and black pepper
1 large tablespoon tomato purée
4 x 14oz cans plum tomatoes
1 tablespoon fresh oregano leaves
a handful of fresh sage leaves
a knob of butter
optional: Parmesan cheese

RISOTTO

If you've made a risotto before you'll know that it takes about forty minutes to cook, so how do restaurants get a risotto to you within ten minutes of you ordering it?

Well, it's quite simple really. The risotto will start off being cooked as normal in bulk, but it will then be stopped halfway through and held until you're ready to put it back in the pan with a bit more stock and any other flavors to finish it off. This way of cooking risotto suits restaurants down to the ground, as it means there's much less work and manpower required in the kitchen at the busiest time and the customer gets their order quicker. But there is another good reason why this trick is a very useful one to know if you're cooking at home ... If you're having people round in the evening and you've made your risotto in the afternoon, then you've done all the hard work beforehand. When your mates arrive, instead of sweating away in the kitchen, you can indulge in a few drinks and a chat with them and then pop back to the stove at the last minute to reheat the rice for the last five minutes to finish your risotto off.

I thought I knew what flavors worked in a risotto. That is until Lloyd (who is now 'The Man' when it comes to risotto) came up with the idea of making one with tomatoes added right at the end. When he told me about it, it didn't rock me to be honest, as I couldn't see how squidgy tomatoes with their skins on could work in the rice, but I asked him to show me. Basically, he put some tomatoes in at the beginning, then added some more cherry tomatoes marinated in oil, vinegar, salt and pepper at the finish. This meant that when you ate the risotto, you got a big hit of fresh tomato and basil. Boy, was it good! It's fantastic to be humbled by the students like that. You can find the recipe on page 126.

A basic recipe for making risotto

Here's the basic risotto recipe. From it I'll show you how to take it in eight different ways, depending on what flavors you fancy, what you've got in the fridge, what time of the year it is, or who's coming round for dinner ... And if you enjoy making these and want to have a go at some more, then have a look in my Italian book, *Jamie's Italy*, as it has a lovely little risotto section.

Now, this recipe will take you up to a point where the rice is 75 percent ready, and all that's left to do is choose one of these recipes and finish it off. The idea is that if you make this base in advance, you can then spread the rice out on a pan until you're ready to use it (or you can launch straight into flavoring it, in which case the pan won't be needed). Remember to have a large clean pan, rubbed with a little olive oil, right by the stove. It's important that it's large, so the rice can be spread thinly, meaning it will cool down faster and not end up cooking itself. If you don't have a big pan in the house, use a couple of small ones instead.

Stage 1: Have a large oiled pan on hand. Bring the stock to a simmer in a saucepan. Put the olive oil and butter in a separate large pan, add the onion and celery and cook very gently for about 15 minutes, without coloring, until soft. Add the rice (it will sizzle!) and turn up the heat. Don't let the rice or veg catch on the bottom of the pan, so keep it moving.

Stage 2: Quickly pour in the vermouth or wine. You will smell the alcohol immediately, so keep stirring all the time until it has evaporated, leaving the rice with a lovely perfume.

Stage 3: Add the stock to the rice a ladle at a time, stirring and waiting until it has been fully absorbed before adding the next. Turn the heat down to low so the rice doesn't cook too quickly, otherwise the outside of each grain will be stodgy and the inside hard and nutty (you don't want to cook it too slowly either, or it will turn into rice pudding!), and continue to add ladlefuls of stock until it has all been absorbed. This should take about 14 to 15 minutes and give you rice that is beginning to soften but is still a little al dente.

Stage 4: Tip the part-cooked rice out on to the waiting oiled pan. Spread it out evenly, about 1 inch thick, on the pan and then put it somewhere cold to cool down. When the rice has lost all its heat, scrape it up carefully with a rubber spatula and store it in a Tupperware container with a lid in the fridge until you're ready to use it. It will keep for a couple of days.

This cooked rice is the risotto base for the following eight recipes, so for each one you will have to refer back to it and make it up to this point first.

serves 8

1¾ pints vegetable or
  chicken stock
2 tablespoons olive oil
1 tablespoon butter
1 large onion, peeled and
  finely chopped
4–5 sticks of celery,
  trimmed and finely
  chopped
1lb 6oz risotto rice
9fl oz vermouth or dry
  white wine

Stage 1

Stage 2

Stage 3

Stage 4

Spicy pangrattato risotto

I love this dish – the rice is cooked so simply that the flavors come out beautifully, and then you get these amazing crispy breadcrumbs on top which are a real shake-up of the senses with their crunch against the incredibly soft rice.

It's a recipe that can be made really cheaply, but when you're eating it you'd never believe that was the case. It just works.

Whiz the lemon zest, dried chillies, garlic, anchovies and bread chunks in a food processor with a bit of oil from the anchovy can until the mixture looks like breadcrumbs. Heat a large frying pan and add a splash of olive oil. Fry the breadcrumbs in the oil until darkened and crisp, then drain them on a piece of paper towel and allow to cool.

Make your basic risotto recipe. Place a large saucepan on a medium to high heat and pour in half the stock, followed by all your risotto base. Stirring all the time, gently bring to the boil, turn the heat down and simmer until almost all the stock has been absorbed. Add the rest of the stock a ladleful at a time until the rice is cooked. You might not need all your stock. Be careful not to overcook the rice – check it throughout cooking to make sure it's a pleasure to eat. It should hold its shape but be soft, creamy and oozy. And the overall texture should be slightly looser than you think you want it.

Turn off the heat, beat in your butter and Parmesan, check the seasoning and add a little salt and pepper if needed. Don't be too generous with the salt because the pangrattato has salt in it too and you don't want to overdo it!

Place a lid on the pan and leave the risotto to rest for a minute. You can now take the pan to the table so that everyone can help themselves, or divide the risotto between individual serving plates and sprinkle the pangrattato over the top. Place a block of Parmesan on the table with a grater and tuck in.

Matt's wine suggestion: Italian white – Verdicchio

serves 8

zest of 1 lemon
3 dried bird's-eye chillies
4 cloves of garlic, peeled
6 good-quality salted
   anchovy fillets in oil
½ a large ciabatta loaf,
   stale if possible, cut into
   chunks
olive oil
1 x basic risotto recipe
   (see page 120)
around 1¼ pints
   hot vegetable or
   chicken stock
7 tablespoons butter
1–2 handfuls of freshly
   grated Parmesan cheese,
   plus a block for grating
sea salt and freshly ground
   black pepper

Asparagus, mint and lemon risotto

This is such a simple, clean and delicious risotto. When buying asparagus, have a look around because there are lots of varieties available now – purple-tipped, white, thin straggly Japanese, wild Spanish and dozens of good English. In this recipe the stalks are finely sliced to an inch below the tips – this will give you lots of flavor from the stalks and you'll then have those whole beautiful tips as a bit of a prize! There are variations on this risotto that I love to do, like sprinkling in a little picked crab or lobstermeat or fresh, peeled shrimp or sliced scallops – all of these work particularly well with asparagus if you fancy a little upgrade. (If you do decide to add any of these seafood suggestions then reduce your Parmesan by half.)

Finely chop your asparagus stalks into tiny discs, keeping the tips whole. Make your basic risotto recipe. Then put a large saucepan on a medium to high heat and pour in half the stock, followed by all your risotto base and the finely sliced asparagus stalks and the tips. Stirring all the time, gently bring to the boil, then turn the heat down and simmer until almost all the stock has been absorbed. Add the rest of the stock a ladleful at a time until the rice and asparagus are cooked. You might not need all your stock. Be careful not to overcook the rice – check it throughout cooking to make sure it's a pleasure to eat. It should hold its shape but be soft, creamy and oozy, and the overall texture should be slightly looser than you think you want it.

Turn off the heat, beat in your butter and Parmesan, mint, almost all the lemon zest and all the juice. Check the seasoning and add salt and pepper if needed. Put a lid on the pan and leave the risotto to rest for a minute. Serve with a drizzle of olive oil, a scattering of lemon zest and a block of Parmesan on the table.

Matt's wine suggestion: Italian white – Pinot Grigio

serves 8

2 bunches of asparagus, woody ends removed and discarded
1 x basic risotto recipe (see page 120)
1¼ pints hot vegetable or chicken stock
7 tablespoons butter
1–2 handfuls of freshly grated Parmesan cheese, plus a block for grating
a bunch of fresh mint, leaves picked and finely chopped
zest and juice of 2 lemons
sea salt and freshly ground black pepper
extra virgin olive oil

Tomato, basil and ricotta risotto

This risotto was inspired by one that Lloyd, Fifteen graduate, made for me. I never thought it would work but was proved wrong when I tasted it. It was absolutely delicious! Two things are especially important when it comes to making this risotto: first, try and get hold of different shapes and colors of tomatoes – there are lots of varieties available these days – and second, make sure you get the right type of ricotta. It should be snow-white and really crumbly. Unfortunately, the ricotta that you tend to get in the supermarkets is a bit like semolina and just horrible, so unless you can get some lovely crumbly white ricotta, then use a mild crumbly goat's cheese instead.

Preheat the oven to 350°F. Marinate your tomatoes in the red wine vinegar, olive oil, and a pinch of salt and pepper. Make your basic risotto recipe, then place the ricotta in a small baking pan, rub it with extra virgin olive oil, sprinkle over the chilli and oregano, season it and place in the preheated oven for 10 minutes until golden brown.

Meanwhile, place a large saucepan on a medium to high heat and pour in half the stock, followed by your risotto base and two-thirds of the tomatoes. Stirring all the time, gently bring to the boil, then turn down the heat and simmer until almost all the stock has been absorbed. Add the rest of the stock a ladleful at a time until the rice is cooked. You might not need all your stock. Be careful not to overcook the rice – check it throughout cooking to make sure it ends up soft, creamy and oozy. And the overall texture should be slightly looser than you think you want it.

Turn off the heat, beat in your butter and Parmesan and tear in the larger basil leaves, reserving the small ones for sprinkling over before serving. Check the seasoning and add salt and pepper if needed, then stir in your baked ricotta and marinated tomatoes. Put a lid on the pan and leave the risotto to rest for a minute before taking it to the table. Either let everyone help themselves, or divide the risotto between individual serving plates. Sprinkle over the little basil leaves, drizzle with a little extra virgin olive oil and put a block of Parmesan on the table for grating over.

Matt's wine suggestion: French white – Chenin Blanc

serves 8

for the tomatoes
4 large handfuls of
   interesting ripe tomatoes,
   seeds removed and flesh
   roughly chopped
a splash of good red
   wine vinegar
a good lug of oil
sea salt and freshly ground
   black pepper

1 x basic risotto recipe
   (see page 120)
9oz crumbly ricotta cheese
extra virgin olive oil
1 dried red chilli, crumbled
1 teaspoon dried oregano
sea salt and freshly ground
   black pepper
1¼ pints hot vegetable or
   chicken stock
7 tablespoons butter
1–2 handfuls of freshly
   grated Parmesan cheese,
   plus a block for grating
1 large bunch of fresh
   basil, leaves picked
extra virgin olive oil

Spinach and goat's cheese risotto

Spinach risotto is a real treat. By cooking your spinach in butter, garlic and nutmeg first, you get a really fantastic, intense flavor going. You can incorporate other light greens such as arugula or watercress if you like, but the real icing on the cake is some really lovely, zingy goat's cheese.

First make your basic risotto recipe, then heat a deep saucepan until medium hot, spoon in a tablespoon of the butter and add a splash of olive oil, the garlic and a good grating of nutmeg. When the butter has melted, add the spinach. Cook for 5 minutes, moving it around in the pan until it's wilted down. A lot of the liquid will have cooked away and you'll have wonderfully dark, intensely flavored spinach. Chop finely or whiz it in a food processor, and season with salt and pepper to taste.

Put a large saucepan on a medium to high heat and pour in half the stock, followed by all your risotto base. Stirring all the time, gently bring to the boil, and cook until most of the stock has been absorbed. Add the rest of the stock a ladleful at a time until the rice is cooked. You might not need all your stock. Be careful not to overcook the rice – check it throughout cooking to make sure it's a pleasure to eat. It should hold its shape but be soft, creamy and oozy, and slightly looser than you think you want it.

Turn off the heat, stir in your spinach and beat in the rest of your butter and the Parmesan. Add a good squeeze of lemon juice, then check the seasoning and add some salt and pepper if needed. Put a lid on the pan and let the risotto rest for a minute, before folding in half the goat's cheese. Sprinkle some lemon zest and the rest of the goat's cheese over the top and drizzle the risotto with a little extra virgin olive oil. Take the pan to the table with a block of Parmesan and a grater and tuck in.

Matt's wine suggestion: Italian white – Sauvignon Blanc blend

serves 8

1 x basic risotto recipe
  (see page 120)
9 tablespoons butter
olive oil
1 clove of garlic, peeled
  and chopped
nutmeg, for grating
5½oz spinach, washed and
  dried
sea salt and freshly ground
  black pepper
1¼ pints hot vegetable or
  chicken stock
1–2 handfuls of freshly
  grated Parmesan cheese,
  plus a block for grating
½ a lemon
7oz soft goat's cheese,
  crumbled
extra virgin olive oil

Mushroom risotto

Mushroom is a classic risotto, really. However, the mixture of mushrooms that you choose will mean the difference between it just being good and being amazing, so feel free to do your best in the mushroom department. But please avoid using button mushrooms as they taste of nothing.

PS For an extra mushroomy risotto, add a handful of dried porcini to your hot stock.

First make your basic risotto recipe, then leave your rice to one side while you get on with your mushrooms. Heat a large frying pan, add a knob of butter to it and when it starts to foam scatter your mushrooms in with a little seasoning. Toss around and cook for a minute, then add your thyme and garlic. Give the pan a good shake and cook for a further 2 minutes, or until the mushrooms are tender, and season to taste.

Put a large saucepan on a medium to high heat and pour in half the stock, followed by all your risotto base. Stirring all the time, gently bring to the boil and then turn the heat down to a simmer. Add the cooked mushrooms and cook until almost all the stock has been absorbed. Add the rest of the stock a ladleful at a time until the rice is cooked. You might not need all your stock. Be careful not to overcook the rice – check it throughout cooking to make sure it's a pleasure to eat. It should hold its shape but be soft, creamy and oozy, and slightly looser than you think you want it.

Turn off the heat, beat in the rest of the butter, Parmesan, parsley and lemon juice, then check the seasoning and add salt and pepper if needed. Put a lid on the pan and leave the risotto to rest for a minute. Serve in the middle of the table or divide the risotto between individual serving plates. Drizzle with a little extra virgin olive oil and put a block of Parmesan on the table for grating over.

Matt's wine suggestion: Italian red – Dolcetto

serves 8

1 x basic risotto recipe (see page 120)
7 tablespoons butter, plus an extra knob
4 large handfuls of wild fresh mushrooms (use chanterelles, porcini, trumpet, oyster, etc.), cleaned
sea salt and freshly ground black pepper
1 tablespoon freshly picked thyme leaves
2 cloves of garlic, peeled and finely chopped
1¼ pints hot vegetable or chicken stock
1–2 handfuls of freshly grated Parmesan cheese, plus a block for grating
a handful of fresh flat-leaf parsley, leaves picked and chopped
juice of 1 lemon
extra virgin olive oil

Squash, sage and amaretti risotto

An incredibly beautiful autumnal risotto. The nearer it gets to Christmas, the more you might be tempted to add some crumbled, roasted chestnuts in at the end with the squash, and maybe some smoked pancetta too.

Preheat your oven to 400°F. In a pestle and mortar pound the cinnamon stick and chilli with a good pinch of salt until you have a coarse powder. Rub the pieces of squash all over with olive oil then rub the smashed spices all over them. Put them in an ovenproof dish and cook for 45 minutes until soft and caramelized. Remove from the oven and put to one side.

While the squash is cooking, make your basic risotto recipe. Then put a large saucepan on a medium to high heat and pour in half the stock, followed by all your risotto base. Scoop the flesh out of the squash skin and break it in. Stirring all the time, gently bring to the boil, then turn the heat down and simmer until almost all the stock has been absorbed. Add the rest of the stock a ladleful at a time until the rice is cooked. You might not need all your stock – be careful not to overcook the rice – check it throughout cooking to make sure it's a pleasure to eat. It should hold its shape but be soft, creamy and oozy, with a texture that's slightly looser than you think you want it.

Turn off the heat, beat in the mascarpone, butter and Parmesan, check the seasoning and add salt and pepper if needed. Put a lid on the pan and leave the risotto to rest for a minute while you heat a medium-sized frying pan with a generous glug of olive oil. Fry the sage leaves for a minute or two until crispy, then remove with a slotted spoon onto some paper towels.

You can now take the risotto pan to the table so that everyone can help themselves or divide it between serving plates. Serve with a sprinkling of crispy sage leaves, a bowl of crushed amaretti biscuits and a block of Parmesan for grating over.

Matt's wine suggestion: American white – Chardonnay

serves 8

1 cinnamon stick
1 dried red chilli
sea salt and freshly ground
  black pepper
1 medium butternut
  squash, carefully
  quartered and seeds
  discarded
olive oil
1 x basic risotto recipe
  (see page 120)
1¼ pints hot vegetable or
  chicken stock
1 tablespoon mascarpone
  cheese
7 tablespoons butter
1–2 handfuls of freshly
  grated Parmesan cheese,
  plus a block for grating
olive oil
a bunch of fresh sage,
  leaves picked
a handful of amaretti
  biscuits, roughly crushed

Leftover stew risotto

One of the easiest and most delicious things to add to a risotto is leftover stew. All you need to do is fork the meat up finely and stir it in. Oxtail stew is my favorite (see page 117), although the beef shin stew on page 151 is also amazing. Very often, when I have leftover stew, I'll put it in a bag and freeze it especially for using in a recipe like this.

First make your basic risotto recipe, then put a large saucepan on a medium to high heat and add your stewed meat. Cook it until hot all the way through. When it comes to the boil, add a ladleful of the stock, followed by all your risotto base. Stirring all the time, gently bring to the boil and cook until almost all the stock has been absorbed. Add the rest of the stock a ladleful at a time until the rice is cooked. Don't worry if you don't use all the stock. Be careful not to overcook the rice – check it throughout cooking to make sure it's a pleasure to eat. It should hold its shape but be soft, creamy and oozy, with a texture that's slightly looser than you think you want it.

Turn off the heat and beat in your butter and Parmesan. Check the seasoning and add salt and pepper if needed. Put a lid on the pan and leave the risotto to rest for a minute, then either take the pan to the table and let everyone help themselves, or divide the risotto between your plates. Drizzle with a little extra virgin olive oil, sprinkle with the thyme and put the block of Parmesan on the table with a grater.

Matt's wine suggestion: Spanish red – Tempranillo

serves 8

1 x basic risotto recipe
  (see page 120)
14oz (about 2 cups) stewed
  meat
1¼ pints hot vegetable or
  chicken stock
7 tablespoons butter
1–2 handfuls of freshly
  grated Parmesan cheese,
  plus a block for grating
sea salt and freshly ground
  black pepper
extra virgin olive oil
a handful of fresh thyme
  leaves

Apple and walnut risotto with gorgonzola

This is like a Waldorf salad! The combo of strong cheese with apples and walnuts just works. If you can get hold of quality gorgonzola, please do – the sweetness of the apples really offsets it. I've used marjoram here, but thyme works just as well.

First make your basic risotto recipe, then put a large saucepan on a medium to high heat and pour in half the stock, followed by all your risotto base. Stirring all the time, gently bring to the boil, then turn the heat down and simmer until almost all the stock has been absorbed. Add the rest of the stock a ladleful at a time until the rice is cooked. You might not need all your stock. Be careful not to overcook the rice – check it throughout cooking to make sure it's a pleasure to eat. It should hold its shape but be soft, creamy and oozy. And the overall texture should be slightly looser than you think you want it.

Turn off the heat, beat in your butter, Parmesan, gorgonzola, goat's cheese, chopped apple and marjoram. Check the seasoning and add salt and pepper if needed. Put a lid on the pan and leave the risotto to rest for a minute so the cheese can really ooze into it. While you're waiting, gently heat the walnuts in a pan. Then either take the risotto to the table and let everyone help themselves, or divide it between individual serving plates. Put a block of Parmesan on the table for grating over. Sprinkle with the walnuts and drizzle with a little extra virgin olive oil before tucking in.

Matt's wine suggestion: Australian white – Viognier

serves 8

1 x basic risotto recipe (see page 120)
1¼ pints hot vegetable or chicken stock
7 tablespoons butter
1–2 small handfuls of freshly grated Parmesan cheese, plus a block for grating
7oz gorgonzola cheese, diced
3½oz soft goat's cheese, crumbled
2 crunchy eating apples, cored, halved, and finely chopped, tossed in lemon juice
a small bunch of fresh marjoram, leaves picked and chopped
sea salt and freshly ground black pepper
a handful of walnuts
extra virgin olive oil

meat

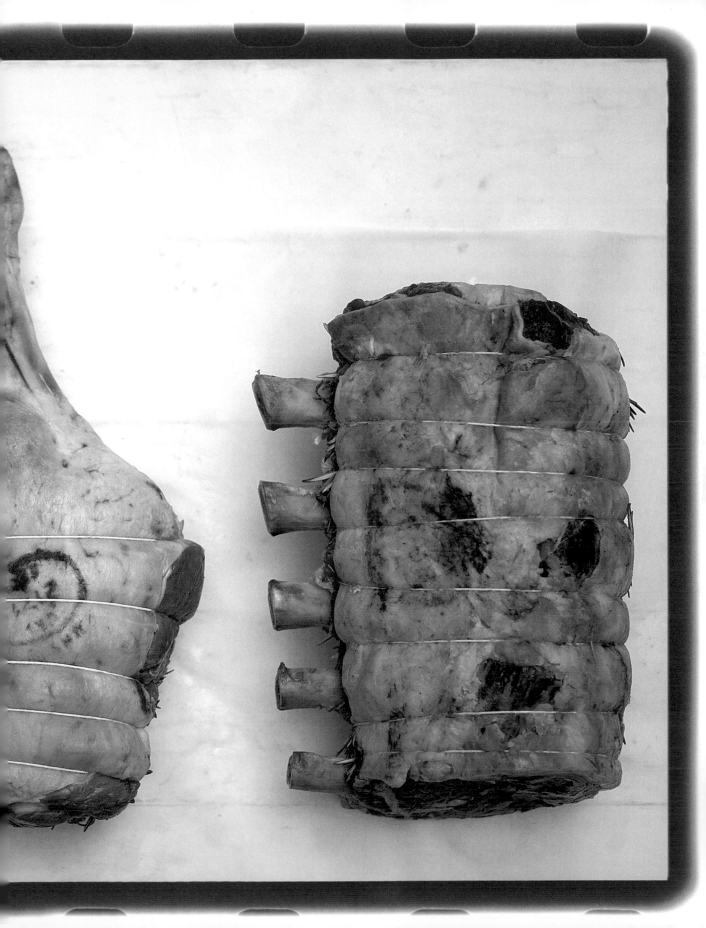

ALL ABOUT MEAT

It's amazing how specific the public are about what they want in return for their hard-earned cash. We are incredibly aware of brands and what they stand for, and of quality and integrity in all kinds of products. People down the pub in any part of the country will immediately pick a very particular brand of beer, and if the pub hasn't got it, then they'll have a second choice, and if the pub doesn't have that one, they probably won't ever go back again! When kids go to buy running shoes, they don't say to Mom, 'Any pair will do, the cheaper the better,' they are totally specific: Adidas, Nike – the ones with the blue stripes, the tag on the back, whatever. We all demand the right clothes, the right car, the right phone, and we kick up a fuss if we don't get it.

And then there's meat. We've forgotten that it's completely normal and healthy to be picky about what meat we buy. You wouldn't be happy with any old beer in the pub, your kids wouldn't be happy with any old sneakers, so why should you settle for any old meat that you're going to put in your and your family's mouth?

The truth is that most people buying meat do not see any value in it, have never thought or wanted to know or even questioned where their meat comes from, how it's been fed, looked after, slaughtered or butchered. You might think, 'Why would I want or even need to know?' Well, you should, because the difference it makes to the quality of your meat is incredible.

So what determines the quality of meat?

Breeds

Once, there were hundreds of different breeds of cows, pigs and chickens around, but nowadays almost all the meat we see in packages in supermarkets or cheap butcher's shops is from a small number of commercial breeds – hybrids they're called, cross-bred to provide animals that have large amounts of muscle on their bodies and reach a good weight in a short space of time. This is done is to provide vast quantities of very cheap meat, but the additional result is that the meat most people eat is predictable and not very interesting.

There are still some of the old breeds left, but nowadays they are so thin on the ground they are called 'rare breeds', and rare-breed meat is hard to find. Now, don't think that because they are called rare breeds we shouldn't eat them. Of course you wouldn't want to eat endangered wild species, but in the case of animals bred for food, it's a good thing. If we create a market for it, hopefully one day we might return to having a wide choice of meats, all with different flavors, shapes, sizes and textures.

Rearing and feeding

If you think all the pigs and chickens we eat spend their lives scratching round farmyards or frolicking in fields, think again. If I took you to an intensive chicken-rearing farm, I reckon I could turn half of you into vegetarians overnight. Try to imagine tens of thousands of birds crammed, twelve to a square yard in huge warehouses with no access to natural light or fresh air. Because the barns are impossible to clean until they're emptied, by the time the birds are fully grown they're up to their knees in their own excrement. The brown speckles on the heels of birds you see wrapped up on supermarket shelves are actually ammonia burns from the sludge they've been standing in all their lives. Imagine that next time you're tucking into a bog-standard chicken for your Sunday lunch!

Intensively produced meat is reared so quickly that the flavor hasn't had time to develop. Chickens, for instance, are often fed a high-protein diet to help them grow quickly, but without much space for moving around they produce meat with a very high fat content – fat that ends up in our bodies, even if we just eat the nice white bits! Animals are often fed antibiotics too, to stop them getting ill from the conditions they live in, and these end up in our bodies as well.

Animals that are raised according to free-range standards have loads more room to move around in. Chickens can go outdoors if they want to through flaps in the sides of the barns, so they can scratch, peck and run around in the open air. If they are raised to organic standards, not only do they have more room and access to the outdoors, they are also fed a diet that's as natural as possible, with no added antibiotics, and they're reared on land that has had no pesticides or fertilizers used on it. I think the organic method of farming is the nearest to what nature intended.

Hanging

Unlike fish, meat that is really fresh actually isn't that nice to eat. It's often tougher, chewier and blander than when it's been hung. You can take the hanging bit quite literally – butchers leave meat to hang on a hook in a big fridge for a while. With time, the fibers of the meat start to break down, making the texture softer and the flavor better. It's a bit like aging red wine in a cellar to make it smoother and fruitier.

It's mostly larger animals that need to be hung, normally about a week for lamb, one to two weeks for pork, and up to three or four weeks for beef. Once meat has been hung to the stage the butcher thinks best, any hard bits are trimmed off and it's cut into roasts, chops and steaks to sell to customers. Hanging takes time, though, and as time is money this explains why most meat nowadays is not hung for as long as it should be.

The way forward

I've been a bit polite in the past and have never tried to push people towards particular products. But now I've learned more about meat, begun to grow my own veg and rear my own animals, I would seriously like you to make better-quality meat a new priority. When you understand what goes into producing meat you soon realize that organic meat isn't overpriced. Rather, standard or economy ranges are cut-price, poor quality and bad value. How the hell did they raise that whole animal and manage to sell it at a profit for a few dollars?

Now, before anyone says, 'It's OK for you,' and starts accusing me of being pretentious, I know not everyone can afford to go out and start spending more money on meat just like that, but what you can do is try it.

Next time you're meat shopping, see if you can't maybe buy free-range or rare-breed meat, or something that's been hung properly. Try to get one out of those three for a start, and if you notice the difference, make two out of three your next goal. The day you buy all three will be the day you never look back.

I just know that once you taste top-quality meat, and once you realize how poor-quality meat is produced, you won't want 'standard' meat any more than a bargain-basement mobile phone, a pair of cheap trainers or a clapped-out old banger of a car. It's time to upgrade!

If you really can't afford to spend more than you're spending at the moment, look at countries like Italy, where people on very low incomes still eat incredibly well. They make the most of pasta, risotto and vegetable dishes, and the two or three times a week they do have a piece of meat, they spend their money on something that's great quality.

The aim of this chapter is to arm you with a basic knowledge of meat – types of meat, where the different cuts come from and how to be a better meat shopper. The world of butchery is pretty complicated, but understanding the basics and knowing a few bits of lingo will mean that your butcher respects you on a completely different level. Not only will you get what you're paying for, but you'll know how to ask for cuts of meat that will make your money go further without compromising on taste or quality.

If you want to learn more about free-range and organic food, have a look at the USDA's National Organic Program's website, www.ams.usda.gov/nop. They are the people who accredit farms and maintain standards across the US.

How to be a better meat shopper

- Look at the windows, walls and floor of your butcher's. If it's dirty, just imagine what the fridge out the back where all the meat is stored looks like.

- Personally, I would never shop in a butcher's that's not clean and where the meat isn't nicely laid out. Different meats should be displayed in different areas and not all piled on top of each other.

- Don't be afraid to ask your butcher where the meat comes from and whether it's organic or free-range. A good butcher can even tell you about the animal's breed, the farm it was raised on, how long it's been hung, or he will certainly find out for you. If you don't get the answers you're looking for, vote with your feet! It's no different than a car salesman knowing nothing about the car he's trying to sell you – would you carry your kids around in it? I don't think so. So why feed them food you know nothing about?

- With the exception of game birds and some meat that has been hung for longer, shop with your nose. If meat has been stored badly, sitting in its own blood or wrapped up in plastic wrap, it's likely the meat will smell sweaty, so don't go near it. Even if it's not too bad when you buy it, just imagine what it'll smell like after an hour in a plastic bag in the trunk of your car while you drive home!

- Whether you are buying chops, steaks or roasts, on or off the bone, you can tell a lot about the quality by just looking at it: bright red pieces of beef or lamb that are wet with blood haven't been hung properly and will probably be tough and tasteless. The surface of the meat should look matte and dry, with a dark, rich red or even slightly purplish color and creamy white fat around the edges.

- Good-quality red meat should be marbled nicely, with thin threads of white or creamy colored fat spread throughout the meat. This is what you want because this fat will melt and keep the meat moist during cooking.

- Pork, too, should be dry-looking with no blood or juices around it, and with a good layer of fat and a thick layer of skin that'll give you good crackling. Don't worry if you see hairs or bristles on the surface of the skin, as these can be cut or singed off before cooking and won't affect the flavor at all.

- Chicken should have a high breastbone and creamy white or yellow skin without any blemishes or bruises. Bear in mind, though, that skin color and shape can depend on the breed of the bird.

How to cook meat

When it comes to cooking meat, you don't have quite as much choice of method as you do with fish, as it depends on how tender or tough it is. In general the parts of an animal that do the most work, such as the shoulders and shins, are the toughest and they need long, slow cooking to tenderize them. The good thing about these cuts, though, is that you will be rewarded with a meltingly soft piece of meat with a really good flavor. The parts that don't really do much work are the back muscles – that means rib, loin, rump and the laziest of all, the fillet. These parts are so tender they can be cooked quickly, most often as steaks, and even served slightly underdone.

Roasting

This method is best used for cooking tender roasts of meat like rack of lamb, fore rib of beef or loin of pork. The roast is seasoned and placed in a hot oven, around 400°F, and cooked, basting as often as possible with the fat that renders out of it, until the meat is done to your liking. Red meat like beef and lamb can be slightly undercooked and served pink in the middle.

Slow-roasting

A great way of cooking not quite so tender cuts like lamb or pork shoulder, or pork belly; cuts that are just a little bit too tough to roast normally. It's the same as roasting except the oven temperature is a little lower, typically 350°F, and the idea is to cook the meat through and then give it a little more time to break its fibers down.

Pot-roasting

This is a gentler method of cooking than straight roasting, and works well with tougher cuts, just like slow-roasting. The meat is browned and cooked in a high-sided pan in the oven, and half-way through cooking, wine or stock is added to keep the meat moist and to make a sauce. It's good to baste the meat with the sauce while it finishes off cooking.

Pan-roasting

This is for tender cuts like rack of lamb and rib of beef that are too thick to fry. Once the meat has browned in the pan, it's popped in the oven to finish off cooking.

Frying and stir-frying

Tender cuts like steaks are often fried in oil or butter in a heavy hot pan, turning every now and then until they are done to the right point. The Chinese use tender cuts of beef for their stir-fries as the cooking process is so quick. Tougher pieces of meat would have no time to break down if cooked this way.

Broiling and grilling

Broiling under a hot broiler or grilling on a grill is a great way to cook steaks. Make sure the broiler is as hot as possible before you put the meat under. If you're cooking meat on a grill, sear your steaks on the hot part first, then cook them out on a medium-hot part of the grill. This will ensure they're crispy on the outside and juicy in the middle.

Poaching

This is a very delicate way of cooking tender cuts of meat. Just like fish, meat can be poached in stock and wine, removed when just cooked and served with dressings or sauces to help lift its flavor.

Stewing or braising

The best way to cook tough cuts of meat like shoulder, shin and brisket of beef. The meat is cooked gently and slowly in a pot, either on the stove or in the oven, with vegetables, flavorings such as herbs and spices and either stock, wine, beer or water, until it's tender enough to eat.

Poultry and game birds

Birds are so versatile they can be cooked by using any of the above methods and you'll get a fantastic result. Older chickens and larger game birds that have toughened up are better when stewed.

Before you start

Make sure your meat is at room temperature. This way, it'll cook more evenly and the timings given in this chapter will work better.

Is it cooked yet?

- Tough cuts of meat are ready when they're meltingly tender and soft, and you can pull them apart with a fork.

- Poultry and pork are ready when the meat's hot in the middle – 175°F – and if the juices run clear when you cut the meat. Good-quality pork and duck can sometimes be eaten slightly pink.

- Steak cuts of beef and lamb can be grilled, fried or pan-roasted to different states of 'doneness', depending on your taste. The pictures on this page will help you tell which page is which. There's no right or wrong way to have your steak, so don't be afraid to experiment with the cooking times until you have it perfect, and cook it or order your steak the way you like it!

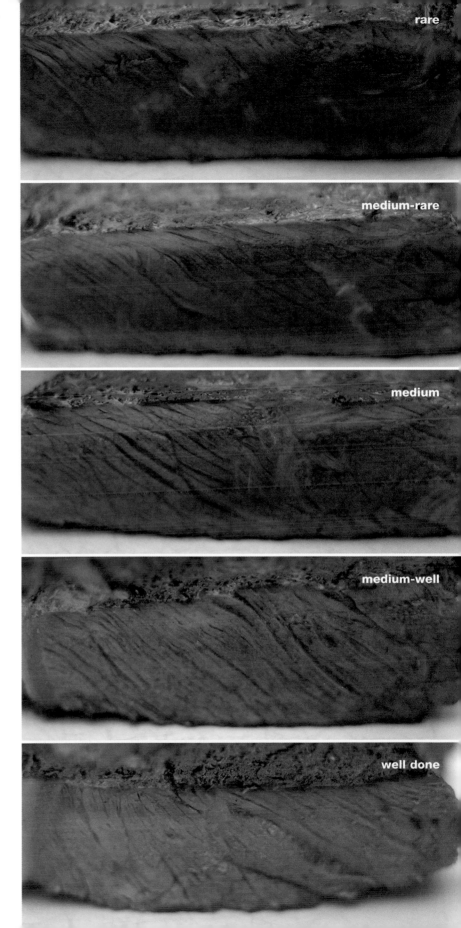

rare

medium-rare

medium

medium-well

well done

CUTS OF BEEF

1. Shoulder
Usually boned and diced for stewing or made into ground meat.

8. Brisket
Another tough but tasty cut of beef. It's fantastic when boiled, braised or very slowly roasted.

7. Shin
This is the toughest cut of beef, but after long, slow cooking in a stew it's meltingly soft and delicious.

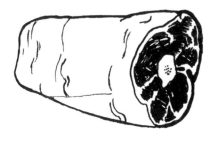

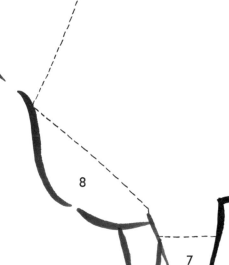

6. Topside
A piece of leg that's cut off the bone and rolled into a roast.

2. Rib steak

Either cut into individual ribs to serve two people or kept together to make a roast. The center of the rib is called the 'rib-eye'.

3. Sirloin steak

Taken off the bone, it can be cut into 'sirloin steaks', or it can be roasted whole and carved.

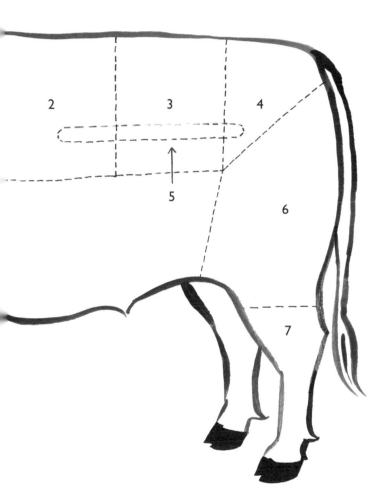

4. Rump steak

This cut is always boneless and, although not as tender as other steaks, it's very juicy and tasty.

5. Fillet steak

The fillet is a long muscle that comes from inside the cow. It's very tender and soft and is often cut into 'fillet steaks' or roasted in one piece.

Melt-in-your-mouth shin stew

Cooking a shin of beef or any good stewing cut this way gives you some really fantastic comfort food. Just letting it slowly blip away in the oven, with the sauce becoming more and more intense, is the nicest sort of cooking there is. Delicious served with some mashed root veg – like carrots, potatoes, a bit of rutabaga, some turnips – but you could also serve it with straight mash, polenta or bubble and squeak (you know, fried veg and potatoes, cockney-London style!) and some nice buttered cabbage or spinach.

Preheat your oven to 350°F. In a heavy-bottomed ovenproof saucepan, heat a splash of olive oil and gently fry the onions, carrots, celery, garlic, herbs, porcini and cinnamon for 5 minutes until softened slightly. Meanwhile, toss the pieces of beef in a little seasoned flour, shaking off any excess. Add the meat to the pan and stir everything together, then add the tomatoes, wine and a pinch of salt and pepper. Gently bring to the boil, cover with a double-thickness piece of aluminum foil and a lid and place in your preheated oven for 3 hours or until the beef is meltingly tender and can be broken up with a spoon. Taste and check the seasoning, remove the cinnamon stick and rosemary sprigs and serve.

Matt's wine suggestion: French red – Côtes du Rhône

serves 4

olive oil
2 red onions, peeled and roughly chopped
3 carrots, peeled and roughly chopped
3 sticks of celery, trimmed and roughly chopped
4 cloves of garlic, unpeeled
a few sprigs of fresh rosemary
2 bay leaves
a small handful of dried porcini
1 cinnamon stick
2¼lb shin of beef, preferably free-range or organic, bone removed, trimmed and cut into 2 inch pieces
sea salt and freshly ground black pepper
1 tablespoon flour
2 x 14oz cans good-quality plum tomatoes
⅔ of a 750ml bottle of Chianti

Ultimate rib of beef with rosemary and garlic roast potatoes

Steaks are so popular these days – on a lot of meat counters, they're all you see. Fillets, sirloins or rib-eyes are often cut into neat portions and packaged; you hardly ever see them on the bone. So what I want you to do for this recipe is go to your butcher's and ask for a single rib of beef on the bone. You only need one rib for two people. It takes a little longer to cook than a normal steak, but when you serve it on a big board in the middle of the table with a pile of rosemary potatoes and the resting juices, and slice it into juicy chunks, you'll never look back. You even get the bone to nibble on!

Put the garlic, lemon zest and the tip of the rosemary brush in a pestle and mortar, add a glug of olive oil and bash together. Use your rosemary brush to rub half the marinade over your rib steak, and leave the steak to marinate for at least an hour.

Preheat your oven to 425°F and get your potatoes parboiled and in the oven. Meanwhile, heat an ovenproof griddle pan on the stovetop until white-hot, and season your steak generously. Put it in the pan and fry for a couple of minutes before turning it over and putting the pan in the oven for 20 minutes for medium. Every 5 minutes, turn the steak over and baste it with some of the remaining marinade, using your little rosemary brush. Cook to your liking – personally, medium-rare to medium is my fave. When done, remove from the oven, squeeze over a little lemon juice, drizzle over a splash of peppery extra virgin olive oil and let the steak rest for 5 minutes. Serve with your perfect roasted potatoes.

Matt's wine suggestion: Italian red – Sangiovese

serves 2

1 x rosemary-roasted cubed potatoes recipe (see page 298)
3 cloves of garlic, unpeeled
zest and juice of 1 lemon
a small bunch of fresh rosemary, tied together at the base to give you a little brush
olive oil
1 x 2lb 11oz rib of beef, preferably free-range or organic, French trimmed
peppery extra virgin olive oil

Rib roast of beef with beetroot and horseradish

This rib roast of beef makes the perfect roast. Even if there are fewer than eight of you it's still worth cooking the whole roast and enjoying the leftovers. Beef and beetroot work so well together. When buying beetroot, try and get hold of some different shapes and colors.

Preheat your oven to 400°F. Wash and scrub the beetroots thoroughly to remove any dirt or grit, place in a pan of cold salted water and bring to the boil, then simmer for about 50 minutes. Meanwhile, put all the marinade ingredients and a few generous pinches of salt in a pestle and mortar or Flavour Shaker, bash them up, add a couple of glugs of olive oil and rub all over your roast. Put the roast on a large roasting pan and into the preheated oven for an hour and a half.

When your beetroot is almost cooked, drain and peel while still warm, then cut each one in half and toss all the pieces in a bowl with the garlic, thyme sprigs, balsamic vinegar and a few glugs of olive oil. After its hour is up, remove the beef from the oven and scatter the beetroot halves all around the meat in the pan. Place the pan back in the oven and cook for a further 30 minutes, by which time the beef should be medium-rare and the beetroot perfectly roasted (feel free to cook the meat to your liking, though). Allow the meat to rest for up to 20 minutes – you may need to keep the beetroot warm in a low oven.

Chop the marjoram or parsley leaves and mix with the crème fraîche and lemon juice. Spike well with the horseradish and season to taste. Carve the beef on to a large platter with the resting juices. Serve with the roast beetroots, flavored crème fraîche and some lovely roast potatoes.

Matt's wine suggestion: Australian red – Shiraz

serves 8

4½lb fresh, different
   colored beetroots
sea salt and freshly ground
   black pepper
olive oil
1 11–13½lb rib roast,
   preferably free-range or
   organic, French-trimmed,
   rolled and tied
2 cloves of garlic, unpeeled
a small bunch of fresh
   thyme
3 tablespoons balsamic
   vinegar
a small handful of freshly
   picked marjoram or
   parsley leaves
11oz crème fraîche
juice of 2 lemons
1½ inch chunk of fresh
   horseradish, peeled and
   grated, or 3 tablespoons
   from a jar

for the marinade
a small handful of freshly
   picked rosemary leaves
6 cloves of garlic, peeled
6 good-quality anchovy
   fillets in oil, drained
zest of 2 lemons

Grilled fillet steak with the creamiest white beans and leeks

This combination of medium-rare beef, with all its lovely resting juices, alongside creamy sweet white beans Is a classic and an absolute must if you've never tried it before.

Sweat the leeks, thyme and garlic with a splash of olive oil and the butter in a heavy-bottomed saucepan on a low heat for 20 minutes until they are soft and sweet. Turn up the heat and add the white wine. Let the wine come to the boil, then add the beans and a splash of water, so that the beans are almost covered. Allow to simmer gently for 5 to 10 minutes until the beans are lovely and creamy. Add the parsley, crème fraîche and a good glug of the extra virgin olive oil and taste for seasoning.

Heat a griddle pan until white-hot, season your steaks and pat with olive oil. Grill a 1½ inch thick steak for 2 to 3 minutes on each side for medium-rare. You can keep them on there for longer, turning as you go, until cooked to your liking. Remove from the grill on to a dish and rest for 5 minutes. Squeeze over some lemon juice and drizzle over some extra virgin olive oil. Carve the steaks into thick slices. Divide the creamy beans between your plates and place the steak on top, drizzling over some of the resting juices.

Matt's wine suggestion: Italian red – Nero d'Avola

serves 4

4 leeks, washed, trimmed and finely sliced
a small bunch of fresh thyme, leaves picked
2 garlic cloves, peeled and finely chopped
olive oil
a knob of butter
a wineglass of white wine
1lb 2oz good-quality canned lima beans, drained and rinsed
a small handful of freshly picked parsley leaves, finely chopped
1 tablespoon crème fraîche
good-quality peppery extra virgin olive oil
sea salt and freshly ground black pepper
7oz well-marbled fillet steaks, preferably free-range or organic, 1–1½ inches thick
1 lemon

Pan-fried sirloin steak with simple Chianti butter sauce and olive oil mash

This simple way of cooking and serving steak is so rewarding. You only need a little of the sauce just to drizzle over the top of the meat and the mashed potatoes. It's great!

Put the potatoes into a large pan of salted water, bring to the boil and simmer until soft and tender. Drain them in a colander and allow them to sit for 4 minutes to steam away any excess moisture. Return the potatoes to the pan and mash them up, stirring in a large glug of olive oil, the Parmesan and butter. Taste, season and then transfer to a bowl, cover with plastic wrap and place over a pot of simmering water to keep warm.

Heat a heavy frying pan, large enough to cook both steaks at once without them touching. Season your steaks and brush them with olive oil. Using a pair of tongs, hold the steaks fatty-edge down in the frying pan to render and color the fat. When the fat is golden, fry the steaks for 8 minutes in total for medium-rare, turning them every minute. Remove from the pan to rest.

Turn the heat down and add a knob of butter to the pan. Fry your shallots and thyme for 4 minutes, then add the wine and reduce by half. Pour in the resting juices from the meat, add the 2 remaining knobs of butter and take the pan off the heat. Stir around to emulsify and make a really simple red wine sauce. Taste, season and serve with your steak and lovely olive oil mashed potatoes with a scattering of watercress and a drizzle of good olive oil.

Matt's wine suggestion: American red – Zinfandel

serves 2

for the olive oil mash
14oz potatoes, peeled and
   halved
sea salt and freshly ground
   black pepper
olive oil
a small handful of freshly
   grated Parmesan cheese
a knob of butter

2 x 7oz sirloin steaks,
   preferably free-range or
   organic, 1 inch thick, fat
   scored
sea salt and freshly ground
   black pepper
olive oil
2 knobs of butter
2 shallots or 1 small
   red onion, peeled and
   finely diced
a few sprigs of fresh thyme,
   leaves picked
1 large wineglass of Chianti
a few sprigs of watercress
good-quality extra virgin
   olive oil

CUTS OF LAMB

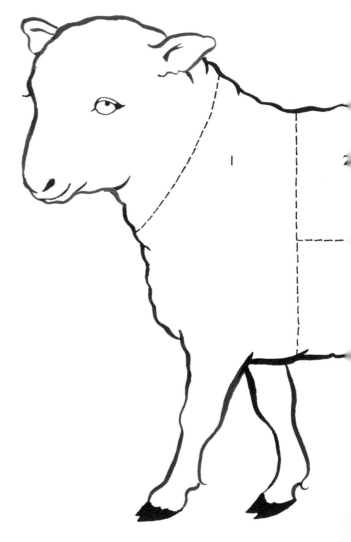

5. Leg
Great roasted whole, or boned and grilled.

4. Rump chop
A really meaty chop with great flavor and texture.

1. Shoulder
Brilliant for stewing or braising and fantastic when slow-roasted.

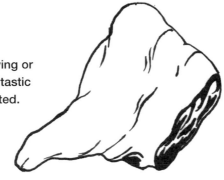

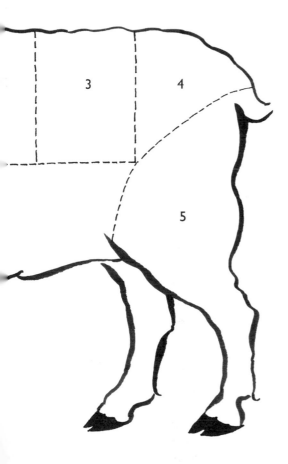

2. Chop
Lovely fried, grilled, or barbecued. When a few chops are kept together in one piece, they make a 'rack of lamb', which is lovely when roasted and cut into chops after cooking.

3. Loin chop
Great for grilling or barbecuing. A few loin chops kept together in one piece, then boned and rolled, make a lovely little roast.

Incredible baked lamb shanks

Many people have a real affection for lamb shanks, thinking of them as a bit of a treat. I've cooked them for years and really love this particular style of baking them because it's so easy and comforting – almost like wrapping up a baking potato to put on the bonfire. By using simple root veg and a flavored butter, and by tightly squeezing the aluminum foil around each shank, the most is made of the flavor of the meat without having to cover it in spices or tomatoes or anything like that. It's very easy to prep the shanks for this dish and I think they look cool enough to be a lovely main course for a dinner party.

The shanks should be eaten with all the veggies and any buttery juices. They're really good served with creamy mashed potato and steamed greens to contrast with the roasting stickiness of the lamb.

Preheat your oven to 400°F. Pick the leaves off 2 sprigs of rosemary, whiz them with the butter, most of the sage and the thyme in a food processor and season with salt and pepper. Using a small knife, take one of the lamb shanks and cut between the meat and the bone from the base of the shank upwards. You want to create a hole big enough to put your finger in, making a sort of pocket. Do this to all the shanks and divide the flavored butter between them, pushing it into the pockets. This will give a wonderful flavor to the heart of the shanks.

Tear off four arm-length pieces of aluminum foil and fold each in half to give you four large-sized pieces of foil. Divide the garlic and veg between them, making a pile in the middle of each square. Rub the lamb shanks with olive oil and season with salt and pepper, then put one on top of each pile of veg and a sprig of rosemary and a few sage leaves on top of that. Carefully pull up the sides of the foil around the shank and pour a swig of wine into each. Gather the foil around the bone, pinching it together tightly. Any excess foil can be torn or cut off with scissors. Repeat for all 4 shanks, then place the foil parcels in a baking pan with the bones facing up. Put in the preheated oven for 2½ hours or until the meat is as tender as can be. Serve the parcels in the middle of the table so that your guests can open them up themselves.

Matt's wine suggestion: Spanish red – Rioja

serves 4

6 sprigs of fresh rosemary
5½oz cold butter
15 fresh sage leaves
2 sprigs of fresh thyme, leaves picked
sea salt and freshly ground black pepper
4 lamb shanks, preferably free-range or organic, crown- or French-trimmed
12 cloves of garlic, unpeeled
2 large carrots, peeled and finely sliced
1 onion, peeled and finely sliced
1 leek, washed, halved and finely sliced
olive oil
2 wineglasses of white wine

Roast rack of lamb with potato and cauliflower dauphinois

A rack of lamb to me is always exciting – it's well behaved, it looks pretty and you can get hold of one in every good butcher shop in the country. And nothing can beat the French-trimmed rack, which just looks amazing when prepared well. To serve with the lamb, I've given a twist to the straightforward dauphinois by adding cauliflower to it. I also like to serve this with some lovely spinach braised with butter and nutmeg.

Preheat the oven to 400°F. Put the cream, milk, the sliced garlic and bay leaves into a saucepan and grate over the nutmeg. Simmer for 5 minutes. Remove from the heat, season with salt and pepper and discard the bay leaves. Get yourself a large earthenware dish and rub it with the butter. Put a layer of potatoes in the bottom, sprinkle over some thyme, then add a layer of cauliflower, another layer of potatoes, and so on, finishing with potatoes. Carefully pour over the infused milk and cream. Oil one side of a piece of aluminum foil and cover the dish, oil-side down, then place in the preheated oven for about 40 minutes or until the potatoes are soft.

While the dauphinois is cooking, rub the lamb with plenty of salt and pepper, pat it all over with a little olive oil and place skin-side down in a large ovenproof pan on a medium heat to begin to render (melt) the fat away from the rack – this should take 4 to 5 minutes. Turn the lamb over in its fat to color on all sides. When it's nicely brown, remove the lamb to a chopping board and sprinkle generously with the finely chopped rosemary. Carefully pour any excess fat out of the pan and put the lamb back in, fat-side down.

Take the dauphinois out of the oven and keep warm. Put your lamb in the middle of the oven and cook for 10 to 20 minutes, depending on how you prefer your lamb to be cooked and the size of the racks. Ten minutes will give you rare meat, 10 to 14 minutes medium (which is what I'm interested in), and 20 minutes will cook it through.

As soon as the lamb goes in the oven, get yourself a dish towel and carefully push down on the dauphinois (remember it's hot!) to make it more compact. Then remove the foil. Feel free to pour a little extra cream over the top if you want, and give it a light seasoning. Finally, sprinkle with a little grated Parmesan, which isn't totally traditional but I like it. Place the dauphinois in the oven below the lamb and within about 10 minutes it will have gratinated and become beautifully golden.

When the lamb is done, remove it from the oven and let it rest for 5 minutes. Turn the oven down to keep the dauphinois warm. To serve, each rack can be cut in half, or you can present the rack whole on a plate, or sliced up into individual little chops.

Matt's wine suggestion: Chilean red – Cabernet Sauvignon

serves 4

for the dauphinois
1 cup plus 2 tablespoons heavy cream
1 cup plus 2 tablespoons milk
4 cloves of garlic, peeled and finely sliced
2 bay leaves
¼ of a nutmeg
sea salt and freshly ground black pepper
a knob of butter
1lb 6oz potatoes, peeled and sliced about ½ inch thick
½ a large cauliflower, trimmed and thickly sliced
a few sprigs of fresh thyme, leaves picked
a handful of freshly grated Parmesan cheese

2 x 8-bone racks of lamb, preferably free-range or organic, French-trimmed
sea salt and freshly ground black pepper
olive oil
a bunch of fresh rosemary, leaves picked and finely chopped

Lovely lamb shank pie

This dish is based on a pretty rock-solid way of braising lamb shanks, but instead of just serving them as stewed meat in their juices, I decided to put them in a baking dish covered with puff pastry. This makes a real change and is delicious, as stewed meat and pastry go so well together. It's best served as you'd serve any pie – with simple boiled vegetables like carrots, broccoli and beans.

To make the sauce, whiz the tomato purée, wine and the tablespoon of flour in a food processor. Heat up a casserole-type pan and add some olive oil. Season the shanks all over with salt and pepper, then put them in the pan and brown them on all sides for a few minutes. Remove them to a plate and carefully discard the hot oil. Add some fresh olive oil to the pan with the chopped carrots, onions, turnip, leek and celery. Cook for 15 minutes on a medium heat until the veg has softened. Add the 2 heaped teaspoons of flour, the wine sauce and the rosemary and thyme. Put the shanks back into the pan and push them down so they are completely covered by the liquid (although it's fine for the bones to stick out). Bring to the boil, put a tight-fitting lid on the pan and simmer for 1½ hours. What you want to achieve is a delicious sauce and meat that is tender but still holding its shape.

While this is ticking away, roll out the pastry on a clean, floured surface to the thickness of a silver dollar, then cut it into strips about 1½ inches wide. Find yourself a high-sided earthenware dish that the 4 shanks will fit snugly into. When the shanks have been simmering for their hour and a half, take them out of the pan and put them into your dish. At the same time, preheat the oven to 400°F. Taste the sauce and season if it needs it. You want it to be thick and stewy – if it's a bit thin, simmer it with the lid off for a few minutes until you get the right consistency, then pour it over the lamb shanks.

Beat the egg and milk together and brush around the rim of your dish. Lay the strips of puff pastry randomly and erratically over the dish (see the picture opposite), criss-crossing and winding them around the shank bones. You will end up with a whole lid of pastry on the top and, when it's cooked, all the goodness bubbling up through the gaps around the bones. Don't worry if you overlap the strips of pastry a few times – you want to keep it rough – and there's no need to trim the edges neatly. Brush your pastry strips with the egg wash.

Bake the pie in your preheated oven for about 20 minutes until the pastry is nicely golden. Serve in the middle of the table with some boiled or steamed broccoli, carrots and cabbage.

Matt's wine suggestion: Australian red – Shiraz

serves 4

for the sauce
2 tablespoons tomato
  purée
¾ of a 750ml bottle of red
  wine
1 tablespoon flour, plus 2
  heaped teaspoons
olive oil
4 lamb shanks, preferably
  free-range or organic,
  French-trimmed
sea salt and freshly ground
  black pepper
3 carrots, peeled and
  roughly chopped
3 onions, peeled and
  roughly chopped
1 medium turnip, peeled
  and roughly chopped
1 leek, washed, trimmed
  and roughly chopped
4–5 sticks of celery,
  trimmed and roughly
  chopped
a small bunch of fresh
  rosemary
a small bunch of fresh
  thyme

1 x 1lb package of puff
  pastry
flour, for dusting
1 large free-range or
  organic egg, beaten
a splash of milk

Roast leg of lamb with eggplant and onions

Many of us are in love with good old roast lamb with all the trimmings – mint sauce, roast potatoes, you know the story! But life is too short to be eating the same thing all the time, so I wanted to show you a fantastic, classic Italian way of cooking lamb with eggplants. The lamb bit is dead simple; what I want you to concentrate on is the seasoning of the eggplants and you'll be laughing.

Preheat the oven to 425°F. Rub your leg of lamb all over with olive oil and salt and pepper and place in a roasting pan. Roast for 30 minutes in the preheated oven. While it's cooking, cut the eggplants in half and then into 2 inch erratic wedges. Toss them with the onion wedges in a little olive oil with a sprinkling of salt and pepper and the dried oregano.

When the lamb has come out of the oven, pour away most of the fat and sprinkle the chopped rosemary on to the lamb. Scatter the eggplant and onion pieces around the lamb in the tray and put it back in the oven for an hour.

Meanwhile, make your tomato sauce. In a saucepan, fry the garlic and chopped parsley stalks in a splash of olive oil for a minute, then add the tomatoes, a pinch of salt and pepper, a good swig of vinegar, the dried chilli and the anchovy fillets. Simmer for 30 minutes. Make a point of checking the veg and lamb after 20 minutes. Turn the lamb over and stir the veggies, making sure they don't go dry – add a splash of water if you need to. Look after them and they'll be fantastic.

When the lamb is cooked, remove the pan from the oven, put the lamb on to a platter with a carving knife and fork and cover loosely with aluminum foil. Leave to sit for 10 to 15 minutes. Pour away any excess fat and then pour your tomato sauce over the roasted eggplants and onions. Place the baking pan on a medium heat, and using a wooden spoon, scrape loose all the sticky bits at the bottom but try not to break up the veg too much. You want it to be a chunky sauce, not a pulp. Add most of your parsley leaves and simmer for a couple of minutes on a gentle heat.

Now taste the sauce – it should be slightly sweet and slightly sour, so it may need another little swig of vinegar. Take a little bit of time and you'll get it just perfect. When you're really happy with the eggplants and you have the same sauce consistency as in the picture opposite, pour the sauce either on to a separate platter or on to the same one as the lamb. Chop your remaining parsley leaves, drizzle with extra virgin olive oil and sprinkle over the parsley. Serve the lamb at the table as is, with delicious warm bread and a little salad.

Matt's wine suggestion: Italian red – Barolo

serves 6

1 x 4½lb leg of lamb,
   preferably free-range
   or organic
olive oil
sea salt and freshly ground
   black pepper
3 round purple eggplants
   or 4 normal ones
2 red onions, peeled
   and each cut into about
   6 wedges
1 tablespoon dried oregano
a bunch of fresh rosemary,
   leaves picked

for the tomato sauce
2–3 cloves of garlic, peeled
   and finely sliced
a large bunch of fresh
   flat-leaf parsley, leaves
   picked, stalks chopped
olive oil
2 x14oz cans good-quality
   plum tomatoes
sea salt and freshly ground
   black pepper
good-quality herb or red
   wine vinegar
1 dried red chilli, crumbled
3 good-quality anchovy
   fillets in oil, drained
good-quality extra virgin
   olive oil

Mad Moroccan lamb

I really love this dish, for its taste and its craziness! Start the lamb on its own in the oven, then transfer it to another pan and completely cover it with the couscous. It may seem a bit of a fuss, but it gives such intense flavor and the lamb will be meltingly tender when you eat it. It's lovely served with a crunchy salad of cucumber and delicate strips of carrot.

Preheat the oven to 425°F. Score the lamb in criss-crosses about 1 inch apart. In a grinder, or in batches using a pestle and mortar, smash up the spices and salt until you have a powder. Rub this all over the meat and push some rosemary leaves into the cuts. Put the lamb in a roasting pan and put that straight into the oven to cook for 2 hours.

Heat some olive oil in a large saucepan and fry your onions, cinnamon and marjoram or thyme with a pinch of salt and pepper for about 15 minutes or until softened. Add the chickpeas with about 3 cups of water and the vinegar. Simmer on a medium heat until nice and thick, then remove from the stove.

In another pan, bring your stock to the boil (you can use water if you like), add your dried fruit and season lightly. Simmer slowly for about 5 minutes, by which time the fruit will have plumped up a bit. Add a good glug of olive oil and the couscous, then remove it from the heat and put to one side to allow the couscous to soak up all the liquid. When it has plumped up and there is no liquid left, pour the couscous out on to a flat tray, drizzle it with olive oil and set it to one side again.

After 2 hours the lamb will be lovely, golden and roasted – a treat. Turn the heat down to 400°F. Take the lamb out of the pan and set aside. Pour away the fat from the roasting pan and put it on a low heat. Add a little water, scrape any sticky bits off the bottom and turn off the heat. Get a large pot or snug-fitting roasting pan with 4–5 inch high sides and rub it with a little olive oil. Sprinkle about 1 inch of couscous on the bottom, some more round the sides, then spoon your chickpeas into the middle, making sure you remove the cinnamon stick. Put your lamb on top, pour the pan juices over it and completely cover with the rest of the couscous. Put the lemon halves around the sides, rub a piece of wet wax paper with oil and drape it over the couscous. Cover with aluminum foil, then put it in the oven for another hour.

Use a knife to pull some of the couscous away and if the meat pulls away from the bone and melts in your mouth, it's done! Keep it wrapped up while you spike your yogurt with the juice from the roasted lemon, which will be sweet and jammy. Bring the pan to the table, cracking open the couscous in front of your guests. It should be lightly crispy on top and fluffy in the middle, with an incredible smell of lamb. Add a dollop of yogurt and sprinkle over some cilantro and chilli. Lovely!

Matt's wine suggestion: Italian red – Amarone, or stick to beer!

serves 6–8

for the lamb
1 x 4½lb shoulder
   of lamb, preferably free-range
   or organic
2 teaspoons cumin seeds
2 teaspoons coriander seeds
2 teaspoons fennel seeds
2 teaspoons black peppercorns
2–3 dried red chillies
2 teaspoons sea salt
a small handful of rosemary leaves

for the chickpeas
olive oil
4 large red onions, peeled
   and sliced
1 cinnamon stick
a bunch of fresh marjoram or
   thyme, leaves picked and
   roughly chopped
sea salt and freshly ground
   black pepper
2 x 14oz cans
   good-quality chickpeas
1 cup good-quality balsamic
   vinegar

for the couscous
2 pints vegetable stock
9oz raisins, dates,
   sour cherries, cranberries
   or apricots, or a mix of
   these, roughly chopped
olive oil
1lb 9oz couscous
2 lemons, halved

for serving
1 pint plain yogurt
a big handful of fresh
   cilantro leaves
1 fresh red chilli, deseeded
   and finely sliced

CUTS OF PORK

1. Shoulder

Can be chopped or diced for stewing. Also fantastic when slow-roasted on the bone.

7. Belly

A fatty but incredibly tender cut of meat which is delicious when slow-roasted.

6. Leg

Usually roasted whole, but it can also be boned and cut into smaller roasts, or thinly sliced to make 'escalopes' for pan-frying.

5. Rump chop

A really meaty chop with great flavor and texture.

2. Rib chop

Great grilled or barbecued. When a few chops are kept together in one piece, they make a brilliant rib roast.

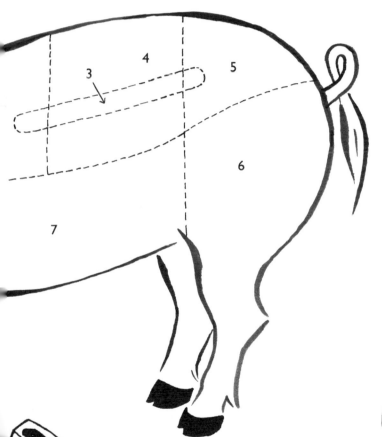

3. Fillet

The fillet or 'tenderloin' is a long thin muscle. It's normally cooked whole or cut into steaks and pan-fried.

4. Loin chop

These lovely lean chops are ideal for pan-roasting and grilling. The loin can be kept in one piece, boned and rolled to make a fantastic roast.

Overnight slow-roasted pork

Pork cooked this way gives you the most meltingly tender meat. This is the last job we do in the evening at the restaurant before we go home, so that when we get to work the next day we have the best roast pork to serve for lunch – you can do the same at home, as it's incredibly easy. This recipe only works with a whole shoulder, so it's an ideal dish to serve on Christmas Day when you have lots of people around (as long as you remember to put it in the oven on Christmas Eve!). Ask your butcher to prepare you a shoulder roast from the whole shoulder as you would a shoulder of lamb.

PS This is a fantastic celebration meal, but before you go out and buy your meat, make sure you've got a pan – and an oven – that's big enough.

Preheat your oven to maximum. Smash the fennel seeds with the salt in a pestle and mortar until fine. Put the roughly chopped vegetables, garlic and thyme sprigs into a large roasting pan. Pat the pork shoulder with olive oil and sit it on top of the vegetables. Now massage all the smashed fennel seeds into the skin of the pork, making sure you push them right into all the scores to maximize the flavor. Put the pork into your preheated oven for 20 to 30 minutes or until it's beginning to color, then turn your oven down to 250°F and cook the pork for 9 to 12 hours, until the meat is soft and sticky and you can pull it apart easily with a fork.

Tip all the wine into the roasting tray and let it cook for another hour to give you a perfect sauce. Once the pork is out of the oven, let it rest for half an hour before removing it to a large board. I like to brush off any excess salt from the meat, then I mash up the veg in the pan using a potato masher. Add the stock to the roasting pan, put it on the heat and boil until you have a lovely, intensely flavored gravy (you can thicken it with a little sieved flour if you like but I prefer mine light). The pork is great served with some good cranberry beans, braised greens, your roast veg mash and tasty sauce.

Matt's wine suggestion: Spanish red – Garnacha

serves 12

2 tablespoons fennel seeds
1 tablespoon sea or rock salt
2 fennel bulbs, trimmed and roughly chopped
4 medium carrots, peeled and roughly chopped
3 onions, peeled and roughly chopped
1 bulb of garlic, cloves unpeeled and smashed
a bunch of fresh thyme
1 x 11–13½lb piece of pork shoulder on the bone, preferably free-range or organic, skin scored
olive oil
a 750ml bottle of white wine
1 pint chicken or vegetable stock

Slow-roasted pork belly with the sweetest braised fennel

Pork belly is a joy to eat but still an underrated cut of meat in Britain. You can slice it about ½ inch thick and grill it until crisp with good results, but for this recipe slow-cooking for 3 to 4 hours is a must. By slow-cooking the fennel as well you get an incredible sweetness. It works so well with pork, and both are great served with mash, polenta or lentils – lovely.

Preheat your oven to its maximum temperature. Get yourself a sharp knife, or even a clean Stanley knife, and score the skin of the pork belly (see opposite).

In a pestle and mortar or a Flavor Shaker, bash up the fennel seeds with a tablespoon of salt until you have a powder, then massage it into the scores on the skin. In a roasting pan, toss the fresh fennel with the thyme, garlic, a good splash of oil and some salt and pepper. Place the pork belly on top and put into the preheated oven. After 10 minutes, turn the oven down to 325°F and roast the pork for a further hour. By whacking the temperature right up at the beginning and then turning it down you will start the crackling off nicely; the meat can then continue to cook slowly.

If you'd like to serve your pork with a lovely salsa verde, make it now and set aside. When the hour is up, take the tray out of the oven, pour away any excess fat, add the white wine and pop back in the oven for another hour. Now remove the fennel and keep warm, while you put the pork back in for a final hour until the skin is golden and crisp and the meat is melt-in-your-mouth tender. If the wine starts to evaporate during this time, add a splash more, or a touch of water, to loosen and make a light gravy.

Allow the pork to rest for 10 minutes and you'll have a beautiful ready-made gravy and lovely sweet, soft fennel. Carve the meat into large chunks and serve with the gravy, salsa verde (if using) and the reserved fennel tops sprinkled on top.

Matt's wine suggestion: French white – Chardonnay

serves 6–8

1 x 4½lb pork belly
  on the bone, preferably
  free-range or organic
2 tablespoons fennel seeds
sea salt and freshly ground
  black pepper
4 fennel bulbs, each cut
  into sixths, herby tops
  removed and reserved
a small bunch of fresh
  thyme, leaves picked
5 cloves of garlic, unpeeled
olive oil
optional: 1 x salsa verde
  recipe (see page 218)
a 750ml bottle of white
  wine

Old-school pork chops with apples and sage

Here is my version of a good English country classic – pork, apple and Stilton. Great pub grub!

Preheat the oven to 400°F. What I like to do is to lay the pork chops out on a board and, using a sharp knife, make 1-inch-deep cuts all along the fatty side of them. Have a look at the picture opposite and you'll see what I mean. You can even ask your butcher to do this for you if you like. It helps to render the fat out and will also make the skin crispy. Sprinkle the chops with salt and pepper.

Pour a glug of olive oil into a hot pan. Carefully place your chops in it and cook them for 2 to 3 minutes on each side until golden brown. If you need to, open out the little pieces of fat along the edge so they don't stick together.

When the chops are nearly done, lift them out of the pan and put them in an oiled baking pan. Add the apple wedges and a knob of butter to the pan and fry until lightly golden. Lay 4 wedges of apple on top of each pork chop. Dress your sage leaves in a little olive oil and top each apple stack with them. Sometimes I like to top it all off with a knob of Stilton or taleggio. Put the baking pan into the oven for 4 to 6 minutes until everything is golden and melted.

These chops are great served with the Savoy cabbage with Worcestershire sauce on page 356 and some simple boiled and buttered new potatoes.

Matt's wine suggestion: Australian white – Viognier

serves 4

4 x 9oz pork chops,
   preferably free-range
   or organic
sea salt and freshly ground
   black pepper
olive oil
2 good eating apples
   (e.g. McIntosh or Cox),
   unpeeled, cored and
   each cut into 8 wedges
a knob of butter
a handful of fresh sage
   leaves
optional: 3½oz good strong
   cheese like Stilton or
   taleggio

Blackened barbecued pork fillets

Although it's hard to define what 'proper' American cooking is, I've been inspired by the food from the Deep South, where there is an incredible amount of smoking, salting, barbecuing and spit-roasting going on – really intelligent cooking. This is a recipe inspired by the kinds of flavors I tasted when I was in Texas.

Skewers are useful for this recipe. They hold the four fillets together, making it easier to turn over when on the barbecue or under the broiler. It also makes serving slightly easier because when you come to slice the fillets up, you can do it between the skewers, giving you pork 'lollipops' of blackened meat, which is quite fun. But if you don't have them, you can just use your tongs.

When you've made this once, I guarantee you'll make it at least once a year as it's so damn good. Great with salad, spiced beans, corn on the cob or rice.

To make your marinade, crush up the cumin, fennel seeds and cloves in a pestle and mortar and mix with the paprika, orange zest and juice, thyme, garlic, ketchup and balsamic vinegar. Season the pork fillets with salt and pepper, then toss them in most of the marinade until completely coated. Feel free to marinate for half a day, but at least an hour. If you have metal or wooden skewers, lay the fillets side by side and skewer them together about 1 inch apart.

When you're ready to cook, simply put the meat on to a barbecue or under a hot broiler for 15 to 20 minutes or until nicely charred. Every time you turn the meat, brush it generously with the leftover marinade so you build up a sticky, blackened glaze. When they're done, put the fillets on a big platter and allow to rest for 5 minutes. Slice the meat between the skewers, or just slice each fillet in half, and sprinkle over some chopped cilantro or squeeze over some lemon juice if you fancy.

Matt's wine suggestion: American white – Viognier, or maybe even a cold beer

serves 8

for the marinade
½ teaspoon cumin seeds
1 teaspoon fennel seeds
2 cloves
1 heaped tablespoon sweet
  smoked paprika
zest and juice of 1 orange
a small bunch of fresh
  thyme, leaves picked and
  very finely chopped
4 garlic cloves, peeled and
  very finely chopped
¾ cup Heinz organic
  tomato ketchup
6 tablespoons balsamic
  vinegar

4 x 14oz pork fillets,
  preferably free-range
  or organic
sea salt and freshly ground
  black pepper
optional: a handful of fresh
  cilantro, leaves picked
  and chopped
optional: juice of 1 lemon

Schnitzel with watercress and spiced apple sauce

'Schnitzel' is an Austrian way of cooking chicken, pork or veal by tenderizing the meat, breadcrumbing the outer surface and then frying it till it's golden and crisp. I learnt to cook this from a famous American chef, David Bouley, who taught me that, apart from the quality of the meat and having good, dry, fine breadcrumbs, the real trick to a good schnitzel is to make sure the coating is not frumpy and thick and also that you're not too stingy with the cooking oil – this is so that you can agitate the pan to allow the bread coating to become light, delicate and crisp.

To make your apple sauce, in a small saucepan gently melt the butter for a minute with the orange zest and juice, the sugar, cinnamon, grated nutmeg and cloves. Stir until the butter foams, then stir in the apples. Place a lid on top and cook for 20 to 25 minutes on a medium to low heat until you have a soft, sludgy sauce. Taste and add a bit more sugar if you want; I quite like mine to be sweet and sour. Keep the apple sauce warm or put to one side to cool – whichever your prefer.

To prepare your meat, put the escalopes on to a chopping board, put a piece of wax paper on top and bat the meat with the bottom of a saucepan to flatten it a little – you want to get it to about ¼ inch thick.

To breadcrumb your meat, get yourself four large plates and lay them out in a line in front of you. From left to right, you want to have your salt and pepper in one, flour in the second, beaten egg in the third and your fine breadcrumbs in the fourth. It's very simple . . . season the pieces of meat and dip them into the flour, shaking off any excess, then put them into the egg, dripping off any excess, and into the breadcrumbs, patting them over both sides and pressing down quite firmly. Gently shake off any excess and put the meat on a board or clean plate ready to be cooked.

Heat a heavy frying pan, add a couple of good glugs of olive oil and, when it's good and hot, put both pieces of pork into the pan. Cook for 2 minutes or so, then carefully start to shake and agitate the pan to cover them in the hot oil. Turn the pork over and continue to cook for a couple of minutes until both sides are crisp and golden brown. Remove to a tray lined with paper towels and season with salt and pepper. Put a schnitzel on to each of your serving plates. Put a little pile of cornichon matchsticks and some watercress leaves on top and serve with a big lob of the apple sauce, a squeeze of lemon juice and a drizzle of extra virgin olive oil.

Matt's wine suggestion: Austrian white – Grüner Veltliner

serves 2

for the apple sauce
a knob of butter
zest and juice of ½ an orange
2 tablespoons of sugar
¼ teaspoon ground cinnamon
¼ of a nutmeg, grated
¼ teaspoon ground cloves
2 good eating apples, peeled, cored and chopped into 1 inch dice
1 cooking apple, peeled, cored and chopped into 1 inch dice

2 x 5½oz pork escalopes, preferably free-range or organic
sea salt and freshly ground black pepper
flour
1 large free-range or organic egg, beaten
3 large handfuls of dry, fine breadcrumbs
olive oil
a small handful of cornichons, drained and chopped into matchsticks
2 handfuls of watercress, washed and dried
1 lemon
extra virgin olive oil

CUTS OF CHICKEN

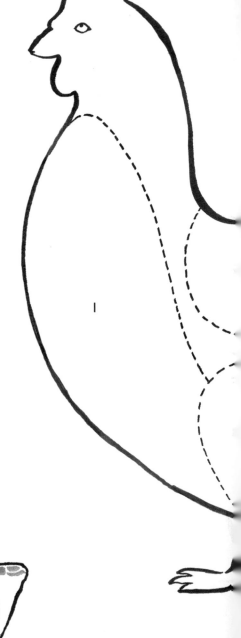

5. Legs

Instead of dividing the legs into drumsticks and thighs, it's just as nice to serve a leg in one piece as a good portion.

4. Thighs

These are the best pieces of the chicken, in my opinion! Their meat is juicy and tasty and they've got a nice bit of crispy skin on top.

1. Breast

Probably the most popular part of the chicken. If you like white meat and no bones, the breast is for you. Try not to overcook it as it sometimes goes a bit dry.

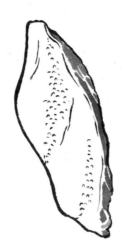

2. Wings

These are the cheapest part of the chicken and fantastic to eat. Whether roasted, grilled or barbecued, they go crispy and delicious.

2

5

4

3

3. Drumsticks

These are the chicken's shins. They're cheap as chips, easy to cook and a big barbecue favorite.

Roasted chicken breast

Make these recipes for one in a snug-fitting baking dish or, to save on washing-up, a little aluminum foil pan.

with cherry tomatoes and asparagus

Preheat the oven to 400°F. Put 1 chicken breast, with its skin left on, in a bowl. Add 8 trimmed sticks of asparagus, 6 halved cherry tomatoes and the leaves from 1 sprig of fresh rosemary plus a whole sprig of rosemary as well. Toss everything together with a pinch of sea salt and freshly ground black pepper and a drizzle of olive oil. Put the veg into an aluminum foil pan and place the chicken and rosemary sprig on top. Season well. Add some white wine and cook in the middle of the oven for 25 to 35 minutes. Serve drizzled with balsamic vinegar.

wrapped in pancetta with leeks and thyme

Preheat the oven to 400°F. Put 1 chicken breast, skin removed this time, in a bowl. Trim and wash a large leek, remove the outer leaves, then slice it into ¼ inch pieces. Add these to the bowl with the leaves of a few sprigs of fresh thyme, a good glug of olive oil, a small knob of butter, a pinch of sea salt and freshly ground black pepper and a small swig of white wine and toss together. Place your leek and flavorings from the bowl into the pan, then wrap the chicken breast in 6 or 7 slices of pancetta. This will not only flavor the chicken but also protect it while it cooks. Try and bend the sides of the pan in towards the chicken so the leeks don't get burned during cooking. Drizzle with olive oil, place a couple of whole thyme sprigs on top and cook in the middle of the oven for 25 to 35 minutes.

with creamy butternut squash and chilli

Preheat the oven to 400°F. Put 1 chicken breast, with its skin left on, in a bowl. Deseed and slice up half a fresh red chilli and add to the bowl with the leaves from a couple of sprigs of fresh marjoram or oregano and a pinch of sea salt and freshly ground black pepper. Toss together. Very carefully cut a medium butternut squash into quarters. Remove the seeds and slice one quarter of the squash as finely as you can. Place the chicken breast and flavorings from the bowl into the pan and snugly fit your squash slices around the chicken. Carefully pour a little heavy cream around the squash (not on the chicken). Season with grated nutmeg and salt and pepper, then drizzle with some olive oil and cook in the middle of the oven for 25 to 35 minutes.

with lemony Bombay potatoes

Preheat the oven to 400°F. Peel a large handful of potatoes, cut them into 1 inch dice and put them into a pan of cold salted water. Bring to the boil, simmer for a few minutes, drain and allow to steam in a colander. Put a heaped teaspoon of turmeric into a bowl and add the zest of 1 lemon, half a teaspoon of ground cumin, 5 sprigs of chopped fresh cilantro, a quarter of a red pepper, roughly chopped, and a 1 inch piece of fresh ginger, peeled and finely sliced into matchsticks. Cut 3 slices off the lemon and set aside. Squeeze the juice from the remainder of the lemon into the bowl. Shake the potatoes up in the colander and add them to the bowl with 1 chicken breast, skin left on. Toss everything around with a splash of olive oil and season well with sea salt and freshly ground black pepper. Remove the chicken, put the potatoes into the pan in one layer, and top with the lemon slices and the chicken. Drizzle with olive oil and cook in the middle of the oven for 25 to 35 minutes.

Matt's wine suggestion: a full-bodied, oaky white – Chardonnay, Semillion or Viognier

Pot-roasted poussins *agro dolce*

This is a fantastic dish with a very delicate *agro dolce* flavor (sweet and sour), and there's something so comforting, deep and dark about it, it just wants to be eaten in the colder months of the year! Poussins are baby chickens. If you can't find them, feel free to use one large chicken instead – the recipe will still work, but you will need to cook the chicken a little longer and a little slower. Both are really nice served with greens and olive oil mash (see page 158).

Preheat your oven to 400°F. Stuff a piece of orange, half a cinnamon stick and a rosemary sprig into the cavity of each bird. In a large ovenproof pan in which the poussins will fit snugly side by side, heat a glug of olive oil and a knob of butter. Add the little chickens and color them gently on all sides for 10 minutes or until lightly golden all over, then remove them to a plate to rest.

Pick the rosemary leaves off the two remaining sprigs. Carefully discard the fat from the pan and add some fresh olive oil and your remaining knob of butter. Over a medium heat, add your onion, celery and rosemary and fry for about 5 minutes until softened. While keeping an eye on the pan, throw the sun-dried tomatoes into a food processor with the wine and whiz them up – this will give you an intense, tangy tomato liquor.

By this time the onion and celery should be soft and nicely colored, so put your chickens back into the pan and turn up the heat. Add the vinegar and sultanas, shake the pan around a bit, and add the tomato liquor. Continue cooking until the liquid has reduced slightly, then put the pan in the preheated oven with a lid on and cook for 30 minutes, turning the birds in the juices a couple of times. Remove the pan from the oven, take the lid off and turn the poussins once more in all the juices. Lay them breast side up and sprinkle the pinenuts over them, then lay your slices of pancetta or bacon over them and cook in the oven for a further 10 minutes until crisp and golden. Allow the poussins to rest in the pan for 10 minutes while you get your guests to the table.

Matt's wine suggestion: New Zealand red – Pinot Noir

serves 4

1 orange, quartered
2 cinnamon sticks, broken in half
6 sprigs of fresh rosemary
4 poussins, preferably free-range or organic
olive oil
2 knobs of butter
2 red onions, peeled and finely sliced
4 sticks of celery, trimmed and finely sliced
1 x 10oz jar sun-dried tomatoes in oil, drained
3 wineglasses of Chianti
6 tablespoons red wine vinegar
a handful of sultanas
a handful of pinenuts
16 slices of thinly sliced smoked pancetta

Grilled spatchcocked chicken with new potatoes, roast asparagus and herby yogurt

This is a lovely summertime, snacky, trattoria, homestyle dish. Your butcher will do the spatchcocking for you if you ask nicely. Spatchcocking is cutting a chicken open through its back and flattening it out so it cooks quickly. It's an ideal way to prepare a chicken for grilling or barbecuing.

Slash the chicken legs about ½ inch deep in a few places – this will help the marinade get into the meat, and the thighs to cook in the same time as the breast.

Mix together the marjoram or oregano, the juice from one of the lemons and a glug of olive oil and rub this all over your chicken. Leave to marinate for half an hour outside the fridge, or a couple of hours in the fridge if you have the time. Don't leave it overnight though, because the lemon juice will 'cook' the meat.

Preheat the oven to 400°F. Heat a griddle pan, season the chicken generously and place skin side down on the griddle. Once it's golden and starts to crisp (after about 4 minutes), turn the chicken over, add a whole lemon to the pan and then put the pan in your preheated oven.

While the chicken is cooking, scrub the potatoes and put them in a pan of cold salted water, then bring to the boil and simmer until nicely cooked. Drain in a colander and put them back into the pan with the butter, a squeeze of lemon juice, and a good pinch of salt and pepper. Pop the lid on to keep them warm.

After 45 to 55 minutes, your chicken should be golden and the meat tender and cooked. You can test it to see if it's ready by pinching the leg meat away from the bone – if it comes away easily you're in business; if not pop it back in for another 10 minutes. When all is good, set the whole roasted lemon to one side, put the chicken on a platter and allow it to rest for 5 minutes in a warm place.

Pour any excess fat out of the griddle pan and put your asparagus into it in a single layer. Griddle for about 3 or 4 minutes until tender. When the asparagus are cooked, toss them in a little olive oil, salt and pepper and a squeeze of lemon juice. I like to pile the asparagus up on a large platter with the potatoes and the beautifully cooked crispy chicken. Cut the whole roasted lemon in half, squeeze the juice into the yogurt, season with salt and pepper and serve in a bowl with your chicken. Scatter your delicate herbs generously over the whole dish – delicious!

Matt's wine suggestion: Spanish rosé – Garnacha

serves 4

for the marinade
a small bunch of fresh marjoram or oregano, leaves picked, or 1 tablespoon good-quality dried oregano
juice of 1 lemon
olive oil

1 small (about 3½lb) spatchcocked chicken, preferably free-range or organic
sea salt and freshly ground black pepper
2 lemons
1¾lb new potatoes
a knob of butter
2 handfuls of asparagus, trimmed
1½ cups plain or Greek yogurt
a handful of fresh soft, fragrant herbs (parsley, mint, chervil or tarragon, or a mix of these), leaves picked

SOME OTHER MEATS I LOVE . . .

Here are a few meats that are absolutely delicious to eat, even though they may not be your obvious, everyday choice. Duck is appearing more and more on restaurant menus and can easily be cooked at home too, while rabbit, in my eyes, is a forgotten treasure. Turkey, of course, is usually saved for Christmas Day, but I dare you to try it another time.

Duck

When cooked in the right way, duck is one of the most delicious things you can eat. Because they spend most of their lives floating about on ponds, ducks have a lovely layer of fat under their skins to insulate them from the cold. It's this fat that keeps the duck meat tasty and moist during cooking. Look for a nice big duck with creamy white skin and make sure you pull the plastic bag with giblets out before you roast it!

Duck meat is so rich and full of flavor – it's great cooked with all kinds of herbs and spices. The Chinese cook duck with soy sauce and five-spice, the French with oranges, and the Italians braise duck with rosemary, garlic, tomatoes and olives and serve it as a pasta sauce. So be bold with your flavorings, the duck can handle it.

- Wild ducks are in season in the autumn and are small, meaty and delicious. They're normally roasted briefly and served pink.

- You can often buy just the duck's breasts – they are best pan-roasted with the skin-side down so the fat renders out and the skin turns nice and crispy.

- Never throw away duck fat. It makes the best roast potatoes ever, so spoon it into an empty jam jar and keep it in the fridge till you need it.

- There isn't as much meat on a whole duck as there is on a chicken. A large duck is just about enough for four people, so if you have more mouths to feed than that, it's best to buy two.

Rabbit

Rabbit used to be a very popular meat, but nowadays not many people eat it. Maybe it's because we've got images of fluffy white bunnies in our heads and we don't like to think of them in the pot – I don't know. What I do know, though, is that people who don't eat rabbit are missing out on one of the cheapest and most delicious meats around.

Both farmed and wild rabbit are available all year round, as there isn't a closed hunting season for rabbit like there is for deer, pheasant or other game. Farmed rabbit is mild in taste and soft in texture, a bit like chicken – you can even grill it on the barbecue or fry it. Wild rabbit has a fuller flavor, and because it's done a lot of running around its meat is a bit tougher and is best stewed or slow-cooked.

- You normally buy rabbit whole from a butcher's. Before he wraps it up, tell him how you're going to cook it and get him to chop it up into suitable-sized pieces for you.

- If the butcher gives you the rabbit liver, either save it for a warm salad (just fry it in a bit of butter or olive oil with some garlic and herbs) or pop it in a stew to turn the flavor up a notch.

- If any of your guests are funny about eating rabbit, just tell them it's chicken. I always do this with Jools and she never knows the difference!

- If you're stewing your rabbit, make sure you tell everyone round the table to watch out for small bones when they eat it.

Turkey

Turkey is an American bird that is traditionally roasted for Thanksgiving dinner every autumn. You might be surprised to learn that turkeys haven't really been around in Britain for very long. In the old days, people used to roast geese, chickens and hams for Christmas Day, but now turkey's the firm favorite and millions of them end up on our tables on December 25.

Like any other meat, turkey is available in standard, free-range or organic form. The difference in flavor is amazing, so if you're used to buying one of those rock-hard frozen boulders every Christmas, why not upgrade to free-range or organic this year? It might cost a little bit more, but isn't your family worth it?

- Always make sure your turkey is at room temperature before you cook it, otherwise cooking times given in recipes might not be accurate.

- Always rest your turkey, covered loosely with aluminum foil, for about 15 to 20 minutes after you have roasted it and taken it out of the oven – the meat will relax and carve more easily. Don't worry about it going cold, it'll keep its heat while you crisp up your spuds and make your gravy.

- Turkey can be a bit dry when cooked, especially its breast. But the good thing is that turkey makes cracking gravy, so I always make sure there's plenty of it to pour over the meat.

The best roast turkey – Christmas or any time

One of the biggest challenges when cooking a turkey is the legs take longer than the breasts. The breasts dry out in the oven while you're waiting for the legs to cook. I like to push stuffing between the turkey's skin and breasts, increasing the thickness of the breasts so they take the same time to cook as the legs. The result? Juicy turkey all round!

Preheat the oven to maximum. Heat a saucepan until medium hot and drop in the butter, sage leaves and 6 of the pancetta or bacon strips. Peel and chop 2 garlic cloves and 1 onion. Add the garlic, celery and onion to the saucepan and fry everything gently until soft and golden brown. Take the pan off the heat, add the breadcrumbs and, while the mix is cooling down, chop the apricots roughly and stir them in. When the stuffing has cooled down, add the pork, lemon zest, nutmeg, egg and lots of salt and pepper, and mix everything together well.

Slice the remaining strips of pancetta or bacon in half and slice 1 peeled garlic clove into thin slivers. Place a rosemary sprig and a garlic sliver on one end of a halved strip of pancetta and roll it up tightly. Repeat with the other pieces of pancetta until you have 12 little rolls. Stab the thighs and drumsticks of the turkey in 6 places on each side. Push a little pancetta roll into each hole until it just peeps out. This'll give your turkey thighs a fantastic flavor and will keep them moist while they cook.

Chop the remaining onions in half and slice the carrots thickly. Give your turkey a good wipe, inside and out, with paper towels, and place it on a board, with the neck end towards you. Find the edge of the skin that's covering the turkey's breasts and gently peel it back. Work your fingers and then your hand under the skin, freeing it from the meat. If you're careful you should be able to pull all the skin away from the meat, keeping it attached at the sides. Go slowly and try not to make any holes! Lift the loose skin at the neck end and spoon the stuffing between the skin and the breast, tucking the flap of skin underneath to stop anything leaking out. Pop the orange in the microwave for 30 seconds to warm it up and stuff it into the cavity. Weigh the stuffed turkey and calculate the cooking time (about 20 minutes per pound).

Place the bird on a large roasting pan, rub it all over with olive oil and season well. Surround with the chopped carrots, onions, remaining garlic, cover with aluminum foil and place in the preheated oven. Turn the heat down right away to 350°F, and roast for the calculated time, or until the juices run clear from the thigh if you pierce with it a knife or a skewer. Remove the aluminum foil for the last 45 minutes to brown the bird. Carefully lift the turkey out of the tray and rest on a board that's covered loosely with foil for 20 minutes while you finish off the veg and gravy. Skim the surface fat from the roasting pan and add the flour and stock. Place the tray on the stovetop and bring to the boil on a high heat. When the gravy starts to thicken, strain it into a bowl. Carve your turkey, serve with the gravy and dig in!

Matt's wine suggestion: French white – Viognier

serves 6–8

- 4 tablespoons butter
- a sprig of fresh sage, leaves picked
- 12 strips of pancetta or thinly sliced bacon
- 1 bulb of garlic, broken into cloves
- 4 medium red onions, peeled
- 2 sticks of celery, trimmed and chopped
- a big handful of breadcrumbs
- a handful of dried apricots
- 10½oz ground pork
- zest of 1 lemon
- a pinch of grated nutmeg
- 1 large free-range or organic egg
- sea salt and freshly ground black pepper
- 12 small fresh rosemary sprigs, plus a few extra
- 9–10lb turkey, preferably free-range or organic, at room temperature
- 2 carrots, peeled
- 1 large orange
- olive oil
- 2 tablespoons plain flour
- 2 pints chicken or vegetable stock

Tender-as-you-like rabbit stew
with the best dumplings ever

This has got to be one of my favorite dinners. Rabbit cooked in this way is absolutely fantastic and such a treat. You can use chicken legs instead but I'd love you to make the effort to buy rabbit from your butcher. It's such a wonderful source of protein and is a meat that used to be so popular. The dumplings really do make the whole dish work for me – I'm not sure which bit I prefer most! Feel free to use this dumpling recipe with any other stew because it's a cracker. This is not a first date kind of dish because you will want to pick up bits of meat and pull them off the bone and it can get a bit messy! It's the kind of food that should be served in all old-fashioned country pubs.

Preheat the oven to 375°F. To make your dumplings, rub together your flour, butter and tarragon with a good pinch of salt and pepper, then, using a fork, mix in enough milk to give you an unsticky dough. Bring it together until it's quite stiff, then flour your hands and knead it into a dough. Roll the dough into a big sausage shape and cut it up into 18 equal-sized pieces. Roll these into little balls in your hands, grate over the nutmeg and place on a tray in the fridge.

Get your rabbit pieces and coat each of them with flour, shaking off any excess. Heat a deep ovenproof pot, about 12 inches in diameter, with a little olive oil and a knob of butter, add the rabbit pieces in batches and cook for about 5 minutes until golden on all sides. After the final batch, return the pieces to the pot, and add a good pinch of salt and pepper and the bacon. Carry on cooking for a couple of minutes until the bacon is crispy, keeping the rabbit moving around the pan at the same time. Add the rosemary sprigs, mushrooms and onions and continue frying for another 10 minutes, by which time the meat will be nicely colored and the veg will be softened.

Mix in a tablespoon of flour, pour in your beer and chicken stock, cover and simmer for half an hour. Then put your dumplings on top of the stew with about ½ inch between them. They will act as a kind of lid, allowing the stew to retain moisture and not to boil dry. When perfectly cooked they will crisp up on the top and stay bun-like and soft on the bottom – delicious! Drizzle them with olive oil and put the pot into the preheated oven for 45 minutes.

For me this is a perfect meal in itself, but if you want to have a veg on the side then look at page 320 for some lovely buttered peas with bacon.

Matt's wine suggestion: Italian red – Barbera, or some more stout or bitter

serves 6–8

for the dumplings
3 cups self-rising flour
14 tablespoons butter
a bunch of fresh tarragon, finely chopped
sea salt and freshly ground black pepper
milk
½ a nutmeg

2 rabbits, preferably free-range or organic, each jointed and cut into 10 pieces
flour
olive oil
a knob of butter
sea salt and freshly ground black pepper
10 slices of bacon, finely sliced
2 sprigs of fresh rosemary
9oz nice mushrooms (field, shiitake, oyster), cleaned and torn
a large handful of baby onions, peeled
2 x 12oz cans Mackeson's or John Smith's or other dark beer
1½ pints chicken stock

Perfectly cooked crispy duck
with spiced plum chutney

I think a lot of people get slightly nervous about cooking duck, yet I know that most of you love it because when we have it on the menu in the restaurant we can't sell enough of it! This recipe is incredibly simple both in its seasoning and its cooking. You will be left with good results every time – melt-in-the-mouth leg meat, unbelievably good breast meat and crispy skin. I've gone slightly Mediterranean with this recipe as I've used sage salt. If you want to go along an Asian vibe instead, simply dust the duck with five-spice and add grated fresh ginger to the cavity instead of the sage salt. Give it a bash – you won't be disappointed.

The spiced plum chutney goes beautifully with this. Make up a batch when you like as it can be served cold or warm, and it will keep well in an airtight jar. Horseradish or Italian pickled mustard fruits – *mostarda di Cremona* – also work really well with duck.

Preheat your oven to 350°F. Get 5 or 6 sage leaves and bash them up in a pestle and mortar or Flavor Shaker with the salt. Rub this all over the skin of the duck, then shove the rest of the sage and the two orange halves inside the cavity.

Get yourself a roasting tray in which the duck and the veg will fit snugly, put the veg and garlic into it and pop the duck on top, breast-side down. Roast in the preheated oven for 2 hours, turning the duck a couple of times during cooking. Halfway through you will probably need to drain away most of the fat that has come out of the bird. Don't throw this away! You can pass it through a sieve and keep it in a jar for a couple of months (as long as it's just the fat; no meat juices) and use it to roast potatoes.

Meanwhile, make your spiced plum chutney. Pour the sugar in a saucepan and add just enough water to dissolve it. Place on the heat, drop in the cinnamon and star anise and bring to the boil.

Simmer the syrup until it reduces right down and the bubbles start to get bigger. As soon as the syrup starts to turn golden, add the chopped plums, orange zest and cumin and turn the heat down to low. The plums will release their sticky, sweet juices and after a few minutes the sauce will cook down to a thicker consistency. Take the pan off the heat, season the chutney with salt and pepper and leave to cool.

For the last half hour, make sure that the duck is breast-side up so the skin gets crispy. To test whether it's cooked, pinch the leg meat and if it comes easily off the bone it's ready. Shred the meat and crispy skin on to plates and serve with some watercress on top, your spiced plum chutney and Scotch stovies (see page 301).

Matt's wine suggestion: French red – Pinot Noir

serves 4

for the roast duck
a small bunch of fresh
   sage, leaves picked
2 teaspoons sea salt
1 duck, preferably free-
   range or organic
1 orange, halved
2 carrots, peeled and
   roughly chopped
2 onions, peeled and
   roughly chopped
2 sticks of celery, trimmed
   and roughly chopped
1 bulb of garlic, cloves
   separated and bashed

for the spiced plum chutney
⅓ cup sugar
½ a cinnamon stick
1 star anise
6 large red ripe plums,
   pitted and chopped
a strip of orange zest
a pinch of ground cumin
sea salt and freshly
   ground pepper

a small bunch of
   watercress, washed
   and dried

fish

THE WONDERFUL WORLD OF FISH

The truth about fish is that, even though we have some of the best fish in the world swimming in our waters, as a nation we are pretty scared of it: eating it, buying it and especially cooking it. I see the faces of people when they queue up to buy it, all of those different shapes, sizes, colors, and varieties – round fish, flat fish, shellfish. The choice seems endless, and daunting! The other day I heard a mother telling her daughter off for buying some trout because she thought she was going to choke to death on the bones. I couldn't believe what I was hearing! Most fish sold today are filleted and you've got more chance of winning the lottery than choking to death on a measly trout bone, so please don't be worried about that. What you should be worried about though, is the amount of fish you eat.

We don't have anywhere near enough fish in our diets. We should be eating fish two or three times a week, to keep healthy, instead of once in a blue moon. During my School Dinners project, I spent a hell of a lot of time with doctors, specialists and nutritionists who all agree that if you want to be healthier, sharper, fitter and more mobile as you get older then fish is the thing to eat.

And the time to eat it is now. It's no good eating smoked mackerel for the first time when you are falling apart at the age of forty. The Japanese eat more fish per head than any other country in the world, and they are healthier and live longer. The amount of fish we eat is tiny by comparison. And here we are, with the first generation of kids in history predicted to live shorter lives than their parents. It's not rocket science.

Every year I see the new students at Fifteen fall in love with cooking fish, and I am convinced you will too. It's amazing what you can do with lovely fresh produce and a bit of imagination. I'm not talking about messing about too much with it, because if ever an ingredient needed to be treated simply and with respect, it's fish. I hope that once you've tried a few of the recipes in this book, you'll see what I mean, as cooking fish is so simple and quick, and the results are delicious.

But before we get cooking, I'm going to give you a little bit of information about the different fish available, and some advice on what to look out for when you're next buying your fish so you know what you're doing and you're never scared of fish again. Guys, welcome to the wonderful world of fish!

Types of fish

To me it's easiest to think of fish in two main groups: round fish and flat fish.

Round fish
So called because of their cross-section rather than their shape, in this group you'll find:

- the pink-fleshed family of salmon, sea trout and trout
- the white flaky family of cod, haddock, hake and whiting
- the oily family of sardines, herring, anchovies and mackerel
- the warm-water family of bass, porgy, mullet and snapper
- the meaty tuna and swordfish brothers

Flat fish
These fish actually are flat and spend most of their time lying on, or flipping along, the seabed.
They are one big family really. Halibut, turbot and flounder are the largest, and Dover sole, lemon sole, fluke and dabs the smallest.

The other few ...
There are a few other common oddballs that don't fit into either of the above categories, but I want to mention them because they are great fish to cook at home. They are:

- monkfish, a very ugly but very tasty deep-sea fish
- skate, which is a member of the ray family
- the spiny and strange-looking John Dory

How to be a better fish shopper

Buying fish isn't rocket science. It's about having a bit of knowledge and trusting your common sense. Below are some bullet points to keep you on the ball when you're next shopping for fish. If you know what to look out for and have a little bit of confidence, you'll end up buying freshly caught fish, not stuff that's been hanging around for a couple of days.

Signs of fresh fish
- Fish should never ever smell fishy. When fish is really fresh, all you can smell is the sea.

- The eyes should be clear, bright and shiny, not cloudy or glazed over. The gills should only be a deep red color. The scales should be neat and intact, not half rubbed off.

- Fish should look moist and shiny, as though it's just come from the sea. There should be a film of slime on it. Dry and hard skin means stale fish.

- Really fresh, whole fish should be stiff. Fillets should be firm and opaque, not all bent and flaking apart.

At the fishmonger's
- Look at the fish on display. Have they been neatly cut and trimmed? Have they been arranged and laid out nicely or just dumped in a pile? A quick glance can tell you all about how much the fishmonger cares about his produce.

- Fresh fish shouldn't smell fishy so neither should your fishmonger's!

- Fish is often kept on a bed of ice. While this is great for whole fish or fish fillets with their skin-side down, sometimes when the meat side of the fillet is rested on the ice, it gets frostbite. So if the meat looks slightly grey and cotton woolly, avoid it.

- Many fishmongers don't scale fish properly. Check your finished product; skin is great to eat, scales are a no-no!

- A good fishmonger's should pinbone your fish fillets for you. This means they take out the small annoying bones that you don't want to end up on your plate.

- Get into the habit of phoning your fishmonger in the morning to see what's come in that day. This way you'll get the best fish and, as an added bonus, you'll be able to pick your order up in a second, rather than having to queue.

- Tell your fishmonger exactly what you want. Be keen and ask questions. If you do have problems with the quality or freshness of your fish, then you must feed it back to your fishmonger honestly. Just do it with charm and a big smile.

- If you're not happy with what's on offer at your fishmonger's, why don't you try a different fish from the same family. So, if the cod's not up to scratch, try whiting, pollock or haddock, and if you don't like the look of the salmon, try trout instead.

- The same goes for fish that's endangered or in short supply. If there are sustainability issues with a particular fish, it's probably a good idea to use something similar in its place.

- If you can't find a great fishmonger's near you then remember that the internet has some fantastic quality companies who can post directly to you in chilled boxes.

- Like you and me, fishermen don't work on Saturdays or Sundays, so don't buy fish on a Sunday or Monday.

- Don't buy all your fish for the whole week in one go. Fresh fish is to be eaten within 36 hours if not that day; it is not a weekly shop product, whatever the sell-by dates tell you.

COOKING FILLETED FISH

First and foremost I thought I'd cut to the chase and show you some different ways to cook, finish and serve a lovely fillet of fish. The great thing about cooking fish fillets is that they're really consistent and well behaved. More than anything, they are so incredibly quick to cook. Most people overcook them, so we'll be concentrating on timing and how to get the skin crispy yet keep the meat juicy and moist. The other day I watched my wife cook some thin slices of salmon, with a little bit of olive oil, some asparagus and a few frozen peas with a squeeze of lemon juice to finish, next to a little pile of couscous, for the kids – minutes from start to finish. And she ain't quick.

If you're a beginner at cooking fish, start with pan-frying a fillet of salmon skin-side down in a tiny bit of oil. To give you a sense of how quickly the fish gets cooked you can literally watch the heat penetrating through the fillet. The meat will turn from an orangey colour to a more pale, opaque pink. Watch and learn, and you'll serve a perfect cooked fillet of fish in no time.

Is it cooked yet?

- Stick the tip of a knife or skewer right into the fillet. Leave it there for eight seconds, then remove it and press it on to your top lip. If it's cold, it isn't cooked yet, if it's warm it probably needs a bit more time, and if it's the temperature of a nice cup of tea (which is about 175°F), it's perfect.

- Some fish, like tuna or wild salmon, are quite nice when they're still slightly undercooked inside. If this doesn't do it for you, cook the fillets right through.

- Cut or carefully break open the fillet on the underside (so you don't see it when you serve). The meat should cut or break away quite easily, and when you have a look at the inside of the fillet, the meat should be the same color all the way through.

Pan-fried red mullet with crispy breadcrumbs and a herby tomato salad

Tomatoes and red mullet just seem to have the most incredible harmony and, as bizarre as breadcrumbs might sound, their surprising crunch with such a fresh and flaky fish will really tickle your fancy.

Remember: only a fool would want to make a tomato salad out of season. Early summer to October is the best time. Make some effort when you buy the tomatoes, and have a look around for green, yellow and cherry tomatoes, a whole mixture. Get some good ones and this dish will blow you away.

Put your chopped tomatoes into a big bowl with a couple of generous glugs of extra virgin olive oil and a splash of vinegar. Season generously with salt and pepper. Now taste, tweak, taste, tweak . . . I usually add a bit more vinegar, salt or olive oil until the tomatoes and their juices sing in my mouth. This is a normal thing to do, so just be confident! Add the basil and fennel tops or dill to your tomato salad and mix in.

Season the fish fillets, then dip them in a little flour to dust them on both sides, shaking off any excess. Heat a glug of olive oil in a medium-hot frying pan and, once hot, place the fish skin-side down in the pan, lightly pressing the fillets down using a fish slice. Fry for 3 minutes or until the skin is bright orangey golden and crisp. Turn the fish over and fry for a minute on the other side until just cooked.

Remove your fish to a plate while you make your crispy breadcrumbs. Add a little extra oil to the juices in the pan, then add your thyme, breadcrumbs, chilli and lemon zest. Toss around and fry until lightly golden and crispy; this will take around 3 or 4 minutes.

Divide the tomato salad between four plates and either lay 2 of your fish fillets over the top of each salad, or break the fillets up and scatter over the tomatoes. I like to put the hot and crispy breadcrumbs in a little bowl with a teaspoon in them and sprinkle it over my guests' plates at the table – delicious.

PS If you want to take this recipe up a notch buy yourself some smoked paprika and mix a tablespoon with your flour at the very beginning. Check out the Spanish flavors – very nice.

Matt's wine suggestion: New Zealand white – Sauvignon Blanc

serves 4

for the tomato salad
3 big handfuls of mixed tomatoes, chopped into irregular chunks
good-quality extra virgin olive oil
red wine vinegar
sea salt and freshly ground black pepper
a small bunch of fresh basil, leaves picked and finely chopped
a small bunch of fennel tops or dill, finely chopped

sea salt and freshly ground black pepper
8 red mullet fillets (about 3½ oz each), scaled and pinboned
flour, for dusting
olive oil

for the crispy breadcrumbs
olive oil
4 sprigs of fresh thyme, leaves picked and finely chopped
3½ cups (about 7oz) stale breadcrumbs
2 dried red chillies, crumbled
zest of 1 lemon

Pan-roasted salmon with purple sprouting broccoli and anchovy-rosemary sauce

Pan-roasting is one of my favorite ways to cook salmon and trout because it really brings out their incredible flakiness and richness. It goes well with the delicate steamed broccoli and intense zingy sauce I've served it with here.

Apart from salmon being a pleasure to eat, it's also high in omega oils, so it's very healthy for you too. A wild salmon lives only on natural food, of course, and is an amazing athlete that has to work very hard to make its way from the deep sea all the way up the rivers. If you ever see it on a restaurant menu, please order it because it's very different from farmed salmon both in flavor and texture. But farmed salmon has come a long way in the last five to ten years and it is probably going to be the more accessible and affordable option for you. If you're going to buy farmed salmon, always go for organic if you have the choice.

Preheat your oven to 400°F, then make your anchovy-rosemary sauce. Pound the rosemary in a pestle and mortar until you have a paste. Add the anchovy fillets and pound again until the paste is dark green. Now add the lemon juice, a couple of glugs of olive oil and some pepper, and mix together until you have a sauce with a good drizzling consistency.

Get a large, ovenproof, non-stick frying pan hot. Pat the salmon fillets with a little olive oil, season them with salt and pepper and cook them in the pan, skin-side down, for 2 minutes. Flip them over, then place the pan in the preheated oven for another 3 to 4 minutes, depending on the thickness of the fillets and the way they've been sliced.

Just after the salmon goes into the oven, put your broccoli into some boiling, salted water for 3 to 4 minutes until perfectly cooked.

To check if the fish is cooked all the way through, you can pull the fillets apart a little bit and look inside. Salmon goes from being an orangey color to an opaque pink, so that's what you're looking for. Please do not overcook them, because, as simple as this dish sounds, it's your mission to 'just' cook the fish so you're rewarded with a soft inside and a slightly crispy outside – heaven!

When the broccoli's perfectly done, drain it, toss it in a little of the anchovy-rosemary sauce and divide it between your plates. Place a salmon fillet on top of each and drizzle with some more sauce.

Matt's wine suggestion: New Zealand red – Pinot Noir

serves 4

for the anchovy-rosemary sauce
a sprig of fresh rosemary, leaves picked and very finely chopped
10 good-quality anchovy fillets in oil, drained and roughly chopped
juice of 1 lemon
extra virgin olive oil
freshly ground black pepper

4 x 7oz salmon fillets, pinboned
olive oil
sea salt and freshly ground black pepper
1lb 2oz purple sprouting broccoli

Chargrilled tuna with oregano oil and beautifully dressed peas and fava beans

The simplicity and flavor of this summer dish are fantastic. Buy your tuna steaks about ½ inch thick rather than going for massive inch-thick ones. That way they cook quickly, giving you a juicy, silky steak that hasn't had a chance to dry out. If you can't get hold of tuna, then shark and swordfish are reasonably good steak-like alternatives.

To make your oregano oil, pound the oregano with a good pinch of sea salt in a pestle and mortar until you have a paste. Add the lemon juice and 8 tablespoons of olive oil and stir until you have a good drizzling consistency.

Bring a large pan of water to the boil, add your peas and cook for 3 to 4 minutes, then remove them with a slotted spoon or sieve. Add the fava beans to the pan and cook for 3 to 4 minutes, depending on their size. Drain and leave to cool, then pinch the skins off any big beans (you can leave the skin on any small or medium ones).

To dress the peas and beans you want the same balance of acid and oil as you would have in a salad dressing. So, put the olive oil and a good pinch of salt and pepper into a large bowl. Chop up most of the mint and throw it in, add the peas and beans and mix everything around. Add lemon juice to taste. You can serve the dressed peas and beans hot or at room temperature.

Heat a griddle pan or barbecue until hot, season your tuna steaks with salt and pepper and pat with some of the oregano oil. Place in the pan and sear for 1 to 2 minutes on each side. Personally I like to keep my tuna a little pink in the middle as this tastes much nicer, but if you're going to cook it through please don't nuke it.

Tear the tuna into 2 or 3 pieces and toss in a large bowl with the rest of the oregano oil. This will give you a lovely combination of flavors. Serve the fish immediately, with the peas and fava beans, scattered with the rest of the mint leaves.

PS Sometimes I love to throw random delicate greens like baby spinach, watercress, even arugula, in with the fava beans for 30 seconds before you drain them. The combination of peppery irony greens, creamy fava beans and sweet little peas makes the veg taste even better.

Matt's wine suggestion: French red – Pinot Noir

serves 4

for the oregano oil
a small bunch of fresh
   oregano or marjoram,
   leaves picked
sea salt
juice of 1 lemon
best-quality extra virgin
   olive oil

4 handfuls of shelled peas
2 handfuls of shelled fava
   beans
2 cups best-quality extra
   virgin olive oil
sea salt and freshly ground
   black pepper
a small bunch of fresh mint,
   leaves picked
juice of 1 lemon
4 7oz tuna steaks, cut
   ½ inch thick

Pan-roasted porgy with a quick crispy fennel salad

With the great-quality farmed porgy and the amazing wild porgy that we have in Britain, this fish is not only one of the tastiest but one of the most accessible. To me it represents the best of British: everyone should eat it. It's great when roasted on the bone and very easy to cook the fillets too, as I did here. Your fishmonger will portion and pinbone the porgy for you if you ask him.

Using a speed peeler, a mandolin slicer or pretty good knife skills, slice the fennel bulbs lengthways very, very finely and put in a bowl of iced water for 10 minutes or so until the slices go crispy and curly.

Lay the fish fillets on a board, skin-side up, then lightly pinch the skin of each one and score it an at angle, about ¼ inch deep, about six times. This will allow the fish not only to cook quicker but to take in the flavors of the seasoning – and it looks pretty too! Sprinkle the fillets with salt, pepper, the fennel seeds and chilli and pat with a little olive oil so all the flavours stick to the fish. Heat a large frying pan and place the fillets in the pan, skin-side down. Fry on a medium heat for about 4 minutes, turning them over when the skin is golden and crisp. Fry them on the other side for a minute or so.

While the fish is cooking, you can finish your fennel salad. Drain and dry the fennel and mix it in a bowl with the herby fennel tops. Add the marjoram leaves – if you prefer oregano use slightly less – and mix with the fennel. When the fish are cooked, divide them between your plates. Dress the fennel salad with the lemon juice, some extra virgin olive oil, the sun-dried tomatoes and salt and pepper to taste. Drizzle the fish with balsamic vinegar and serve with some salad piled on top.

Matt's wine suggestion: Italian white – Orvieto

serves 4

for the crispy fennel salad
2 fennel bulbs, herby
   tops reserved
a small bunch of fresh
   marjoram or oregano,
   leaves picked
juice of 1 lemon
extra virgin olive oil
8 sun-dried tomatoes in
   oil, drained and finely
   chopped
sea salt and freshly ground
   black pepper

4 7oz porgy fillets,
   pinboned
sea salt and freshly ground
   black pepper
2 teaspoons fennel seeds,
   bashed
1 dried chilli, crumbled
olive oil
good-quality thick balsamic
   vinegar

Pan-fried lemon sole fillets with salsa verde

I just love the speed with which you can turn some sole fillets, tossed in flour, salt and pepper and fried in butter and olive oil, into a lovely little dinner with some nice greens and a squeeze of lemon juice. Put a few other side dishes with it if you feel a bit greedy – new potatoes, asparagus, broccoli – the ultimate fast food. Brilliant!

To make your salsa verde, finely chop the garlic and put in a bowl. Add the capers, gherkins, anchovies, parsley, basil and mint. Mix in the mustard and 1 or 2 tablespoons of red wine vinegar, then 3 good lugs of olive oil, adding more if needed to make a loose mixture. Balance the flavors with pepper and, if necessary, salt and a little more red wine vinegar.

Put your new potatoes into a large pan of salted, boiling water and cook for 12 minutes with the lid on. Put the sole fillets into a clean plastic bag and season nicely with salt and pepper and a small handful of flour. Toss around until all the fillets are well coated. Just before you start cooking the fish, put your broccoli into a colander, place on top of the potato pan, cover with the lid and steam for 4 minutes or so until cooked.

While the broccoli is steaming, heat a glug of olive oil in a large non-stick frying pan and quickly but carefully put your fillets into them so they all cook at the same time. Cook for a couple of minutes until beautifully golden, then, starting with the fillet that went in first, turn them all over. Once you've done that, add the butter to color and flavor the fillets. Cook for no more than another 2 minutes. When the fillets are golden on both sides, remove the pan from the heat. Wait for 20 seconds before squeezing in the juice of ½ the lemon and shaking the pan about, otherwise the lemon juice will burn black and ruin the whole thing.

Divide the fish fillets between your plates with some of the juices from the pan. Drain the potatoes and divide them and the broccoli between the plates. Spoon the salsa verde over the fish and veg, put a lemon wedge beside each and tuck in – heaven!

Matt's wine suggestion: German white – Riesling

serves 2

for your salsa verde
1 clove of garlic, peeled
a handful of capers, drained
a handful of gherkins,
   drained and finely chopped
6 good-quality anchovy fillets
   in oil, finely chopped
2 bunches of fresh flat-leaf
   parsley, finely chopped
a bunch of fresh basil,
   leaves picked and finely
   chopped
a bunch of fresh mint, leaves
   picked and finely chopped
1 tablespoon Dijon mustard
red wine vinegar
good-quality extra virgin
   olive oil
sea salt and freshly ground
   black pepper

10½oz new potatoes,
   scrubbed or peeled
4 double sole fillets, pinboned
sea salt and freshly ground
   black pepper
flour
10½oz purple sprouting
   broccoli
olive oil
a knob of butter
1 lemon

Poached salmon steak

Poaching is a classic way to cook fish steaks, or darnes, by immersing them in very gently simmering liquid and lifting them out carefully the moment they're cooked through. The brilliant thing about poaching is that the liquid can be flavored with things like vegetables, herbs or wine to complement the flavor of the fish.

Look, you've caught me out; I'm in the filleted fish section and I've included a darne of salmon (a portion of fish on the bone). Let me dig myself out of the hole and say that this is a cut of fish you can cook in the same way as a nice thick fillet of salmon. Darnes are best either pan-roasted or poached, as I did here.

Put all the poaching liquor ingredients into a large saucepan. Fill it up with cold water and bring to the boil. Add your salmon steaks and when the water comes back to the boil, turn the heat straight down. Simmer for 5 minutes then turn the heat off and allow the fish to sit in the liquor for 5 minutes so the residual heat can slowly penetrate the fish right through to the bone.

A fantastic optional extra is to add beetroot to the poaching liquor. The beetroot will bleed into the water and color the fish, so that it looks amazing.

Drain off the poaching liquor after the 5 minutes, and serve the fish with the veggies.

PS There are loads of things that you can do with poached fish once you've cooked it. Here are a few ideas . . .

Flake it into mashed potato with some chopped parsley to make delicious fishcakes; flake it into farfalle, with peas and cream, for a simple pasta dish; whiz it up in a food processor with crème fraîche and lemon juice and serve on toast as a pâté; add it to a pan of boiling water or stock, with peas, asparagus and noodles, for a delicious broth; use it in a fish pie; flake it into couscous and add chopped fennel, olives and chilli.

Matt's wine suggestion: French red – Beaujolais

serves 4

for the poaching liquor
2 carrots, peeled and sliced
1 fennel bulb, sliced
1 onion, peeled and cut
  into eights
2 sticks of celery, trimmed
  and roughly chopped
2 tomatoes, halved
4 sprigs of fresh thyme,
  leaves picked
2 bay leaves
a few fresh parsley stalks
a small glass of white wine
a glug of white wine
  vinegar
a small pinch of sea salt
1 teaspoon black
  peppercorns
optional: 1 large beetroot,
  peeled and sliced

4 7oz salmon steaks,
  pinboned

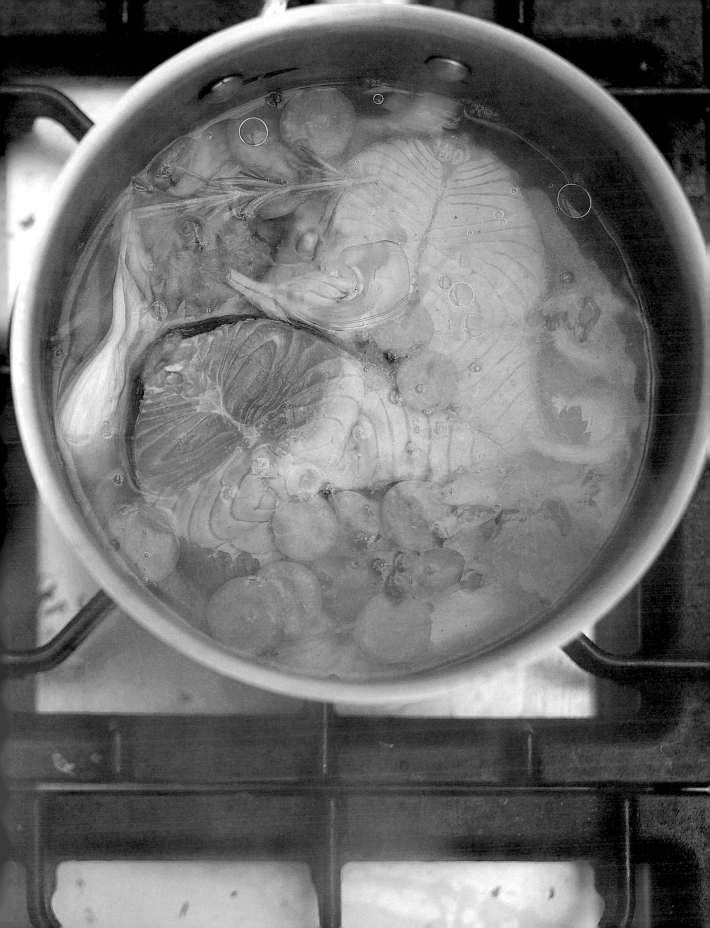

Delicious roasted white fish wrapped in smoked bacon with lemon mayonnaise and asparagus

This combination is a complete win-win. Any robust white fish like haddock or monkfish will work brilliantly, as would whiting and pollack, as they are all wonderful carriers of flavors and can handle the stronger tastes of crispy bacon and rosemary. I love this recipe because it treats the fish almost like a piece of meat, with crispy and soft, flaky textures together.

Preheat your oven to 400°F. Season your beautiful fish fillets with the rosemary, finely grated lemon zest (no bitter white pith, please) and pepper – you don't need to use salt because we're going to wrap the fish in the lovely salty bacon. Lay your slices of bacon or pancetta on a board and one by one run the flat of a knife along them to thin them and widen them out. Lay 4 slices together, slightly overlapping, put a fish fillet on top and wrap the bacon around it.

Lightly heat a large ovenproof frying pan, add a splash of olive oil and lay your fish, prettiest side facing up, in the pan. Fry for a minute, then place the pan in your preheated oven for 10 to 12 minutes, depending on the thickness of the fish, until the bacon is crisp and golden.

While the fish is cooking, you can make your simple lemon mayonnaise. I do this by mixing homemade mayonnaise with a nice amount of lemon juice and pepper. Or, if you'd rather sit down for five minutes with a glass of wine, use some ready-made mayo instead! You want to add enough lemon juice to make the flavor slightly too zingy. This is because, when you eat it with the asparagus and the fish, it will lessen slightly in intensity. And don't worry if the mayo looks a little thinner than usual when you've added the lemon juice – think of it as more delicate.

The asparagus is a great accompaniment because, like the fish, it also loves bacon. You can either boil or steam it; either way it's light and a nice contrast to the meatiness of the fish. When cooked, toss it in the juices that come out of the fish. Simply serve the fish next to a nice pile of asparagus, drizzled with the lemon-spiked mayonnaise. And if you're feeling very hungry, serve with some steaming-hot new potatoes.

Matt's wine suggestion: Australian white – Semillon

serves 4

4 7oz white fish fillets, cut 1 inch thick, skinned and pinboned
2 sprigs of fresh rosemary, leaves picked and very finely chopped
zest and juice of 2 lemons
freshly ground black pepper
16 slices of thinly sliced bacon or pancetta
olive oil
4 tablespoons mayonnaise (see page 26)
2 large bunches of asparagus, trimmed

Grilled or roasted monkfish with black olive sauce and lemon mash

Monkfish is a lovely meaty fish to cook. However, it does contain a lot of milky juices. This can sometimes be a pain because they tend to come out during cooking, so instead of roasting, grilling or frying, you end up almost boiling the fish in its own juices. So what I tend to do to stop this is season the fish with salt about an hour before cooking. This draws out any excess moisture – then I just pat it dry and get cooking. If you want to grill your monkfish, ask your fishmonger to butterfly the fillets for you.

In a pestle and mortar or Flavor Shaker, smash up 2 tablespoons of salt with the lemon zest and rosemary and rub this all over the fish fillets. Put the fillets in a dish in the fridge and let them sit there for an hour.

Now make your black olive sauce by mixing all the ingredients except the vinegar together. You want the sauce to have the consistency of a coarse salsa. Then carefully balance the flavors with the vinegar to taste.

If you're roasting your monkfish, preheat your oven to 425°F just before the fish comes out of the fridge. Pat the fish dry with some kitchen paper and then pat it with a little olive oil.

Peel and halve your potatoes. Put them into a pot of salted, boiling water and cook until tender. Then drain and mash up with 6 tablespoons of olive oil and a good swig of milk. Season to taste with salt, pepper and lemon juice. If you want to get your mash really smooth and creamy you can use a spatula to push the potato through a sieve once or twice. It doesn't make it taste any better but it will make it silky smooth, shiny and lovely. Just depends if you can be bothered, really. If it needs thinning with a little extra milk, feel free.

To roast the monkfish, heat a large ovenproof frying pan, add a splash of olive oil and fry the fillets in the pan for 2 minutes. Then turn them over and put the pan in your preheated oven for 6 to 8 minutes, depending on the thickness of the fillets.

To broil, place the the butterflied fillets on a hot griddle pan and cook for about 3 minutes on each side, depending on the thickness. Whichever way you cook it serve the fish and the juices with a good dollop of the mashed potato, the black olive sauce and a little arugula dressed with the extra virgin olive oil, lemon juice and salt and pepper. Really, really good.

Matt's wine suggestion: French white – Sancerre

serves 4

sea salt
zest of 2 lemons, plus a
  little juice
a sprig of fresh rosemary,
  leaves picked
4 7oz monkfish fillets
olive oil
2 bunches of arugula,
  washed and drained

for the black olive sauce
2 large handfuls of good
  black olives, pitted and
  very roughly chopped
½ a fresh red chilli,
  deseeded and finely
  chopped
a small handful of fresh
  herbs (basil, marjoram and
  parsley), finely chopped
1 celery heart, yellow leaves
  chopped
1 clove of garlic, peeled
  and finely chopped
juice of 1 lemon
freshly ground black pepper
a couple of glugs of extra
  virgin olive oil
balsamic vinegar

for the lemon mash
2lb 3oz floury potatoes
sea salt and freshly ground
  black pepper
extra virgin olive oil
milk
juice of 1 lemon

My black cod with steamed pak choi and cucumber

Japanese restaurant Nobu in London is known for a famous dish called black cod, which is absolutely delicious. For my version, I've played around with various fragrant ingredients which really transform meaty white fish; even salmon. For the best results you do have to marinate the fish for at least 24 hours. As this dish will be quite rich, I've decided to serve it with something really clean and fresh – steamed pak choi (Asian greens) and cucumber – to give a great contrast.

There is only one ingredient that you might have to duck and dive to find for this dish and that is miso (a salty-sweet soybean paste), which you can get in any good Asian store or good supermarket. It's out there, it just needs hunting down.

So, the day before you want to cook this, start on the marinade. Remove the outside layer of the lemongrass and discard it. Smash the lemongrass up using the back of a knife to release its lovely fragrance, then chop it. Put it in a pestle and mortar or Flavor Shaker with the chilli, ginger and a pinch of salt and bash up. Place in a pan with the sake or white wine and the honey and bring to the boil, stirring in the miso paste little by little. Simmer until lightly golden. Pour it out into a baking pan and shake it out flat so it cools down quickly.

Once the miso marinade is cool, put the fish into a clean plastic bag, pour in three-quarters of the marinade and gently shake so all the fillets get coated. Squeeze the air out of the bag, tie a knot in the top and place in the fridge. Put the rest of the marinade into a pot in the fridge until needed.

On the day of cooking, heat your grill up good and hot. Put the fish in an appropriately sized oiled roasting pan under the broiler and cook until the top of the fish has caramelized slightly and is nice and golden. Check it every now and again. This will only take about 6 to 8 minutes, depending on your oven. Meanwhile, lay the quarters of pak choi in a steamer or large colander above a pan of boiling water. Slice your cucumber into long, angled ½ inch strips and put these in with the pak choi. Steam until the pak choi is tender and cooked.

Take your leftover marinade from the fridge and stir in enough lime juice to loosen it slightly and turn it into a kind of dressing. Serve the fish next to your greens with a few drizzles of soy sauce and the miso dressing on the side.

Matt's wine suggestion: French rosé – Champagne

serves 4

1 day before cooking
2 stems of lemongrass
1 fresh red chilli, deseeded
  and chopped
1 inch piece of fresh ginger,
  peeled
  and chopped
sea salt
a wineglass of sake or
  white wine
2 tablespoons runny honey
10½oz miso paste
4 7oz cod steaks, pinboned

on the day of cooking
4 bulbs of pak choi,
  quartered
1 cucumber, peeled, halved
  and deseeded
juice of 1 lime
soy sauce
optional: 1 container of
  watercress, snipped

Steamed Thai-style sea bass and rice

This is one of those dishes that's really exciting to eat – the flavors are really fragrant and light. Steamed fish and rice is always a winner, especially with Thai flavors. If you've got a good fishmonger, using other fish like red snapper, shrimp or squid to mix things up a bit is a great idea. It's easy to put together and loads of fun to serve the tray at the table.

Preheat the oven to 400°F. In a food processor or blender, whiz up the cilantro stalks, half of the cilantro leaves, the ginger, garlic, halved chillies, sesame oil, soy sauce, lime juice and zest and the coconut milk. This will give you a lovely fragrant Thai-style paste.

Cook your rice in salted, boiling water until it's just undercooked, then drain it in a colander. Scoop it into a high-sided roasting tray. Pour your Thai paste over the rice and mix it in well, then shake it out flat. Lay the sea bass fillets on top, scatter over the sugar snap peas, then cover the dish tightly with aluminum foil and put it in the preheated oven for around 15 minutes. Remove the foil and sprinkle over the spring onions, the sliced chilli and the other half of the cilantro leaves. Divide between your plates with a wedge of lime.

Matt's wine suggestion: German white – Riesling

serves 4

for the Thai paste
2 large bunches of fresh
  cilantro, leaves picked
  and stalks reserved
2 thumb-sized pieces of
  fresh ginger, peeled
3 cloves of garlic, peeled
2 fresh red chillies, halved
  and deseeded
2 teaspoons sesame oil
6 tablespoons soy sauce
juice and zest of 2 limes
1 x 12oz can coconut milk

14oz basmati rice
sea salt and freshly ground
  black pepper
4 6oz sea bass fillets,
  pinboned and
  skin scored
a handful of sugar snap
  peas or snow peas
a bunch of spring onions,
  outer leaves discarded,
  trimmed and finely sliced
1–2 fresh red chillies,
  deseeded and finely sliced
1 lime, quartered

COOKING WHOLE FISH

Cooking fish whole, on the bone, is great, as the bones give the meat a better flavor and make it lovely and moist. To quote my mate's dad, who was a bit drunk the other night, 'The closer to the bone, the sweeter the taste.' Profound and true!

It's not difficult to cook whole fish – all it requires is a little bit of common sense. Basically, you don't want to cook it too fast; you need a lower temperature and a longer cooking time so the heat gradually works its way through to the middle. It's easy to tell if your fish is cooked or not – if it

doesn't fall or come off the bone, it's not cooked! Genius. Here are my tips to help you get it right first time, followed by a few notes about the different types of fish that are amazing cooked whole, with a few suggestions for their best friends in the flavor department.

Tips for cooking whole fish

- Don't forget to ask your fishmonger to take the gills out of your whole fish. Not only do fish with gills take longer to cook, the end result will taste horrible!

- Make sure you cook your whole fish in a snug-fitting pan. This will help hold any juices that run out while the fish is cooking.

- To make the fish taste great loosely stuff the belly cavity of your fish with finely sliced vegetables, herbs and spices. Carrots, celery, fennel and parsley are all great to use for stuffing fish, as are thyme, sage, rosemary, garlic, sliced chilli, fennel seeds, nutmeg or citrus zest. You can also lay things like fennel branches or slices of lemon over or under the fish while it's cooking, to flavor it even more.

- Try and find yourself a big fish kettle for poaching large fish. I can't think of anything more exciting than having a dinner party for a bunch of people and having a whole poached fish, served with a pungent aïoli or a thick spicy tomato sauce, some lovely bread and a glass of wine. Such a simple thing to cook, and yet a real event. If you don't have a big fish kettle, you could use a high-sided roasting pan.

Good fish for cooking whole

- **Sea bass** is such a fantastic fish. It's nice cooked in any way, but especially baked whole. It goes really well with Mediterranean flavors like fennel, lemon and tomato, and can even stand up to stronger things like olives, capers and garlic.

- **Bream** (porgy or grouper) is a good fish on which to practice before you move on to something bigger and more expensive. Small ones will feed one person and those around 2lb 3oz will make a lovely supper for two. This fish goes well with any of the flavors suggested above for sea bass.

- **Red mullet** is similar in size to bream but has a slightly stronger flavor. It can handle just about anything flavor-wise, even strong herbs like sage, rosemary, thyme and bay. Unlike that of many fish, its color becomes even better when cooked, and it always looks amazing on a plate.

- **Salmon and trout** are really user-friendly fish – easy to cook, easy to bone after cooking and forgiving if you overcook them a little. They're great cooked whole, whether roasted, poached or baked in salt. I like to team salmon with rosemary, slices of orange and a little grated nutmeg. You'll find another lovely whole salmon recipe on page 232.

- **John Dory** is a strange-looking fish, bristling with spines and sharp bony bits – so it's wise to be very careful when handling it! An interesting fact: unlike other fish, it has six fillets instead of just two! Like a flat fish, it doesn't have any scales and it's almost always sold already gutted. John Dory likes the same sort of flavors as sea bass – olive oil, olives, tomatoes, lemon zest, parsley and any other fragrant herbs. It's slightly less forgiving from an overcooking point of view.

Roast salmon with fennel, parsley and tomato

Whole salmon is amazing to cook and it's a really forgiving fish because, even if you overcook it, its fat content makes sure it stays juicy. I get excited every time I cook it, and I'm sure that once you've tried this recipe you'll feel the same.

Preheat your oven to 400ºF. Rub the salmon with a little olive oil and season, inside and out, with salt and pepper.

Toss the fennel, tomatoes, parsley and lemon together with a splash of olive oil and a pinch of salt. Stuff the salmon with as much of the mixture as will fit, pile the rest in a roasting pan and sit the salmon on it.

Drizzle with some more olive oil, sprinkle with the fennel seeds and bake in the preheated oven for 45 minutes. Leave to rest for 10 minutes before serving, and eat with a few spoonfuls of the lovely, juicy lemony fennel and tomatoes cooked underneath the fish.

Matt's wine suggestion: French white – Chardonnay

serves 8-10

1 7lb whole salmon, scaled, cleaned and gutted
olive oil
sea salt and freshly ground black pepper
2 fennel bulbs, finely sliced
6 ripe tomatoes, roughly chopped
a small bunch of fresh flat-leaf parsley, coarsely chopped
2 lemons, very thinly sliced
1 teaspoon fennel seeds

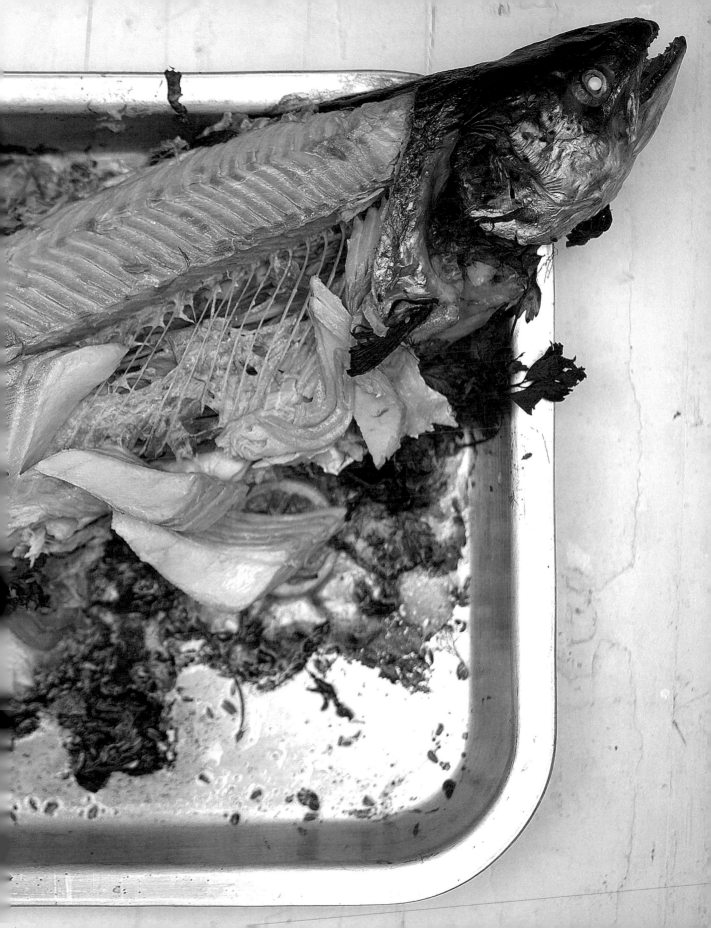

Grilled and roasted red mullet
with pancetta and thyme

Although mullet is quite a small fish, it's got a big flavor and can easily handle things like thyme, bacon and anchovies. This dish would be great with purple sprouting broccoli, a squeeze of lemon and a good olive oil.

Preheat your oven to 425°F and get your griddle pan nice and hot.

Rub the fish with olive oil and season them, inside and out, with salt and pepper. Stuff each cavity with sprigs of thyme or marjoram and some of the lemon slices.

Place the fish on the hot griddle and sear them for 1 minute, on both sides, then lay them on a chopping board. Wrap each fish in 2 strips of pancetta and top with an anchovy fillet. Put in a roasting pan, sprinkle over any extra thyme or marjoram, drizzle with olive oil and pop in the preheated oven for 8 minutes or until cooked through.

Matt's wine suggestion: French white – Chenin Blanc

serves 4

4 red mullet, scaled, cleaned and gutted
olive oil
sea salt and freshly ground black pepper
a large bunch of fresh thyme or marjoram
2 lemons, sliced
8 slices of pancetta or bacon
4 good-quality salted anchovy fillets in olive oil, drained

Whole fish baked in a salt crust

Now don't panic at the sound of this – you don't actually eat any of the salt! The idea is that you encase the fish in damp salt before putting it in the oven. During cooking, the salt dries out again, forming a hard crust right around the fish, meaning that all the moisture is kept inside the fish as it cooks. After cooking, the crust breaks away in big pieces and you're left with a really juicy fish to eat. Using a bit of egg white and water to moisten the salt helps keep the crust in bigger, easier-to-handle pieces.

Fish must be whole to be cooked in salt, so don't make any cuts in your cleaned and gutted fish. If you do, the salt will get into the flesh and it will be too salty to eat. Don't worry about the cut in the fish belly – it will be protected from the salt by the herbs you've stuffed in. The good news is that you don't need to scale or trim your fish at all before baking, as you don't eat the skin of a fish that has been cooked in salt. I'm using bream in this recipe, but feel free to use any of the fish I've mentioned on page 231.

Preheat the oven to 400°F. Whisk the egg whites to soft peaks and stir into the salt. Add a few tablespoons of water and mix until the salt is damp throughout but not wet. Pack half your salt into the bottom of a baking dish, making a layer about ½ inch thick. Rub your fish all over with olive oil and stuff each cavity with a few rosemary and thyme sprigs. Don't go overboard with the rosemary, though, as it can dominate the flavor of the fish. Lay the fish on top of the salt and completely cover it with the rest of the salt, patting it down and patching it in places where you can still see bits of the fish skin. If your roasting pan seems a little too small to hold both fish, don't worry. You can leave the head and tail sticking out of the salt at either end; it's the body of the fish that needs to be buried.

Put the fish into the preheated oven. A couple of 1lb 2oz fish, as here, need about 20 minutes; for a 2lb fish, you'll need to give it 30 to 35 minutes. Once cooked, remove from the oven, take the tray to the table and let the fish rest – for a couple of minutes for a small fish, and up to 10 minutes for a larger fish. To serve, crack the salt crust open and brush any excess salt away. Remove the herbs from inside each fish and peel the skin off the body, leaving it on at the head and tail.

Fish cooked in this way is always best served with simple things like salads (shaved fennel salad is particularly good), spinach, or braised zucchini.

Matt's wine suggestion: Spanish white – Albarino

serves 2

2 egg whites
9lb coarse rock or
   sea salt
2 x 1lb 2oz whole porgy or
   grouper, cleaned and
   gutted
olive oil
a bunch of fresh rosemary
a bunch of fresh thyme

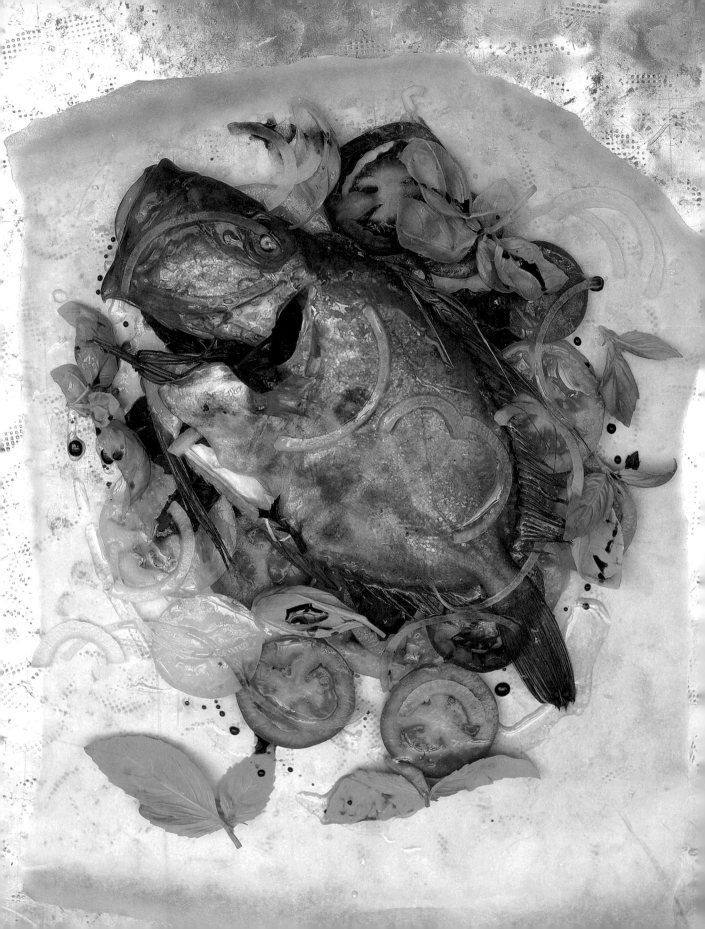

Baked John Dory in the bag with tomatoes and balsamic vinegar

This is such a win-win combo of flavors with so many fish – try it with cod, haddock or even skate wing. It works beautifully served with a big bowl of spaghetti with some chopped parsley, olive oil and lemon zest.

Preheat your oven to 425°F. Tear off a yard or so of wide aluminum foil or wax paper and fold it in half so you get a double sheet 20 inches long. Fold it in half again and open it out – it should look a bit like an open book.

Toss the tomatoes, garlic, chilli, onion, balsamic vinegar and basil with a good glug of olive oil, salt and pepper in a bowl. Spoon the mixture on to one side of your foil or paper and place the fish on top.

Brush the edges of the foil lightly with the beaten egg and fold the foil over the fish. Seal two of the three edges by folding them over a couple of times. Add a splash of water before folding the final edge tightly, making sure the bag is tightly sealed and there are no gaps anywhere.

Place the parcel on a flat metal baking tray, pop the tray in the preheated oven and bake for about 20 minutes.

Remove the bag from the oven and allow to rest for 5 minutes before you put it on a clean plate and open at the table.

Matt's wine suggestion: New Zealand white – Pinot Gris

serves 2

4 or 5 ripe tomatoes, different colors if possible, sliced
1 clove of garlic, peeled and thinly sliced
1 fresh red chilli, halved, deseeded and chopped
½ a small onion, peeled and finely sliced
6 tablespoons balsamic vinegar
a small bunch of fresh basil
olive oil
sea salt and freshly ground black pepper
1 large John Dory, about 1lb 6oz, scaled, cleaned and gutted
1 large free-range or organic egg, beaten

Granddad Ken's crispy grilled trout
with parsley and lemon

My granddad used to take me fishing when I was about six years old. He has sadly passed away, but it was only the other day that I laughed my head off thinking of him, cheating at fly-fishing by putting a secret maggot at the end of his rod – and breaking English fishing etiquette – then reporting to have caught only two fish when we had at least ten. The one thing I thank him for is teaching me not to be scared of bones when eating fish.

Preheat your broiler to full whack. Slash each trout with a knife, about ten times on each side. Each slash should be about ¼ inch deep. Rub the trout with olive oil and season with salt and pepper. Stuff the cavities with plenty of chopped parsley and the lemon slices. Place the fish side by side on a baking rack over a roasting pan.

Put the lemon zest on top of the fish and place the lemon halves on the tray too. Dot the trout with the butter and place it 6 inches from the heat. Cook for around 6 minutes on each side until crispy and golden.

Squeeze the roasted lemon over the top of the fish and serve with a simple crunchy side salad (see page 28).

Matt's wine suggestion: Spanish white – Albarino

serves 2

2 10½oz whole trout,
    scaled, cleaned and gutted
olive oil
sea salt and freshly ground
    black pepper
a large bunch of fresh flat-
    leaf parsley, leaves picked
    and chopped
2 lemons, 1 zested and
    sliced, 1 halved
a few knobs of butter

SCALLOPS

Scallops are delicious, and easy to open and to cook. They grow on the sand at the bottom of the sea and are either harvested by hand by divers, or by a dredging boat that rakes the seabed for them. Dredged scallops are cheaper than hand-dived ones, but they are often damaged by clumsy harvesting, along with loads of other creatures that live next to them on the seabed. You can tell if you have bought dredged ones as they will be full of sand and muck when you open them up.

Look out for scallops still in the shell, and ask your fishmonger to prepare them for you. When he has finished, he should present you with a nice, clean, round piece of white meat with a floppy orange lobe attached to it. This orange bit is called the coral; it's perfectly edible – some people like it, some don't – so you can leave it on or take it off as you like. Wash your trimmed scallops carefully in cold water and pat them dry before cooking them.

- Scallops used to be served with chips in fish and chip shops in the UK, but now they're rightly recognized as one of the finest foods the sea produces and they're found in all sorts of fancy restaurants.

- They can be eaten raw, either as sushi or with just a squeeze of lemon juice and a pinch of salt, and they're also great pan-fried, grilled or steamed.

- Like a good fillet steak, they're best served a little rare in the middle, but if this isn't for you feel free to cook them through like my wife, but don't blame me if they're chewy and rubbery!

- Scallops go really well with garlic, chilli, bacon and of course lemon or lime juice.

Shell-roasted scallops

If you're lucky enough to be able to buy some lovely scallops in their shells from a good fishmonger, which isn't as hard as you'd imagine these days, ask him to remove the scallop, prep it and clean it up for you, and to give you the roe and the shells to take home. Baking things like scallops, lobster and crab in their shells is a great way of cooking because the shells contain lots of flavor. I love the naturalness and old-fashioned feel of cooking in the shell, even though the finished dish might look like 1980s retro campness on a plate!

Here are three of my favorite ways to bake scallops in their shells. For me these are not main courses, they're starters or snacks, allowing 2 large or 3 small scallops per person. If you want to embellish any of them there is plenty of room in the shells to add a few shrimp or bits of flaked lobster or crab. A little chopped-up spinach is also nice. But please only have a go at these recipes when you can get hold of really fresh scallops, and remember to give the shells a good scrub before using them.

Matt's wine suggestion: Scallops are quite rich and generally you'll need a white wine with a bit of weight to match. Most importantly, you need to consider the ingredients used in the toppings and try to find wines with a similar character.

the old-school French way

Scatter a good layer of salt or rice over the bottom of a roasting pan and flatten down. This is going to keep the shells upright and prevent them moving around on the pan. Leave your scallops to one side, out of their shells, while you make the flavored butter. Peel and grate 4 cloves of garlic into a bowl, add a handful of finely chopped fresh flat-leaf parsley, the finely grated zest of 1 lemon and 7 tablespoons unsalted butter. Mix together, using your clean hands, with a good pinch of sea salt and freshly ground black pepper, and grate in ¼ of a nutmeg. Put a little chopped spinach in the deep side of each shell (scallop shells have a deep side and a flatter side), and lay 2 scallops on top. Smear a little knob of your flavored butter on top of the scallops (any leftover butter is great smeared over a roast chicken), and drizzle with extra virgin olive oil. Place the flat sides of the shells on top and bake in your pan in the oven at 325°F for about 12 minutes, until the butter is bubbling. Serve with lemon wedges.

Matt's wine suggestion: French white – Chablis

with sweet tomato and basil sauce

Scatter a good layer of salt or rice over the bottom of a roasting pan and flatten down. This is going to keep the shells upright and prevent them moving around on the tray. To make the sauce, all you need to do is get a large handful of really ripe fresh tomatoes, get rid of the seeds and add them to a blender or a food processor with ½ a clove of garlic, peeled, a handful of fresh basil, a swig of balsamic vinegar, a good pinch of sea salt and freshly ground black pepper and a knob of butter. Whiz up, then spoon 3 tablespoons of the sauce into the deep half of each scallop. Lay 2 scallops on top of the sauce and top with a piece of pancetta. Place the shells side by side in the roasting pan and drizzle with a little extra virgin olive oil. Place the flat sides on top.

At this point you can keep them in the fridge for a few hours, if you're doing a dinner party, or you can cook them straight away. Preheat the oven to 325°F, cook for about 15 minutes. This might sound like a long time, but it will take a little while for the heat to penetrate the cold sauce and fish.

Matt's wine suggestion: Chilean white – Sauvignon Blanc

with ginger, soy and cilantro

Lay 2 scallop shells with their scallops on the roasting pan. Peel and grate a 1 inch piece of fresh ginger into a bowl and mix it with 2 tablespoons of soy sauce, the finely grated zest and juice of a lime, 1 teaspoon of sugar, 1 teaspoon of sesame oil and a few sprigs of finely chopped fresh cilantro. Mix up and divide the sauce over your scallops. Drizzle with a little extra virgin olive oil, then place the flat shells on top and bake in the oven at 325°F for 12 minutes. If you fancy trying something else on this Asian vibe, a couple of lugs of coconut milk in the mix works well.

Matt's wine suggestion: German white – Gewürztraminer or Riesling

Pan-fried scallops with lentils, crispy pancetta and lemon crème fraîche

This is a dish that we've had on the menu at Fifteen for years because customers just love it! Smoky, crispy bacon alongside soft, sweet, fresh scallops that have cooked in some of the bacon fat – a win-win combo in every way. The recipe might seem a bit of a bother at first sight, with things going in and out of the pan, but make it once and it truly is the simplest fun cooking.

In a saucepan, cover the lentils with water and, to give them great flavor, add the bay leaf, garlic cloves, potato and tomato. Bring to the boil and simmer for around 20 to 25 minutes (topping up with water if necessary) until the lentils are tender but holding their shape (i.e. not mushy). Drain off 90 percent of the water, discard the bay leaf, tomato skin and garlic skin and mash the potato, tomato and garlic into the lentils with a fork. Add the parsley and around 2 tablespoons of vinegar and 4 tablespoons of olive oil. Mix into the lentils and season carefully to taste.

Season the crème fraîche or yogurt with salt, pepper and just enough lemon juice to give it a twang – the juice of 1 lemon will probably be enough.

Cut the last 2 inches off the asparagus stalks at an angle and discard. Now's a good time to get your plates out and round your guests up. Get a very large non-stick frying pan (or two medium ones) hot and lay the pancetta or bacon in it with a little drizzle of olive oil. Once golden and crisp, remove to a platter. Add the asparagus and your lightly seasoned scallops to the pan and cook over a high heat until the scallops are golden on both sides. Remove these to the bacon platter too. Finally drizzle in a little more olive oil and lay in your sage leaves. Fry on both sides for 40 seconds or so until crisp and remove to the platter.

Divide your lentils between four plates and place 3 or 4 scallops per person on top. Scatter the bacon over the top of the scallops, with the sage leaves and asparagus sprinkled around the plate. Serve with a good dollop of your lemon crème fraîche.

Matt's wine suggestion: French white – Chardonnay

serves 4

10½oz Puy lentils
1 bay leaf
2 cloves of garlic
1 potato, peeled
1 tomato
a small handful of fresh flat-leaf parsley, leaves picked and finely chopped
herb or red wine vinegar
good-quality extra virgin olive oil
sea salt and freshly ground black pepper
5 heaped tablespoons crème fraîche or thick, natural plain yogurt
juice of 1 lemon
2 handfuls of asparagus
12 slices of pancetta or bacon
olive oil
12 large or 16 small scallops, shelled and trimmed
24 sage leaves

MUSSELS AND CLAMS

Mussels and clams are part of the shellfish family. They are small sea creatures that live inside shells and should actually be alive when you buy them with their shells tightly closed – if you see any with open shells, tap them gently and they should close up; if they don't, they're dead, and because you don't know how long they've been dead, you shouldn't buy them or eat them.

Fresh mussels and clams are cheap and accessible and such a pleasure to eat. Their brilliant salty-savory flavor means that just a few of them in a fish stew, a soup or a pasta sauce will not only look beautiful but make all the difference to the finished dish. They taste of the sea, they're delicious and meaty.

- To prepare mussels or clams, give them a good wash in plenty of clean, cold water and scrub any dirty shells lightly with a scrubbing brush, pulling off any beardy bits you might find on them.

- The key to a fantastic dish of mussels or clams is not being tempted to overcook them. Keep them plump, juicy and fresh. As soon as those shells have opened, get them in those bowls and tuck in.

- All you really need to do to cook them is drop them into a deep pot with a little boiling liquid in the bottom, cover them with a lid and cook for a few minutes until all their shells open. The liquid they give off is the basis of a great sauce which can then be flavored with various things. My favorites are: softened onion, white wine and parsley, grated apple, cider and cream, and spicy tomato sauce and olives. Don't forget the crusty bread to mop up the juices, and the finger bowl.

Mussels steamed with fennel and crème fraîche

This is my version of the incredible French dish, *moules marinière*. All I've done is added the fragrance of fennel and the crème fraîche, which gives it a rich, delicately sour, creamy sauce. Many people walk past fennel in the supermarket, but it goes so well with fish dishes. Try and buy one with a bushy, herby top. If you go to a local farmers' market you'll probably find they have some great ones to offer.

Finely chop half the fennel and the onion. At home I tend to do this very quickly by pulsing them in my Magimix until fine – this stops me crying too! Slowly sweat the fennel, onion, thyme, garlic and chilli, with a pinch of salt and pepper, in a large heavy-bottomed saucepan over a medium-low heat for about 10 minutes, until soft and sweet. Finely shave the rest of the fennel with a speed peeler.

Turn up the heat to full whack. As it starts to get noisy and the veg begins to color a little, add the mussels, wine and crème fraîche. Mix everything together with some force, then put a tight-fitting lid on top and let the thing cook for a couple of minutes. At this stage have a look inside, turn the mussels over and give the pan a good shake. Depending on the size of the mussels, and how big your pan is, it will take around 3 or 4 minutes for them to open. This is where you have to be careful, because the difference between soft, plump, juicy mussels and dry, chewy ones is about 2 minutes of overcooking. Don't panic, though. Just look at what's going on in the pan.

When all the shells seem to have opened, have one final stir up and throw away any mussels that remain closed. Season with some pepper and perhaps a little salt, although you may not need any as the mussels are naturally salty. Using a slotted spoon, divide the mussels between two bowls, or put them into one big one. If your sauce is perfect, pour it on top of the mussels; if it could do with being a little thicker and more intense, put it back on the heat. Don't even think about pouring that sauce over the mussels unless you've seasoned it to utter perfection! When you pour it over, get the sauce going into the little half shells as they will act like saucers. Before eating, sprinkle with the fennel tops and shaved fennel, and drizzle with really good olive oil and sprinkle with the fennel tops. Serve with some warm crusty bread and the rest of the white wine.

Matt's wine suggestion: Portuguese white – Vinho Verde

serves 4

1 large fennel bulb, herby tops reserved

1 large white onion, peeled

2 sprigs of fresh thyme, leaves picked

4 cloves of garlic, peeled and finely chopped

1–2 dried red chillies, crumbled

sea salt and freshly ground black pepper

2½lbs mussels, washed, scrubbed and beards removed

a large wineglass of good white wine

1½ cups crème fraîche

good-quality extra virgin olive oil

The nicest clam chowder, Essex girl style

I started making chowder when I was a kid and my dad had it on the menu at his pub. I wasn't keen on eating clams at the age of eight, but I absolutely adored this soup. There are thousands of chowder recipes out there, but for me the key is to balance the cream with the chilli and the smokiness of the bacon.

In America they tend to use canned clams, which is fine, but I think that if you're going to do it, you may as well do it properly. Similarly, you could use canned or, better, frozen corn, but the true sweetness is only achieved by using fresh corn.

Heat up a little olive oil in a large soup pan and cook the bacon bits until lightly golden. Add the onion, celery, garlic, potatoes and bay leaves and cook very, very gently for 15 minutes, making sure the onion doesn't color. Meanwhile, stand each corn up tall and carefully run a knife down the cob to cut off the kernels. Drop the corn kernels into the pan, add the thyme and stock and simmer for 20 minutes.

While that is ticking away, get a pot with a lid on to a high heat. When really hot, add the clams with a splash of water and slap the lid on. Leave to boil and steam for a few minutes until the clams have opened. Hold a sieve over the soup pan, then pour the clams into the sieve, making sure any cooking liquid ends up in the soup pan. Discard any clams that remain closed, then add the meat from the clams that have opened to the soup, with the chilli, parsley and a squeeze of lemon juice.

Remove about half the soup to a blender, discarding the bay leaves, and whiz up to a purée. Pour your whizzed-up soup back into the soup pan, stir in the cream, warm through and season carefully to taste. You now have a creamy yet chunky chowder. Ladle the hot soup into serving bowls. I guarantee you'll be back for second helpings!

Matt's wine suggestion: Australian white – Chardonnay

serves 6–8

olive oil

4 slices of bacon, finely sliced

1 small onion, peeled and finely chopped

4 sticks of celery, trimmed and finely sliced

4 cloves of garlic, peeled and finely sliced

14oz floury potatoes, peeled and cut into ½ inch dice

2 fresh bay leaves

5 ears sweet corn, husks removed

1 tablespoon fresh thyme leaves

2 pints chicken stock

2lb 3oz clams, cleaned and debearded

2–3 fresh red chillies, deseeded and finely chopped

a small bunch of fresh flat-leaf parsley, leaves picked and chopped

½ a lemon

3 tablespoons heavy cream

sea salt and freshly ground black pepper

SHRIMP

Shrimp, like lobster and crab, are crustaceans with hard shells on the outside of their bodies for protection. Ideally they should be alive when you buy them, but if they're not they should be bright and shiny and smell of nothing but the sea.

- Shrimp are found all over the world, mainly in warmer waters, and these days they're extensively farmed. They come in different sizes, from tiny ones you can eat in one bite, shell and all, to great big ones that are a meal in themselves. You can buy them cooked or uncooked, frozen or fresh, shell on or off. Like most other crustaceans, they turn a lovely pink color when they're cooked, but when they're raw they're either silvery grey and translucent or bluey green.

- To peel a shrimp, pinch its head between your thumb and forefinger and pull and twist it until it detaches from the tail. Pick the legs off the underside of the shrimp, then gently peel the shell off with your fingers, leaving the meat inside in one piece. Don't throw anything away – shrimp heads and shells are dynamite for stocks and sauces!

- Small shrimp are ready to cook or eat as they are, but with shrimp the size of your finger, or bigger, you need to lay the peeled shrimp tail on its side and make a shallow slit down its back from its neck to the end of its tail to expose a small black vein – this is the intestine. Remove this with the tip of a knife – it only takes a second and can be done either before or after cooking.

- Nothing beats a pint of shell-on shrimp. Shell the tails as you eat them, pulling the heads off and sucking out the rich juice inside. To cook them like this, just drop your shrimp into salted boiling water for a few minutes until they curl up, turn pink and are hot all the way through.

- Shell-on shrimp are fantastic grilled or just boiled and eaten with mayonnaise. Shelled shrimp are fantastic for stir-fries and curries, and you can grill or broil them, but make sure you don't overcook them. As soon as they turn pink and they're hot all the way through, they're ready.

- Shrimp are great tossed in a bit of flour spiked with crumbled dried chilli and deep-fried – lovely eaten as crisps with a pint of cold beer.

Fabulous fish stew

It's worth trying to get hold of saffron for this one – it's available from most specialty shops and good supermarkets. It's not cheap, but bear in mind you won't need much at all to spice up a dish. Make sure you use a wide pan so all the fish is in contact with the tomatoey broth. If you haven't got one, try using a high-sided roasting pan instead, with a baking sheet as a lid.

To make the saffron aïoli, smash a clove of garlic, a tiny squeeze of lemon juice, and the saffron (if using) with a small pinch of salt in a pestle and mortar or a Flavor Shaker until it turns into a mush. Add a tablespoon of mayonnaise and pound again. Stir in the rest of the mayo. Taste and season with a little more lemon juice, salt and pepper.

Give the mussels and clams a good wash in plenty of clean cold water and scrub any dirty ones lightly with a scrubbing brush, pulling off any beardy bits. If there are any that aren't tightly closed, give them a sharp tap. If they don't close up, throw them away. (For more information on mussels and clams, see page 252.)

Heat a large, wide saucepan or stewing pot and pour in a splash of olive oil. Slice up the rest of the garlic and fry it in the oil until lightly golden. Add the wine and the tomatoes and the basil stalks and bring to the boil. Simmer gently for 10 to 15 minutes, until the liquid has reduced a little.

Add all your fish and shellfish in a single layer and season with salt and pepper. Push the fish down into the liquid and put the lid on. Cook gently for about 10 minutes or until all the clams and mussels have opened and the fish fillets and langoustines or shrimp are cooked through. (Discard any clams or mussels that don't open.)

Toast the bread on a hot griddle pan and get out the serving bowls. Put a piece of toast in each bowl and ladle the soup over the top, making sure the fish is divided more or less evenly. Top each bowl with some fennel tops, basil leaves, a drizzle of extra virgin olive oil and a big blob of saffron aïoli.

Matt's wine suggestion: French rosé – Grenache

serves 2

2 cloves of garlic, peeled
optional: a small pinch of saffron
sea salt and freshly ground black pepper
1 x mayonnaise (see page 26) or 1 cup ready-made mayonnaise
lemon juice
12 mussels
20 clams
olive oil
a small wineglass of white wine
1 x 14oz can good-quality plum tomatoes
2 small fillets of seabass or bream, cut in half
2 small fillets of red mullet or snapper, cut in half
2 small fillets of monkfish or other firm white fish
4 langoustines or tiger shrimp, shell on
2 thick slices of crusty bread
a small handful of fennel tops
extra virgin olive oil
a small bunch of fresh basil, leaves picked and stalks chopped

Crispy fragrant jumbo shrimp

When I was a kid, just about every other pub in the area, apart from my old man's pub, served scampi in a basket. I came to realize that very often what was inside the 'scampi' was some weird concoction of unrecognizable fish, and this meant I was always a bit put off by fish in breadcrumbs ... until I had it in Italy last year. It's a really good way of celebrating nice medium to large shrimp – don't bother making it with small ones. And if you can make breadcrumbs out of good-quality stale bread, it's a wonderful way of protecting the shrimp while they cook. The best thing is having the crunchiness on the outside and the soft shrimp inside – perfect snack, perfect starter.

When it comes to making breadcrumbs I always remove any thick crusts and cut the bread into chunks before whizzing them in a food processor until nice and fine. And make sure you save yourself a job by asking your fishmonger to shell the shrimp and butterfly them.

Preheat the oven to 425°F. Rub a baking pan with olive oil and put it to one side. Put the breadcrumbs into a bowl, add your parsley, lemon zest, a glug of olive oil and your Parmesan, mix it all up and spread the mixture on a baking sheet to dry.

Toss the shrimp in the flour so they're nicely coated and shake off any excess. Dip them into the egg, letting any excess drip off, then put the shrimp on to the sheet of breadcrumbs. Shake the tray to coat each prawn, using your hands to press the breadcrumbs and flavors into each one – you want them to be completely coated. Put the shrimp in your oiled baking pan and bake them in the middle of the oven for about 10 minutes or until crispy and golden.

When done, sprinkle the shrimp with a little salt and divide between your plates. Lightly dress the arugula with olive oil and lemon juice and season. Add a handful to each plate, and serve each with a quarter of lemon.

PS If you like this recipe you can always try breadcrumbing other types of seafood like squid, scallops or sardines. They all work well.

Matt's wine suggestion: Italian white – Prosecco

serves 4 as a starter,
2 as a main course

olive oil
3 large handfuls of
  breadcrumbs
a handful of fresh flat-leaf
  parsley leaves, finely
  chopped
zest and juice of 1 lemon,
  plus 1 to serve
a handful of freshly grated
  Parmesan cheese
8 large king shrimp, peeled,
  heads removed and
  butterflied
a small bowl of seasoned
  flour, for dusting
2 large eggs, cracked into
  a bowl and whisked
sea salt and freshly ground
  black pepper
4 handfuls of arugula,
  washed and dried

Shrimp cocktail

Here's my way of making the ultiimate shrimp cocktail. I've tweaked the old recipe a bit to make it more interesting. If your fishmonger has got some nice crab or lobster, just a little bit mixed in with your shrimp makes it even more exciting! Remember if you're using frozen shrimp to let them thaw out overnight. However, if you've been caught out, and you need to thaw them quickly, put them in a bowl and run cold water over them. This will take away some of their sweetness, but after 15 minutes you'll have thawed shrimp and you'll be ready to rock and roll.

Separate the lettuce leaves from the cores. Wash and spin all your lovely leaves and put them to one side. Drain your fresh or thawed shrimp.

The Marie Rose sauce is an interesting one, because on paper it sounds disgusting – mayo, ketchup, brandy – but it actually works really well and it's unquestionably delicious! So, simply mix together the mayo, ketchup, Worcestershire sauce and brandy until loose and pink. Have a taste. It should be halfway there. I like to cut my Marie Rose with a tang of lemon juice – add to taste.

Now for the pangrattato. Put your bread slices into a food processor and pulse until you have coarse breadcrumbs. Pour a good lug of olive oil into a frying pan, add a pinch of salt and pepper, then add the breadcrumbs and fry until golden and crisp. Lay them on paper towels to drain off the oil.

To assemble, score the avocados in half and twist them to separate the 2 halves. Make sure you put them down on a board to stone them – you want to click the knife into the pits and twist them out. (Cuts from pitting avocados are one of the most common injuries in hospitals, so be warned, you nutters!) Remove the skin, slice them up roughly into 3 or 4 wedges and divide between your four plates.

Divide your shrimp up and pile them on top of the avocado. I like to lightly dress the salad leaves with a little squeeze of lemon juice, a pinch of salt and pepper and a drizzle of olive oil. Toss them together and place a nice pile of leaves next to and around the avocado and shrimp.

Gently spoon over your ridiculous but tasty cocktail sauce, ideally so there is one reasonably fine layer of sauce over most of the shrimp. Flick over a pinch of cayenne, half on the shrimp and half on the salad. Serve with a wedge of lemon on the side and your pangrattato in a separate bowl for sprinkling over. You will definitely, definitely enjoy it!

Matt's wine suggestion: Spanish rosé – Garnacha

serves 4

1 Boston lettuce
1 little butter lettuce
optional: a container of
    watercress, snipped
1lb 6oz small, sweet,
    good-quality fresh or
    frozen shrimp
2 ripe avocados
sea salt and freshly ground
    black pepper
cayenne pepper
1 lemon, cut into wedges,
    plus a little extra juice

for the Marie Rose sauce
3 heaped tablespoons
    mayonnaise (see page 26)
1 heaped tablespoon
    tomato ketchup
a splash of Worcestershire
    sauce
1 tablespoon good brandy
1–2 lemons

for the pangrattato
4 slices of good stale
    white bread
olive oil
sea salt and freshly ground
    black pepper

CRAB

Crabs are crustaceans, like shrimp and lobsters, but they have a slightly different shape and so are cooked and prepared in a different way.

You very often find crabs ready-cooked these days, but if you pre-order from your fishmonger you'll get one fresh and alive, and then you'll need to kill and cook it (see the next page). Watch out for its claws – a big angry crab can give you a bone-crushing pinch if you're not careful!

- Crabs are found all over the world in a variety of shapes and sizes. In Europe the crabs are quite large, with thick brown shells and big heads. Elsewhere, spider crabs and snow crabs are prized for their long meaty legs and mud crabs for their delicious claws.

- Normally we boil the crab whole first and then pick the cooked meat out. In parts of Asia, crabs are chopped up with a cleaver while still raw and braised or stir-fried in the shell.

- Soft-shell crabs are baby crabs that have just shed their outer shell to grow a slightly bigger one, in which case the shell doesn't need to be removed before the crab is cooked and eaten. They are fantastic deep-fried!

- Crab is delicious in a sandwich with crusty bread and butter, or in a salad with chilli, lemon and parsley or even with spaghetti or linguine.

How to prepare and boil a whole live crab

Dealing with killing a crab is quite a controversial thing. Some people believe you should just drive a sharpening steel or skewer straight through it, which kills the crab instantly. I have always put mine into a great big stock pot, seven or eight of them at a time, layered up with some nice bits of fennel, peppercorns, etc., then covered them with cold water and turned the heat on, so by the time it comes up to temperature they should have gone to sleep and won't know what's going on.

If you prefer to kill the crab first, place it upside down on a chopping board and feel for the bony flap on the underside of its body. Pull it back, poke a sharpening steel or a thick skewer into the hole you see there, and thump the top of it with your hand so it shoots right down into the crab. This crushes the crab's central nervous system, killing it immediately.

To cook your crab, fill a deep pot with cold water and stir in salt, a teaspoon at a time, until it tastes about as salty as seawater. Drop your crab in the pot and make sure it's completely submerged. Put the pot on the stove and bring the water slowly to the boil, then turn the heat down and simmer gently for about 10 minutes to make sure the heat has penetrated the thick shell and cooked the meat inside. Lift the crab carefully out of the hot water, using a slotted spoon or a pair of tongs, and leave it on a plate to cool down.

How to pick cooked crabmeat

Once the crab is cold, pull off the claws and legs, crack them with a pair of lobster crackers or the back of a heavy knife and pick all the meat out with a crab pick or the handle of a teaspoon. Pull the head shell away from the body of the crab and with a small spoon scoop out the brown meat that's tucked against the inside. The hen (female) crab tends to have a lot more of the rich brown meat than the male. Keep the brown meat separate from the white for now and throw away any plasticky membranes you might have spooned out with the meat. If you're lucky enough to find a few orange lumps inside the crab's head, these are roe from a hen crab and are really delicious!

Around the body of the crab are a dozen or so grey spongy bits. These are the crab's gills. Like fish gills, they're not edible, so just pick them off and throw them away. With your crab pick or teaspoon handle, pick out all the white meat from the nooks and crannies in the crab's body, trying not to break off any small pieces of bone as you go. Don't throw away your crab shells, as they'll make a fantastic stock for a shellfish soup.

Check through your two piles of picked white and brown crabmeat for little pieces of shell that might have got in there. It would be a shame after all your hard work to have a guest crack a tooth during dinner!

Cooked crab can be used in loads of ways. I like to take some of the brown and the white meat and mix them together, so that it still looks white but tastes a bit more robust. I mix any leftover brown meat with butter and put it in the freezer so that when I make a seafood pasta (in the restaurant we often make a linguine using crabmeat – see page 74) I add a slice of this crab butter at the end of cooking for a fantastic hit of flavor. Mixed with olive oil, lemon and herbs, crabmeat is great in a salad or on a piece of grilled bruschetta. It's also fantastic stirred into a risotto, and crab spaghetti with a little chopped fresh red chilli is a big favorite in Italy. In Britain, crabmeat is most often packed back into the head shell, decorated with boiled egg and chopped parsley, and sold as 'dressed crab'. Or it will be served in chunks, still in the shell, with crusty bread and butter and mayonnaise.

Old-fashioned potted crab

Once upon a time potting meat and fish was pretty common in Britain and the results were regarded as highly as the French regard their pâtés. I think this recipe is really interesting because it uses a pestle and mortar to smash up the crabmeat with the butter, and it's a great one for serving at dinner parties or for cooking in advance. It's also a short-term method of preserving as it can be kept in the fridge for up to a week. As for the pots, once made up they're great for picnics. They're also lovely served at home with hot toast! Once you've had a go at making this recipe a few times, try potting shrimp instead, or smash up some other flavorings like dill or chives and add these to the butter. I'm pretty sure that once you've tried, you'll really get into it!

In a pestle and mortar or a Flavor Shaker, smash up the fennel seeds, chilli and lemon zest. Put in a large metal bowl with half the butter and the brown crabmeat. Using your pestle or the end of a rolling pin, gently scrunch until well mixed and slightly softened. Grate in the nutmeg and stir in the flaky white crabmeat. This is a good time to try some on a bit of toast – taste it and slightly over-season it with salt and pepper. (Chefs are always trained to slightly over-season food that is going to be served cold, like a pâté or a terrine, because otherwise when you come back to it a few hours later, or the next day, it can be a bit bland.)

You can serve this in one larger appropriately sized shallow dish, or find some classic individual pots (3½ inches in diameter and 2 inches high) and divide the crab mix between them. Flatten it down with a spoon and make sure that it doesn't quite reach the top of the dish or the pot. Melt the rest of the butter and spoon this over the crab mixture – when it sets this will act as a 'lid'. Sprinkle with a little chopped fennel or parsley and place in the fridge to set (anything from 1 hour to 5 days). When you're ready to eat it, serve with hot toast and a nice glass of chilled white wine.

Matt's wine suggestion: Italian white – Soave

makes 4–6 pots

½ teaspoon fennel seeds
1 small dried chilli
zest of 1 lemon
butter, softened tablespoon
2¾oz brown crabmeat
8oz picked white crabmeat
⅓ of a nutmeg
sea salt and freshly ground white pepper
1 heaped tablespoon fennel tops or fresh flat-leaf parsley, chopped

Delicious crab crostini

This is one of my favorite ways of eating crab – simply on a slice of hot, grilled ciabatta. You can't beat it!

Put all the crabmeat into a bowl. Add most of the chopped fennel tops, the chilli, a squeeze of lemon juice and a good lug of extra virgin olive oil and mix. Taste it and season accordingly. Think about the balance of flavor – you want to taste the fragrant fennel alongside the sweetness of the crab, with just enough lemon juice to lift and lighten the whole story. I like to taste and balance the flavors at the last minute before serving, but feel free to do it 20 minutes before – no longer than that, though, or the lemon juice will take away the sweetness of the crab.

Make your aïoli by pounding the garlic and salt together in a pestle and mortar until you have a paste. Spoon in a tablespoon of the mayonnaise and pound again. Fold the garlicky mixture into the rest of the mayo. Put your griddle pan on a high heat to chargrill your ciabatta slices, or you could use a toaster. Take your grilled or toasted ciabatta slices, divide the crabmeat on to them and spoon over a dollop of the garlic aïoli. Feel free to eat these with your fingers as posh nibbles, or you could serve them on bigger plates with a little fennel and arugula salad on the side if you want a more complete snack.

Matt's wine suggestion: Italian white – Soave

serves 4

14oz picked white
  crabmeat
5½oz picked brown
  crabmeat
a handful of fennel tops,
  finely chopped
1 fresh red chilli, deseeded
  and finely sliced
1 lemon
extra virgin olive oil
8 slices of ciabatta
sea salt and freshly ground
  black pepper

for the aïoli
1 small clove of garlic,
  peeled
½ teaspoon sea salt
4 tablespoons mayonnaise
  (see page 26)

Southern Indian crab curry

If you fancy a really different, quick and tasty treat, you must have a go at this curry. I've included a whole array of different spices, yet they're so light and fragrant that you still get to appreciate the lovely sweet crab. And by using the brown meat in the base of the sauce and sprinkling the delicate white meat in at the end you'll get a lovely depth of flavor and still be able to taste the crab because you won't have cooked the life out of it. Best served with steamed rice.

Heat 2 tablespoons of olive oil in a large pan and add the fennel seeds, mustard seeds, cardamom pods, cumin seeds, ginger, garlic, onion and chilli. Fry on a medium heat for 4 to 5 minutes until lightly golden, then add the turmeric, butter and brown crabmeat. After a minute or so, pour in the coconut milk and a can of water. Let it simmer away for 5 minutes so all the flavors develop. Then add the lemon juice and simmer for another 10 minutes, or until the sauce resembles heavy cream in consistency.

Just before you stir in the white crabmeat, check that all the shell has been picked out, then add half the cilantro, simmer for 4 more minutes and taste. Season carefully with salt and pepper and a little more lemon juice if you think it needs it. Serve with some fluffy white rice, sprinkled with the rest of the cilantro leaves.

Matt's wine suggestion: South African white – Viognier

serves 4–6

olive oil
3 teaspoons fennel seeds
2 heaped teaspoons black
  mustard seeds
5 green cardamom pods,
  crushed and husks
  removed
1 teaspoon cumin seeds
a thumb-sized piece of
  fresh ginger, peeled and
  finely sliced
2 large cloves of garlic,
  peeled and finely sliced
1 medium white onion,
  peeled and finely sliced
2–3 fresh red chillies,
  deseeded and
  finely sliced
2 heaped teaspoons
  turmeric
1½ tablespoons butter
9oz brown crabmeat
1 x 12oz can coconut milk
juice of 2 lemons
1lb 2oz picked white
  crabmeat
a good bunch of fresh
  cilantro, leaves picked
sea salt and freshly ground
  black pepper

LOBSTER

Lobsters are not as hard to get hold of now as they were twenty years ago – you can even order them in good supermarkets or fishmonger's. With their juicy shell-covered tails and strong meaty claws, they're halfway between shrimp and crabs, with the best of both worlds. Live lobsters are a beautiful navy blue with creamy patches underneath. When sold, they normally have their pincers bound with strong elastic bands. If you see them without, be careful – their pincers are as dangerous as a crab's.

- Lobsters can be boiled or steamed whole; halved and grilled; roasted or chopped up and stir-fried, Chinese stylie.

- Lobsters go really well with chilli, garlic and lemon, just like shrimp. Americans love them with hot melted butter.

- Like shrimp, lobsters turn pink when cooked and are most often sold pink and cooked in supermarkets or fishmonger's.

- All you need to do to eat a cooked lobster is shell the tail like a shrimp and crack the claws like a crab, but a nicer way to present it is to part-crack the claws and chop the lobster lengthways right through the head and tail, giving half a lobster to each person.

- Cooked lobstermeat can be used in exactly the same way as crabmeat.

● Lobstermeat that's hot or at room temperature is sweet and tender. The colder it gets, the more rubbery it can be.

How to prepare a live lobster

You can of course boil a lobster whole, but I love to prepare it like this – it allows you to cook it in so many more ways. So if you have a live lobster and you plan to grill, roast, steam or barbecue it, this is what you'll need to do. First, you'll need to kill it and cut it in half. Place the lobster on a big chopping board and look for the small cross mark on its shell, just at the back of its head. Taking great care, place the tip of a large chopping knife at the center of the cross and quickly and confidently push the tip of the knife straight through the shell, chopping right down through the head to the board underneath. This kills the lobster immediately, and if the legs continue to wriggle afterwards, don't worry; it's just a reflex reaction and will stop after a while.

Turn the lobster around and chop lengthways right down through the tail so you've cut the lobster in half. Pull out the little gritty stomach sac in the lobster's head and throw it away. Give the claws a crack in a couple of places with the base of a saucepan or a pestle – this will allow the heat to penetrate the shell more easily so that the claws cook in the same time as the tail. Your lobster is now ready to be drizzled with a little oil or dotted with some butter, seasoned with salt, pepper and herbs, and cooked to your liking.

How to steam a lobster

Find yourself a wide, deep saucepan with a lid and place either some pastry cutters or a small metal cake tin upside down in it – this is to rest your lobster on. Pour in just enough water to cover the saucer or bowl and bring to the boil. Season the cut-side of the **lobster** with a little sea **salt** and freshly ground black **pepper**, sprinkle with **lemon** zest and dot with **butter**. Place it on a plate that will fit inside your saucepan and sit the plate on the upturned saucer or bowl. Be careful not to burn your fingers! The plate should be above the level of the water so the lobster steams and doesn't boil. Cover with the lid and steam for about 10 to 15 minutes until the lobster's cooked through. Lift the lobster out of the pan, drizzle with lemon juice, sprinkle with chopped **flat-leaf fresh parsley** and dot with more butter before serving.

Matt's wine suggestion: Whether you're steaming or grilling a lobster, you'll need a full-bodied white wine. Grape varieties like Chardonnay, Semillon and Viognier are worth a look.

How to pan-grill a lobster

Heat a griddle pan big enough to fit your lobster. Season the cut-side of the **lobster** with sea **salt** and freshly ground black **pepper** and rub with a little **olive oil**. Cook the lobster cut-side down in the hot griddle pan, pressing down with a lid to make sure the lobster meat touches the hot ridges of the griddle. The lid will also turn the griddle into a mini oven, helping the top of the lobster to cook at the same time as the bottom. After about 5 minutes, turn the lobster over, sprinkle with a little chopped **garlic** and chopped **fresh red chilli**, then turn back again and cook for 5 minutes more. Turn over once more and grill for 5 minutes on the shell side. At the same time place 2 **lime** halves cut-side down on the grill with the lobster. When the lobster's cooked through, serve it with more chopped chilli, plenty of fresh torn **mint** leaves and the grilled lime.

Sticky fingers lobster

Part of me definitely thinks that lobster simply boiled or steamed, or halved and roasted with just a little bit of olive oil, parsley and lemon, is the best way to go. However, sometimes you fancy a luxury taste experience instead. Which brings me to this recipe ... When I made it up I was inspired by the incredibly confident way that the Keralans wok-fry crab using copious amounts of black pepper instead of chilli, and then offset that heat with the juiciness and fragrance of ginger and cilantro. As it works so well with crab I figured it would also be brilliant with lobster too. Even though you can have this sticky lobster as a main course, I prefer it best as a sociable sharing-type starter with a couple of finger bowls. Don't forget some cold white wine. It's damn messy but damn tasty!

I'd really love you to have a go at preparing your live lobsters, but if you don't feel ready to do this just yet, feel free to ask your fishmonger to do it for you.

Preheat your oven to 425°F. In a pestle and mortar or a Flavor Shaker, smash the black peppercorns up until nicely ground, then put into a large bowl with the ginger, garlic, spring onions and salt. Add a couple of lugs of olive oil, the honey and the lemon juice and mix up with your hands. Rub all over your 4 lobster halves until nicely coated. Reserve any of the spring onions that may not have stuck to the lobsters.

Lay the lobsters next to each other on an appropriately sized roasting pan. Cook for 12 to 15 minutes in the oven, then remove and serve in a big bowl sprinkled with the chilli, any extra slices of spring onion and the cilantro. Serve with finger bowls for your sticky fingers!

Matt's wine suggestion: French white – Gewurztraminer

serves 4

1 heaped tablespoon black peppercorns
a thumb-sized piece of fresh ginger, peeled and finely chopped
4 cloves of garlic, peeled and finely sliced
a bunch of spring onions, trimmed and finely sliced at an angle
a good pinch of sea salt
olive oil
2 tablespoons honey
juice of 1–2 lemons
2 medium-sized live lobsters, prepared as on page 278
1–2 fresh red chillies, deseeded and finely sliced
a small bunch of fresh cilantro, leaves picked

SQUID

Squid is neither a shellfish nor a crustacean, but a strange boneless creature that is found in seas just about all over the world. It's easy to prepare and cook and it has a good flavor and a meaty texture. Because it's accessible to so many people, just about every country has different and interesting ways of cooking it.

Did you know that in some parts of South America squid can grow to the size of a car? Over the years, there have been lots of fishermen's tales about sailors being eaten by these giant creatures. Even though squid are quite placid, when angered they have been known to eat each other. Their beaks are as hard as porcelain, which makes for an incredibly sharp cutting machine. But, hey, don't be worried about all this, because we can only get little ones.

- When buying squid, make sure it's an icy blue-white color – this means it is nice and fresh. Sometimes, if cheeky fishmongers are trying to sell their squid off cheap, they'll be a blushing pink color, which looks nice but means it's old.

- Squid can be chopped up and fried, stuffed and braised, steamed like the Chinese do, and everyone loves it bread-crumbed and deep-fried with some good old mayonnaise (see recipe on page 26).

- Squid goes well with just about anything. It's great in fish soup, it's nice in a mixed fish grill, it's lovely with pasta and even goes well with chicken and shellfish in a paella.

- Please don't think squid is rubbery and chewy. If you fry or grill it quickly, or steam or stew it slowly, it can melt in your mouth.

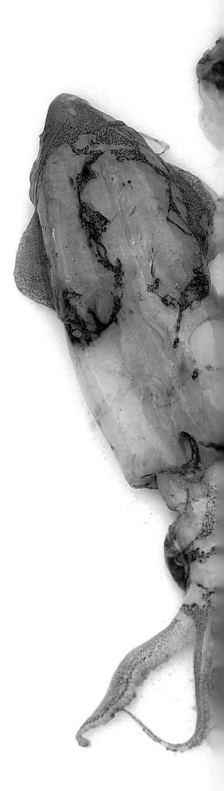

How to prepare squid

Squid can be bought ready-prepared from your fishmonger, but if you want to have a go at preparing it yourself, here's what to do. Place the squid on a clean chopping board and pull its tentacles straight so they're all in a line pointing away from its body. Trim the two longer tentacles so they are the same length as the other ones, and then cut the clump of tentacles off just below the eye. If there's a small hard lump in the middle of the tentacles, pull it out and throw it away. This is the squid's beak and it isn't edible. The eyes are attached to the squid's insides, which are tucked inside its large, tubular head sac. If you pull the eyes gently, they should come away and bring all the insides with them. In the head, there should also be something that looks like a transparent plastic feather. This is the quill and it needs to be pulled out and thrown away with the guts. Pull all the icy blue-white membrane off the outside of the squid, give it a good rinse inside and out and pat dry.

It can now be stuffed, if that's what you plan to do with it, but if you want to grill or fry it, it's a good idea to open the squid out and score it. This tenderizes it and makes it curl up nicely when cooked. To do this, lay the squid head flat on the chopping board and push a knife inside it until it can't go any further. Cut open one side of the squid's head, as if you were opening a book, and it should open out in one piece on the board, with the inside surface facing up. Very lightly score this surface with a sharp knife, making sure you don't cut right the way through. It's now ready to go.

My favorite crunchy squid with lime and chilli mayonnaise

When you're deep-frying, you can use a thermometer to find out if your oil is at the right temperature, but the potato method (see below) works just as well. And as usual, don't go off to do something else and leave the oil on the heat, don't let the kids get too close, and don't get drunk! I usually put the oil on 6 or 7 minutes before I'm ready to feed my guests. You don't want to stink your house out too much either, so wait as long as possible before doing the actual deep-frying bit. (In fact, I'll let you into a secret … I keep a deep-fat fryer outside in my shed and make it there. That way I don't get a rollicking from Jools for making the house smell!)

First make your flavored mayonnaise. Put the mayonnaise, chilli and lemon and lime zest into a bowl, mix together and add a good pinch of salt and pepper. Add all the lime juice and half the lemon juice, mix up and taste – you should have a nice creamy, zingy, slightly hot flavor going on. When you feel the citrus flavor is good and prominent, add a couple of extra squeezes of lemon juice so that when you dip your crispy hot squid into the mayonnaise it should balance to perfection.

Get yourself a sturdy, thick-bottomed pot, about 12 inches in diameter, and fill it with 1½ inches of sunflower oil. Put the heat on high and chuck your small piece of potato into the oil. When the potato is golden, floating and frying this is a sign that your oil has reached around 350°F, the perfect temperature for deep-frying. Make sure you discard the potato. Toss your squid in the flour, shake off any excess and carefully place in your deep-fat fryer. You may have to do this in batches, depending on the size of your fryer. After 2 minutes, when the squid is crispy and golden, remove it using tongs or a slotted spoon and leave to drain on some paper towels. Season generously with sea salt, slice up at an angle and serve with your incredible mayo and ½ a lemon or lime each.

PS Great with a root veg salad (see page 43).

Matt's wine suggestion: British white – sparkling wine

serves 4

for the flavored mayonnaise
4 heaped tablespoons
  mayonnaise (see page 26)
2 fresh red chillies,
  deseeded and finely
  chopped
zest and juice of 1 lemon
zest and juice of 1 lime
sea salt and freshly ground
  black pepper

sunflower oil
a small piece of potato,
  peeled
1lb 6oz squid, cleaned,
  scored and tentacles
  removed (see page 286)
1¾ cups seasoned flour
2 lemons or limes, for
  serving

Squid with black pudding stuffing and sticky tomato sauce

I know this sounds a bit strange, but squid is often cooked with meat – the great Spanish paella is a good example. Here I've combined the squid with blood sausage. You can serve the squid tubes whole with the tomato sauce on top, or take them out of the pan, slice them thickly and pop them back into the sauce if you prefer.

Heat a splash of olive oil in a wide saucepan and add the bacon or pancetta. When it's sizzling, add the onion and thyme and cook gently until the onion is soft. Stir in the blood sausage, then turn the heat up a little and fry until everything's crisp and hot. Tip the contents of the pan into a food processor, add the bread and lemon zest and pulse everything together. Season with salt and pepper and put to one side to cool.

Spoon the cooled blood sausage mixture into the squid tubes (don't stuff them too full) and secure the open ends with cocktail sticks. Rub the stuffed squid with a little oil, salt and pepper.

Sear the squid tubes and tentacles in a little oil on a medium heat until light brown on all sides. Add the chilli and garlic, and when the garlic is golden brown, add the tomatoes. Cover with a lid and simmer gently for about 10 minutes, until the tomatoes have cooked into a lovely sticky sauce and the squid is hot all the way through.

Taste the sauce and season with salt and pepper if it needs it. Great with spinach on the side.

PS Remember to take the cocktail sticks out before you tuck in!

Matt's wine suggestion: Australian white – Chardonnay

serves 4

olive oil
3 slices bacon or pancetta, chopped
1 small red onion, peeled and finely chopped
1 tablespoon fresh thyme leaves
7oz blood sausage, peeled and chopped
2 handfuls of good-quality stale bread
zest of 1 lemon
sea salt and freshly ground black pepper
8 small or 4 medium squid, prepared as on page 286, leaving the tubes whole
1 dried red chilli, crumbled
2 cloves of garlic, peeled and finely sliced
1lb red and yellow cherry tomatoes, sliced in half
extra virgin olive oil

vegetables

CELEBRATING VEG

It's a fact that human beings aren't going to like everything. There are plenty of things – like gizzards – that I'll eat but actually don't float my boat. But in the vegetable world there are so many ways that you can cook everything, from a cauliflower to a pea, that there is something beautiful for everyone. Yet most people nowadays have hardly gone beyond the usual pretty plainly cooked carrots, potatoes, cabbage and leeks.

The problem is we don't get excited about vegetables. For so long we have thought of dinner as meat and two veg – but those veg are just a token, something boiled or steamed, that's it. I see it all the time filming *Jamie's School Dinners*: boiled cabbage, boiled broccoli, boiled greens, boiled cauliflower, boiled leeks . . . even if they are al dente, if they're not dressed, seasoned or given a bit of love and attention, they're pretty miserable. Whereas in Italy, France or Spain, where they are more in touch with the seasons, the minute fava beans, asparagus or artichokes appear, they have multiple uses for them: they will toss some with olive oil, butter and herbs, smash some up to make fritters, put them in soups, stews, in pasta, and preserve some. Everything goes back to the days before freezers and microwaves when you had to be resourceful and make the most of those vegetables until you could see them again next year. And because there are so many ways to prepare everything, you will always find something you like.

Plain boiled or steamed leeks: boring. But cut them up, put them in a pan over a medium to low heat with a little bit of olive oil and butter, a few sprigs of thyme and a good pinch of sea salt and freshly ground black pepper and let them cook slowly, turning them over every ten minutes or so, and you will see how beautiful and sweet and incredibly big-flavored they become. Even if you just cook some broccoli and toss it in a bit of butter and extra virgin olive oil and maybe a squeeze of lemon, then sprinkle it with some Parmesan or Gruyère, it will be so much more interesting and exciting.

There are so many vegetables to choose from that it was never going to be possible to cover every single one in this chapter, so I decided to cut to the chase and pick the ten most popular vegetables in the UK, plus a couple of my personal favorites. I wanted to give you a handful of great recipes that are not only delicious in their own right but, most importantly, really very simple to learn how to do properly – kind of 'day one at college'. I've also given you a little bit of background history and information for each vegetable – facts that I think are pretty fascinating. And at the end of this book are some guidelines on how to chop up your veg (see pages 430-31).

We're in the middle of very exciting times at the moment, as good supermarkets and farmers' markets are not only protecting and selling some original varieties of vegetables but are also offering fantastic choices and variations in shape, color and flavors of all sorts of different vegetables – from asparagus to potatoes to beetroots. There is absolutely no need to settle for one type of each veg any more and that is incredibly exciting! I suppose what I'm trying to say is that if, like all of us, you're a little bit guilty of buying the same old veg every time you go shopping, week in, week out, then try and get into the habit of having a browse and looking around for different variations. You'll be amazed at what's already out there, just under your nose. Real cooks and really good chefs, in my opinion, are those who embrace vegetables and do fabulous things with them – so let's get started . . .

POTATOES

Let's start with the good old potato. Originally from South America, potatoes have only been around in Britain for the last 300-odd years, which is amazing when you think how many of us eat them every day of our lives – mashed, roasted, boiled or even as fries or chips!

There are hundreds of varieties of potato – large, small, yellow, white, purple – and even an average supermarket will have three or four types for you to choose from. But all these varieties fall into two basic categories: waxy and floury. Waxy potatoes, also called all-purpose potatoes, have a firm, smooth texture. They grow more quickly than floury potatoes and are harvested and eaten earlier in the year. Waxy potatoes like red gold, Yukon gold, Pink Fir and blue potatoes are fantastic for

boiling and for salads, and make the best dauphinois (see page 164). Floury potatoes, also called baking potatoes, grow more slowly and are picked later in the year when they are larger and their skins are thicker. Russet potatoes, called Idaho sometimes, are great for baking, mashing or roasting.

The first of the new potatoes – the Jersey Royals – arrive in April. They're so young they hardly have any skin, so they just need to be rubbed clean before they're cooked. They're followed by Maris Piper, King Edward and Desiree (red-skinned ones). Although you can cook these any way you like, thin-skinned new potatoes are at their best when boiled and buttered, served in salads or sliced thinly in gratins.

As well as energy-giving carbohydrates, potatoes contain all sorts of vitamins, including vitamin B6, which your immune system needs to produce antibodies that keep you from getting ill. Most of these vitamins are actually found in, or just under, their skins, so to get the most nutrition out of a potato, eat it with the skin on!

- When you have peeled your potatoes, cover them with water till you are ready to cook them or the air will turn them brown.

- Potatoes are brilliant roasted with garlic and woody herbs like rosemary, thyme and sage.

- New potatoes are lovely boiled and buttered, but they are also great roasted in their skins with plenty of salt, rosemary and olive oil.

- If potatoes turn green, throw them away as they're mildly poisonous and will give you a tummy ache.

Rosemary-roasted cubed potatoes

I love these incredibly quick roast potatoes. Cutting them into small cubes means they cook so much quicker than normal-sized roasties – sometimes I don't even bother peeling them if they have nice skin. Feel free to use different woody herbs, like thyme or sage, in place of the rosemary. For a twist, I also love to add some roughly chopped onions, halved mushrooms or big chunky fatty bacon lardons to the tray.

Preheat your oven to 425°F. Place your potato cubes in a large pan of cold, salted water and bring to the boil. Drain them immediately in a colander and allow them to steam for a couple of minutes until they dry out a bit. Bash up the rosemary leaves in a Flavor Shaker or pestle and mortar.

Heat some olive oil, or duck or goose fat, in a roasting pan. Add the garlic cloves, potatoes and rosemary oil. Season and toss together until well coated. Place in the oven for about 20 to 25 minutes, shaking the tray every so often, until the potatoes are golden and crispy.

serves 4

1lb 6oz all-purpose
  potatoes, peeled or
  scrubbed and cut into
  1 inch cubes
sea salt and freshly ground
  black pepper
a sprig of fresh rosemary,
  leaves picked
olive oil, or duck or
  goose fat
5 cloves of garlic, skin on
  and smashed

Scotch stovies

Scotch stovies is a classic potato dish from up north and, like in parts of Italy, different areas think that they have the best recipe! This is one of my favorite ways of doing it as I think it brings the best flavor out of the potatoes; and the celery leaves and watercress give a lightness which means it's good with fish dishes. If you've never tried them, you must give these a bash.

Very slowly fry the onions with the butter or lard and the olive oil, thyme and a little salt and pepper for 10 to 15 minutes until lightly golden and soft. Add your potatoes and a pint of water. Simmer with a lid on and stir occasionally until the potatoes have gone mushy. Stir and scrape any sticky bits off the bottom of the pan and mix them in. You can mash the mixture up if you like, or leave it as it is with bigger and smaller lumps. Correct the seasoning, then stir the watercress and celery leaves through the mash and serve.

serves 4

2 onions, peeled and
  finely sliced
lard or butter
olive oil
a few sprigs of fresh thyme,
  leaves picked
sea salt and freshly
  ground black pepper
2¼lb floury potatoes,
  peeled and
  cut into chunks
a bunch of watercress,
  washed and dried
a handful of celery
  leaves, chopped

Potato rösti

Potato rösti was one of the classic potato dishes of the 1980s. However, to be honest, a lot of the ones I ate when I was a teenager were rubbish – either made with grated potato, which made them gluey and wet, or with flour, which I didn't think was necessary either. So in my recipe I've decided to stay away from both of these things. The potatoes should be cut by hand or by using a mandolin to give you matchsticks, but don't get too concerned about being precise. The trick to cooking a rösti is to make the top and bottom crisp and golden while the inside stays soft, so this is what you're aiming for.

Preheat the oven to 400ºF. In an ovenproof non-stick frying pan, about 8 inches wide, heat a splash of olive oil. Add the butter and toss the potatoes in it with a pinch of salt and pepper, the rosemary leaves and the whole garlic cloves. Fry on a medium heat for about 10 minutes, stirring all the while, until the potatoes start to soften a little. Then place the pan in the oven and cook for about 25 minutes or until the potatoes are lightly golden, both on the top and the bottom.

Take the pan out of the oven and cover it with a piece of damp wax paper. Wrap your hand in a tea towel, or use a perfectly sized plate, and press down on the paper to flatten and compact your rösti. Remove the wax paper and place the pan back in the oven for 25 minutes. Cut into slices and serve.

serves 4

olive oil
a small knob of butter
1½lb floury potatoes,
   peeled and
   cut into matchsticks
   (see page 431)
sea salt and freshly ground
   black pepper
a few sprigs of fresh
   rosemary, leaves picked
6 cloves of garlic, peeled

Baked potatoes stuffed with bacon, anchovies and sage

I once saw a version of this dish being cooked in Italy where baking potatoes were being stuffed with chopped-up pieces of quail and finches, and the odd sage leaf. As bizarre as this might sound, it was delicious because all the flavor from the birds cooked into the potato, giving you a double whammy of flavor. I really love my combination of flavors in this recipe (and remember, if you don't like anchovies then don't worry because I promise that you won't taste them – you will just get an incredible richness from them). I've enjoyed eating these stuffed potatoes on their own or as a side to things like lamb chops or roasted sausages. Smaller stuffed potatoes are great when served alongside a delicious cheese platter.

Preheat your oven to 400°F. Stick one end of a pineapple or apple corer, or a conventional peeler, into your potato and twist it round and round as you cut through, as if you were coring an apple – essentially you're trying to carve out a tube from inside the potato. Keep the cores as you will use them as plugs later. Prick each potato a few times with a fork and rub them in a little olive oil and sea salt.

Lay out the stuffing for each potato: a slice of bacon topped with 2 sage leaves, an anchovy fillet and a sliver of garlic. Grate over some lemon zest. Fold and twist the stuffing together into a little sausage shape and stuff into each potato. Don't worry if you have bits sticking out at either end.

Cut the potato plugs in half and stuff them back in either end of each potato to keep the stuffing in place. They will stick out a little but this is fine. Put the potatoes on to a baking tray and bake in the preheated oven for about an hour, turning them every so often, until crisp, golden and cooked.

serves 4

4 medium-sized waxy
   potatoes, skin left on
olive oil
sea salt
4 slices of bacon
8 fresh sage leaves
4 good-quality anchovy
   fillets in oil, drained
1 clove of garlic, peeled
   and sliced lengthways
1 lemon

April's rosemary straw potatoes
with lemon salt

My friend April, who's the chef at the Spotted Pig gastropub in New York, serves these with her famous blue cheese hamburger. She calls them shoestring fries, but in classic old-English game cooking they're called straw potatoes. They're a pretty common side dish to roasted grouse or partridge, or you might have pommes gaufrettes (which are comparable to crinkly fries). By cutting the potatoes in this recipe nice and fine – around ¼ inch thick – you can cook them until golden and crisp first time round in a fryer or large pan of frying oil. For the last 30 seconds I like to put a nice big handful of rosemary in with them – this will flavor the oil and the potatoes in the most incredible way.

A quick word about deep-frying: don't disregard the importance of being incredibly careful and remember a) not to leave the pan alone as it might catch fire and b) not to leave kids in the same room on their own with the pan.

To make your lemon salt, bash and mix together the lemon zest with the salt in a pestle and mortar or Flavor Shaker until the salt is flavored, colored and fine. Place in a dish. Use whatever you need right away or allow it to dry out for a couple of hours before storing it. It might go hard, so just crush it up a bit before putting it into a jam jar.

Heat 2–3 inches of sunflower oil in a sturdy pan and bring to deep-frying temperature. You can do this by using a thermometer, or by placing a small chunk of potato into the cold oil before you begin to heat it. When the potato is floating and a dark golden brown the temperature will have reached 350°F and you're ready to begin frying (remember to remove the piece of potato before you begin).

Pat the julienne strips dry with some paper towels to remove any excess starch. Making sure you've got a slotted spoon or spider (which is like a flat colander with a handle) and a big pile of paper towels to one side, carefully place some of your potatoes into the pan of oil (don't overcrowd it) for a couple of minutes until golden brown and crisp. Cook the potatoes like this in batches until they are all used up. Add the rosemary for the last 30 seconds. Remove the chips and rosemary to the paper towels to soak up any excess oil, and then dust with your lemon salt. Serve straight away.

serves 4

for the lemon salt
zest of 1 lemon
4 tablespoons sea salt

sunflower oil
1¾lb potatoes, peeled and cut into fine matchsticks (see page 431)
a few sprigs of fresh rosemary, leaves picked

CARROTS

Did you know that carrots were originally purple, not orange?! According to Tony Booth, top veg supplier at Borough Market in London, the orange variety we see everywhere today was originally bred to match the colors of the Dutch royal family. You can still find the purple varieties around if you try, and also look out for golden, yellow and white carrots.

Carrots contain a lot of sugar and this makes them ideally suited for roasting, as the sugar turns to caramel and makes them sticky, brown and delicious! They are also often used in stews, soups and stocks to give a basic sweetness to a dish, and are even sweet enough to be used in a cake – if you haven't tried carrot cake yet, you really must (see page 387).

Baby spring carrots pop up in May or June and are either picked then or left until later in the year when they are a little bigger. Baby carrots are so tender and sweet that they don't need peeling and can be eaten raw, or boiled and buttered.

Carrots have a reputation for improving your eyesight and this is because they contain large amounts of beta carotene, which our bodies use to make vitamin A – good for the retinas of our eyes. Carrots also contain alpha carotene, which helps protect against cancer and heart disease, and vitamin C, which is good for your skin and immune system.

- Try scrubbing carrots instead of peeling them before cooking – the skins are full of vitamins and they keep you regular.

- Carrots go well with cumin, ginger, orange juice and zest, and coriander seeds and leaves.

- Carrot soup is quick, easy to make, delicious, and kids love it.

- Raw baby carrots and a pot of hummus with some chopped red chilli and a splash of lime juice stirred in makes a brilliant lunchtime or TV-time snack.

Sticky saucepan carrots

There's something about this dish that is really brave and brash – I love the way the carrots are packed into the pan all stood up like little soldiers! And I also love the fact that by the time the water or stock has reduced down, the carrots will just be cooked and then the bottoms will have started to caramelize – absolutely fantastic.

Chop the carrots across into 2¼ inch lengths, then find yourself an appropriately sized pan in which the carrots will fit snugly when they stand up side by side, as in the picture opposite. Once your carrots are snugly packed in, put your knob of butter on top of the carrots, tuck the bay leaves between them and season well with salt and pepper. Then add enough water to come halfway up the carrots and put them on the heat. Bring to the boil, then turn the heat down and cover with a lid. Simmer for about 20 minutes or until the carrots are cooked.

Take the lid off and let the liquid reduce until there isn't any left. This will take about half an hour. Let the carrots sizzle gently in the butter for about 5 minutes until the bottoms of the carrots are sticky-brown. Turn them out on to a plate and serve – and watch out for the hot butter!

serves 4

1¾lb medium-sized
   carrots, peeled
a large knob of butter
a few bay leaves
sea salt and freshly ground
   black pepper

The best whole-baked carrots

I love cooking any type of carrot in this way. By cooking them first covered by aluminum foil, they steam and exchange flavors with the herbs and garlic. Then when you remove the foil they start to roast and sweeten. A really simple method but one that gives incredibly delicious results!

Preheat your oven to 400°F. Toss your carrots with a good glug of olive oil, a splash of vinegar, salt and pepper, the thyme sprigs and the garlic cloves. Place in a roasting pan or earthenware dish, cover tightly with foil and cook for 30 to 40 minutes until just tender. Remove the foil and cook for a further 10 minutes until the carrots have browned and caramelized nicely.

serves 4

1lb 10oz young bunched
   carrots, different colors if
   possible, washed and
   scrubbed
olive oil
herb or red wine vinegar
sea salt and freshly ground
   black pepper
a few sprigs of fresh thyme
3 cloves of garlic, crushed

Dinner-lady carrots

Last year I saw some dinner ladies cooking carrots like this. They were using one of those industrial slicing machines to knock out hundreds of finely sliced carrots and then throwing them into those classic dinner-lady pans with the metal lids. The pans were buttered and then they just kept layering the carrots with little bits of butter and some salt and pepper. I've tweaked the recipe by adding herbs and a tiny bit of wine, but essentially these are 'dinner-lady carrots'! You'll be amazed at how quickly this dish cooks as the carrots are sliced so finely. Make a change by putting these in the middle of your table with a Sunday roast.

Preheat your oven to 350°F. Mix the garlic with the orange zest and parsley, then chop the mixture some more until fine. Rub your baking dish or tray generously with butter and scatter over some of the parsley and zest mix. Add a layer of carrots to your baking dish, followed by a small pinch of salt and pepper, a drizzle of extra virgin olive oil and a sprinkling of the parsley and zest mix. Continue layering like this until you run out of carrots. Squeeze over the orange juice, pour in the white wine and enough stock to cover. Lay a large sheet of damp wax paper on top and tuck in around the edges of the dish. Bake in the preheated oven for 20 to 25 minutes, or until the carrots are perfectly cooked. The cooking time will depend on how thinly you have sliced the carrots.

serves 4

a good knob of butter
3 cloves of garlic, peeled
   and chopped
zest and juice of 1 orange
a handful of fresh flat-leaf
   parsley, leaves picked
   and chopped
1lb 10oz carrots, washed,
   peeled and very finely
   sliced
sea salt and freshly ground
   black pepper
extra virgin olive oil
a small wineglass of
   white wine
¾ cups vegetable
   or chicken stock

PEAS

Peas come from southern Europe and Asia and were first cultivated by the ancient Greeks and Romans. The season for peas is the late spring and is quite short, but they dry very well and dried peas have been used in winter soups and stews for hundreds of years. However, dried peas aren't used so much any more because we all have freezers and peas freeze amazingly well too. When picked, their high sugar content quickly starts to turn into starch, so if they're frozen immediately they are actually sweeter than fresh peas that have been hanging around for a while.

You can't beat fresh peas in summer, though. When picked and eaten straight from the pod, they're really delicious (as are the tender, curly shoots on the ends of pea branches) and are great tossed raw into a salad.

Frozen peas are best when cooked, and are lovely stirred into risottos or pasta dishes, soups and omelettes. When they're mashed, they're great with fish and chips.

Peas are high in protein, which your body needs to build muscles, and they're one of the few vegetables that are sources of vitamin B1, which your body needs to break down carbohydrates and turn them into energy.

- Always have a bag of peas in your freezer – they last for ages and they always come in handy.

- Adding a handful of peas to your stews, soups and pasta sauces for the last few minutes of cooking really livens things up.

- Before you buy fresh peas, bust open a pod or two and eat a few peas to make sure they are not too big, turning pale, splitting or horrible and floury.

- If you're making pea soup or risotto, boil the pea pods with your stock to get loads of extra sweet flavor.

Braised peas with spring onions and lettuce

This is my version of a classic French dish and, apart from it being delicious, what I love about it is that you can make it in literally a few minutes from start to finish. And I can guarantee you that practically everyone who turns their nose up at having some lettuce in with their peas ends up being converted.

Slowly heat the butter and a good glug of olive oil in a pan. Add the flour and stir around, then slowly pour in the stock. Turn up the heat and add the spring onions, peas and lettuce with a pinch of salt and pepper. Put the lid on and simmer for 5 minutes or until tender. Taste, correct the seasoning and squeeze in a little lemon juice. Serve drizzled with a splash of good oil. It's fantastic served with a piece of fish.

serves 4

a knob of butter
olive oil
1 heaped teaspoon flour
1 cup chicken or vegetable
   stock
6 spring onions, trimmed,
   outer leaves discarded,
   and finely sliced
14oz fresh or frozen peas
2 little butter lettuces,
   sliced
sea salt and freshly ground
   black pepper
juice of 1 lemon
good-quality extra virgin
   olive oil

Buttered peas with crunchy bacon

This is an incredibly simple way to transform a bowl of good old peas with their best mate, bacon. They can be eaten on their own or added to pasta dishes or risottos.

Quite simply, place the peas into boiling water and cook for 3 or 4 minutes until tender. Fry the bacon slices in a tiny bit of olive oil until golden and crisp, then remove them to a dish and keep the pan with all the juices left in. Drain your peas, reserving a little cup of cooking water, and add them to the pan with the bacon fat, but don't put the pan back on the heat as you don't want to fry them. Add a knob of butter, a tiny squeeze of lemon juice and a little sea salt and freshly ground pepper to taste. Add a little splash of cooking water to delicately coat and glaze the peas. Serve them in a bowl mixed with the crispy bacon bits on top – scrummy yum yum!

serves 4

4 big handfuls of fresh or
   frozen peas
5 slices of bacon, finely
   sliced
olive oil
a knob of butter
1 lemon
sea salt and freshly ground
   black pepper

Minted peas under oil

This is a fantastic way of cooking peas. In Italy it's known as *sott'olio*, which literally means 'under oil', and generally, when served in this way, they will be cool or at room temperature, as it's a summer dish. You may think I'm being over-generous with the amount of oil, but just go with me!

Add the peas to a cold pan. Put the small bunch of mint on top of the peas, then boil the kettle. Pour just enough boiling water over the peas and mint to cover them, then put the pan on a high heat with a lid on. Bring back to the boil and cook until the peas are just perfect and tender – this should only be a couple of minutes. Immediately drain in a colander, then place the peas and mint into a salad-type bowl. Sprinkle with a little sea salt and freshly ground black pepper and a good squeeze of lemon juice or a swig of good-quality red or white wine vinegar. Cover the peas and mint with the olive oil (it's important to use the best you can get, as the better the quality, the better the dish) and mix around. Put to one side for half an hour, after which the flavors will really have started to develop.

There are so many things you can serve these peas with: from grilled fish to bruschetta or crostini, roasted or grilled lamb cutlets or pork, or served next to a hearty roast chicken. It's always exciting to see lovely green peas under golden green oil.

serves 4–6

4–6 big handfuls of fresh or frozen peas
a small bunch of fresh mint
sea salt and freshly ground black pepper
1 lemon or red or white wine vinegar
about 1 cup good-quality extra virgin olive oil

Cheesy peas

Peas and Parmesan – it couldn't be more simple, and if your kids won't eat their peas this way then they probably never will. Boil the peas until perfect, then remove from the heat and drain in a colander, saving a small cup of the cooking water. Put the peas back in the pan with some of the reserved water and add a knob of butter. Stir around, then sprinkle in the Parmesan cheese and stir again until every single pea is lightly coated in the sweet, delicately melted cheese. You may need to add a bit more water to loosen the peas – you want them to be oozy (almost like a risotto consistency). A small squeeze of lemon juice always lifts the peas and cuts through the cheese, and a sprinkle of white pepper is nice too.

This dish is best made quickly at the very last minute as, like a risotto, the moment those peas begin to cool down things start getting a little claggy and rubbery and you definitely don't want that.

serves 4

4 big handfuls of fresh or
  frozen peas
a knob of butter
a big handful of freshly
  grated Parmesan cheese
1 lemon
ground white pepper

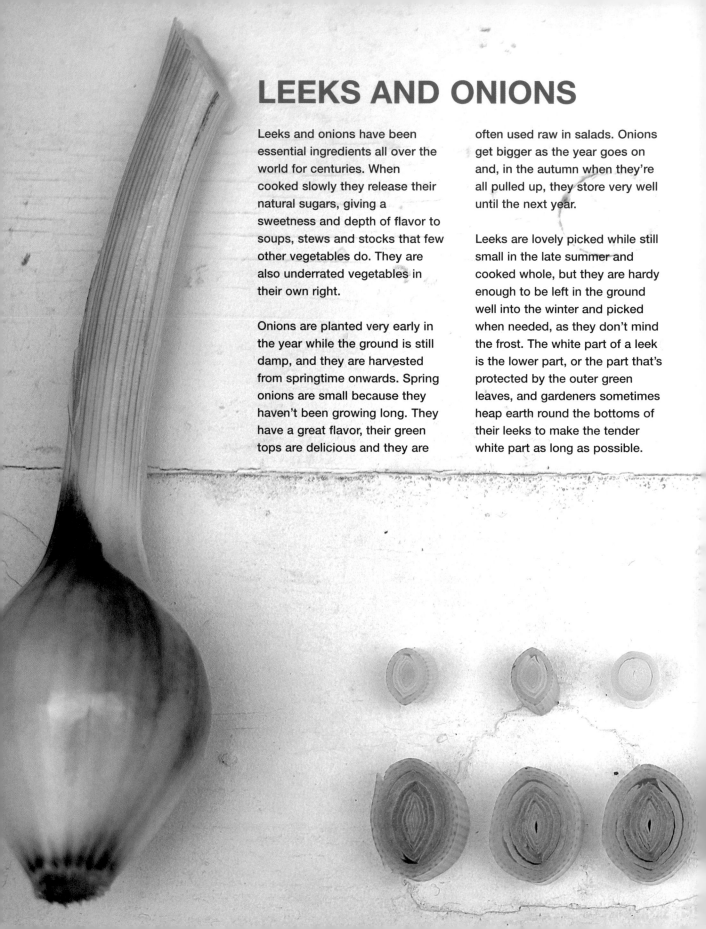

LEEKS AND ONIONS

Leeks and onions have been essential ingredients all over the world for centuries. When cooked slowly they release their natural sugars, giving a sweetness and depth of flavor to soups, stews and stocks that few other vegetables do. They are also underrated vegetables in their own right.

Onions are planted very early in the year while the ground is still damp, and they are harvested from springtime onwards. Spring onions are small because they haven't been growing long. They have a great flavor, their green tops are delicious and they are often used raw in salads. Onions get bigger as the year goes on and, in the autumn when they're all pulled up, they store very well until the next year.

Leeks are lovely picked while still small in the late summer and cooked whole, but they are hardy enough to be left in the ground well into the winter and picked when needed, as they don't mind the frost. The white part of a leek is the lower part, or the part that's protected by the outer green leaves, and gardeners sometimes heap earth round the bottoms of their leeks to make the tender white part as long as possible.

Because leeks have lots of layers of leaves, they often get mud in between them so they need to be washed well in plenty of cold water before cooking.

Onions and leeks contain allicin, a natural antibiotic that helps your body fight infections, and sulphur, which helps your liver detox – a good thing to eat after a big night out! They also thin your blood and help to lower your blood pressure.

- When buying leeks, always pick the thinner ones – they are softer and sweeter.

- Leeks go well with thyme and they are great friends with mushrooms and chicken.

- I don't like to mix leeks and onions in cooking – they are from the same family so it gets a bit too much.

- Red onions have a stronger flavor than normal ones, which are milder and sweeter.

- If chopping onions makes you cry, use a food processor or wear swimming goggles and a snorkel like I did when I was young!

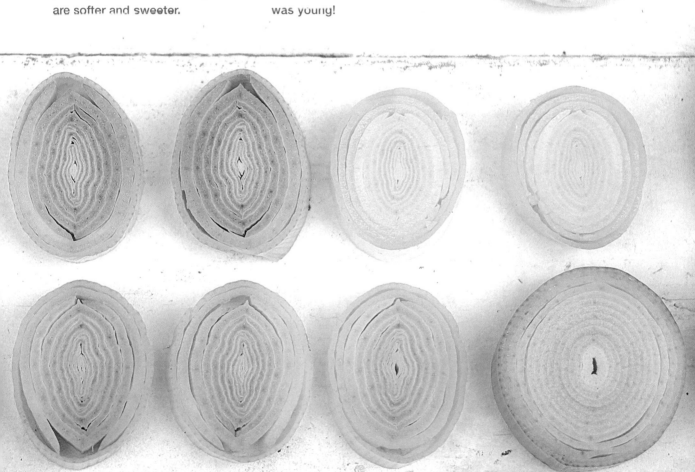

Slow-cooked leek soldiers with bacon

I love cooking leeks in this way as I find that by keeping them whole you get to taste their true flavor, and by finely slicing the outer leaves you get a really leeky intensity as a bonus! This is a great one for dinner parties or alongside your Sunday roast.

Preheat your oven to 400°F. Ideally you need a 10 inch buttered ovenproof dish about 1½ inches high. Trim the ends of the leeks and discard the outer two or three layers. Cut off the dark green top part of the leeks, leaving the remaining pale green and white sections in 2 inch pieces. Finely slice and wash the dark green pieces, and put them in a frying pan with a glug of olive oil, the garlic, thyme and butter. Cook for about 10 minutes until softened and spread them out in the bottom of your dish.

Stand the remaining pieces of leek upright next to each other in the dish. Pack them in really tightly so that the flavors from underneath, and from the bacon that you're going to put on top, will cook subtly and evenly through the leeks.

Add the wine and stock and lay the bacon over the top. Get a big strip of wax paper, wet it under the tap and scrunch it up, fit it snugly over and around the leeks and bacon, then cover with a layer of aluminum foil. Place the dish in the oven for about an hour. The leeks should be nice and tender by this point, but if not, give them a little longer – it will depend on the size and age of the leeks. Once tender and soft, remove the foil and wax paper, and put the dish back for 20 minutes or until the bacon is crisp and golden. Remove the bacon, finely chop it, taste the juice in the dish for seasoning and adjust if need be. Serve the leeks at the table sprinkled with the crispy bacon.

serves 6–8

12 leeks
olive oil
4 cloves of garlic, peeled and finely sliced
a small bunch of fresh thyme, leaves picked
a knob of butter
a wineglass of white wine
1 cup chicken or vegetable stock
8 slices of bacon

Roasted baby leeks with thyme

Baby leeks are just small leeks and there are two things that are exciting about them: a) the fact that they haven't had the time to develop many green leaves or the fibrous structure that can sometimes make them stringy, and b) they're definitely sweeter. For me, they signify late spring to summer cooking. The purpose of quickly boiling them in water and then roasting them, as I've done in this recipe, is to make them deliciously soft and then to caramelize them so they develop a robustness that makes them wonderful served over or next to fish and meat. They will also add an interesting flavor to pastas or soups. When I have friends round for dinner, I do everything in the method below in advance apart from roasting them, so all I need to do is flash them in the oven for 10 minutes.

Preheat your oven to 400°F. I like to serve 4 or 5 baby leeks per person, depending on their size. Lightly trim both ends and peel back the first or second layer of leaves and discard. Drop the leeks in a pan of boiling salted water for 2 to 3 minutes to soften – this is called blanching. Drain them well (if there's too much water in them they won't roast properly) and toss in a bowl with a good glug of olive oil, a splash of red wine vinegar, the chopped thyme leaves and the garlic. Arrange the leeks in one layer in a baking pan or earthenware dish and roast in the preheated oven for about 10 minutes until golden and almost caramelized. Keep your eye on them – I've seen many chefs burn baby leeks when cooking them this way and it drives me mad!

serves 4

20 baby leeks
olive oil
red wine vinegar
1 teaspoon chopped fresh
  thyme leaves
2 cloves of garlic, peeled
  and sliced

The best onion gratin

I always think it's a pleasure to write a recipe that celebrates onions as vegetables in their own right, and not just treat them as something that you use as the base of a stew or soup. Make this gratin and it's bound to be the talk of the meal because it's got ballsy flavor and sweetness. To rev the recipe up a bit, try using a mixture of white, red and button onions or shallots. But I'll leave that up to you.

Preheat the oven to 400°F. Break the onion quarters apart to give you little 'petals'. Place these in an ovenproof glass or earthenware oven dish. Drizzle with a couple of glugs of olive oil and a pinch of salt and pepper, and toss in your thyme and garlic. Mix up well, add your white wine, cover with a double layer of aluminum foil, wrap tightly and place in the preheated oven. Bake for 45 minutes, then remove the dish from the oven, take the foil off and pop the dish back in the oven for 15 minutes to start caramelizing. Once the onion is looking lightly golden, stir in your crème fraîche and sprinkle over your Gruyère and Parmesan. Turn the oven down to 350°F and let the gratin tick away for about 15 minutes or until golden and gorgeous. You can eat this straight away, or cool it down and flash it under the broiler later.

serves 4

4 medium red onions, peeled and quartered
olive oil
sea salt and freshly ground black pepper
8 sprigs of fresh thyme, leaves picked
2 cloves of garlic, peeled and sliced
a small wineglass of white wine
4 tablespoons crème fraîche
1¾oz Gruyère cheese, grated
1¾oz Parmesan cheese, grated

BROCCOLI AND CAULIFLOWER

Broccoli was originally a wild Mediterranean vegetable, but has been bred into several different types over the years in various countries. These days the two main types available are the large-headed 'Calabrese' and the smaller headed 'purple sprouting'. Calabrese is pretty much available all year round, but purple sprouting broccoli is a treat that is only available from the end of winter to the spring.

Broccoli is full of vitamin C, which is vital for your skin, gums and immune system, and protects against illnesses like colds and flu, and some say even cancer. It's also a good source of fiber and is one of the only veg to contain vitamin K, which is great for your blood, and for maintaining healthy bones.

There are many ways to cook broccoli, but if you want to get the most out of it nutritionally, it's best to steam or boil it for just a few minutes, keeping it green and slightly crunchy. Remember, the stalk is just as good to eat as the florets, so don't waste it – chop it up and cook it too!

Broccoli's sister, cauliflower, is an honest, humble, no-frills vegetable, but when cooked carefully and mixed with the right things, it can definitely be one of the most delicious. There are few things more comforting and warming on a cold winter's day than a cauliflower soup or a good cauliflower cheese. Nowadays cauliflower is grown all year round, as there are different varieties for each season.

Cauliflower is easy to prepare. All you have to do is trim the coarse leaves off, trim the bottom of the stalk and it's ready to chop into chunks. Cauliflower is normally steamed or boiled in salted water, but it's truly amazing when parboiled and roasted, and it can even be eaten raw as part of a nibbles plate with a few tasty dips. Don't forget to trim up the stalk and use it as well, and the smallest yellow leaves on the stalk are delicious.

- Broccoli is great friends with things like anchovy, soy sauce and Parmesan cheese.

- Don't buy broccoli that's turned yellow – look for firm, dark green heads.

- Broccoli is more delicate than you think, so keep an eye on it when it's cooking and don't overcook it.

- Cauliflower is friends with fennel seeds, cinnamon, cheese and chilli, and is very comfortable in a curry.

- If you like making cauliflower cheese, try experimenting with different types of cheese, like blue cheese, Gruyère or even taleggio.

Steamed broccoli with soy and ginger

From a cooking point of view this is an interesting recipe because you have the light flavors of the steamed broccoli but then the fragrant yet toasty and intense sesame and garlic dressing, which is a real joy to eat. This dish sits quite nicely as a side to simply cooked fish or meat or, of course, with Asian-style cooking.

Cut off the dry end of the broccoli stalk, then remove the florets really close to the stalk. By doing this you'll be left with lovely small florets of broccoli and the stalk. You don't want to throw the stalk away as it's absolutely delicious to eat, so peel it using a speed peeler then cut it in half and finely slice it up. It will now cook at the same time as your florets. Feel free to either steam or boil the florets and stalk; just cook them so they're soft enough but not overdone and mushy.

While the broccoli is cooking, toast and toss your sesame seeds in a dry pan until golden and then put them to one side. Add 3 tablespoons of olive oil to the pan, heat it up and slowly fry your garlic until golden and crisp; like mini crisps. I find that if I angle my pan so that the oil pools in one side, the garlic will fry really nicely. Make sure you don't let it burn as it will taste bitter. When done, remove the garlic chips with a slotted spoon and put them next to the sesame seeds.

Now, instead of giving yourself another bowl to wash up, make your dressing in the pan – you don't need the heat on, so turn it off and let the pan cool down a little. You only need to use about 2 tablespoons of the garlicky oil, so discard any extra, then add the soy sauce and sesame oil to the pan and swill it around. Add the juice from one of your limes, then grate your ginger with a fine grater and press it into a sieve with a wooden spoon to extract as much juice as possible and add this. At this point taste it – you should have a balance of nuttiness, saltiness and a lovely zing from the lime. If it needs more soy sauce, olive oil or lime juice for perfect harmony then feel free to adjust to your taste.

Serve the steaming broccoli in a bowl drizzled with your dressing (which you'll need to keep shaking in the pan before serving so it doesn't divide), and sprinkle with the garlic chips and sesame seeds – gorgeous.

serves 4

1 large head of broccoli
2 heaped tablespoons
    sesame seeds
olive oil
5 cloves of garlic, peeled
    and sliced
3 tablespoons soy sauce
½ teaspoon sesame oil
juice of 1–2 limes
a thumb-sized piece of
    fresh ginger, peeled

Indian-style broccoli with spiced yogurt

My latest fave Indian restaurant in London is called Amaya. We went there for a night out and had an incredibly simple and brave steamed broccoli dish that I'm pretty sure had been broiled just before it was served. It arrived at the table with a dollop of yogurt which had some fragrant yet intense spices mixed into it. I don't really know how they made it, but here's my version and I'm really pleased with it. It's a delight to eat, whether as part of an Indian meal or with simply cooked meat or fish.

Blanch the broccoli in boiling, salted water for about 4 minutes until tender, then drain in a colander. Toss in a little olive oil then place on a hot griddle pan or under a hot grill for a couple of minutes to char it slightly. Meanwhile, toast your spices in a hot pan for 2 minutes then bash them up in a pestle and mortar or Flavor Shaker. Stir most of the spices into the yogurt, together with the lemon zest and juice and a little salt and pepper. Taste and balance the flavors by adding a little more salt, pepper or lemon juice. Serve the broccoli in a bowl with the spiced yogurt spooned over the top. Sprinkle with the remaining spice mix.

serves 4

1 large head of broccoli, broken into florets
sea salt and freshly ground black pepper
olive oil
2 teaspoons cumin seeds
2 teaspoons fennel seeds
5 cardamom pods, seeds removed and pods discarded
1 generous cup natural plain yogurt
zest and juice of 1 lemon

Steamed broccoli with beurre blanc

Beurre blanc is one of the first things I was asked to make in a commercial kitchen. It's a French sauce that is surprisingly delicate, and it goes well with any green veg, like asparagus, broccoli or snow peas. There are many ways of making it, so I thought I'd show you the two that I find most convenient.

Put your wine, shallot, herbs and peppercorns into a small pot and bring to the boil, then simmer slowly for 3 or 4 minutes or until reduced by half and remove from the heat. The first way to make your beurre blanc is to pour the flavored wine through a sieve into a metal bowl. Place the bowl over a pan of water on a very low heat, whisk, and add the cubes of butter one at a time, whisking them in until all the butter has been used. The sauce will emulsify and look like a very loose custard. Use the beurre blanc immediately or keep whisking it over your pan of water. If you leave it too long, the sauce may split.

The second way, and this is my favorite, is to pour some boiling water into a thermos flask to preheat and clean it. Pour the water away and then sieve the flavored wine into the thermos, adding all of the butter. Put the lid on tightly, place a tea towel over the lid and shake the thermos around for a few minutes. Open it very carefully (in case of any hot steam escaping) and you should have a nice beurre blanc sauce. The best thing about this method is that you can keep it in the flask and it will keep warm until you're ready to serve the food.

Steam or boil your broccoli florets until they're soft but not overdone and mushy. Correct the seasoning of the beurre blanc and pour it over the steaming broccoli. For dinner parties it's quite nice to send out your plain steamed broccoli first, then if you've used a thermos, take it out and pour it over – everyone will think you're mad. Happy days!

serves 4–6

1 cup good white wine, preferably Chablis
1 shallot or ½ a red onion, peeled and finely chopped
a few fresh flat-leaf parsley leaves and a little fresh tarragon (if you've got any)
1 bay leaf
4 black peppercorns
2 heads of broccoli, broken into florets
¾ cup cold unsalted butter, diced
sea salt and freshly ground black pepper

Roasted cauliflower with cumin, coriander and almonds

When most people think of ways to cook cauliflower they will come up with either boiling or gratinating – I'm sure this is the same for you. It may seem strange, but cauliflower is absolutely fantastic when lightly roasted, especially with herbs, spices, cheeses or breadcrumbs. It develops a really incredible flavor that I'm well impressed by. Here's a recipe I made up that is Indian-ish in style. But, hey, it's not about points for authenticity – it's about whether it's delicious or not and I think it is! Please try this one.

Preheat your oven to 400ºF. Blanch the cauliflower in salted boiling water for a couple of minutes then drain in a colander, allowing it to steam dry (you don't want any water left in your cauliflower or it won't roast properly). Toss it in a good glug of olive oil and the butter. In a pestle and mortar, bash your spices and chillies with a pinch of salt, then mix them with your almonds and put in a hot, dry ovenproof pan to slowly toast them. After a couple of minutes, add the cauliflower. When it gets a nice bit of color on it, add the lemon zest and juice and mix around well. Fry for about a minute longer then pop the pan into the preheated oven for about 15 minutes to crisp up.

serves 4

1 head of cauliflower, outer
  green leaves removed,
  broken into florets
sea salt
olive oil
a knob of butter
2 teaspoons cumin seeds
2 teaspoons coriander
  seeds
1–2 dried red chillies
a handful of blanched
  almonds, smashed
zest and juice of 1 lemon

Whole baked cauliflower with tomato and olive sauce

This is a great way to cook cauliflower because it half steams and half boils in the delicious sauce. It's really nice served at the table in the pan it has cooked in, as it looks so different to any other conventional way of cooking cauliflower, but if you prefer you can serve it in a dish like I did in the picture. Even though I made this recipe up, it feels quite Mediterranean in style to me.

First of all, find yourself a pan in which your whole head of cauliflower will fit, leaving an inch around the outside of it – this is important, otherwise it won't cook in the way it's supposed to. I use my regular porridge-for-four-people pan and it works a treat! Add the onion, garlic, chopped cauliflower stalk and a glug of oil to the pan and slowly fry for 10 minutes until softened and with a little color. Add the olives, anchovies and parsley stalks and fry for another couple of minutes. Add your tomatoes, then half-fill one of the cans with water and add that to the pan, with a good swig of red wine vinegar. Stir everything together, breaking the tomatoes down with a spoon to make sure there are no big lumps, and bring to the boil.

Take your cauliflower and gently push it down into the sauce. If you've got the size of your pan right, half of the cauliflower will be in the sauce, half above it. Drizzle with olive oil, put the lid on and let it tick over on a low heat for 50 minutes. Serve sprinkled with the parsley leaves. Again, this is a pretty well-behaved dish when it comes to cooking it in advance and then reheating it just before you want to serve it. Lovely with roast lamb, and it's also a delicious main course for a vegetarian if you leave out the anchovies.

serves 4

1 red onion, peeled and sliced
5 cloves of garlic, peeled and chopped
1 large head of cauliflower, outer green leaves discarded, stalk chopped
olive oil
a handful of black olives, pitted
4 good-quality salted anchovy fillets in oil, drained and sliced
a handful of fresh flat-leaf parsley, leaves roughly chopped, stalks finely chopped
2 x 14oz cans good-quality chopped plum tomatoes
red wine vinegar

SQUASH

Squash originally came from America, but nowadays they are grown all over the world. You can find all kinds of varieties in supermarkets and farmers' markets around the country.

Squash plants start growing in the summer, spreading their long branches along the ground. By autumn, the fruits are big, dense, sweet and delicious. Squash are brilliant when cooked as a vegetable accompaniment – roasted, mashed or baked – and in risottos, soups and curries. Make sure you choose a nice firm one, as some of the softer ones are a bit stringy inside.

Squash contain lots of energy-giving carbohydrates, and fiber to keep you regular! They also contain folic acid to help your body produce red blood cells and build up your nervous system. Pregnant women need lots of folic acid, especially in the early stages of pregnancy, to help the development of their babies.

Squash seeds are rich in fatty acids and are very good for your skin and brain. They also provide you with zinc, a mineral that keeps your naughty bits in tip-top condition; so if you want to get it up, then get some down you!

- Squash is great friends with chilli, nutmeg, cheese and bacon, and its favorite herb is sage.

- The squash recipes in this book are all made with butternut squash, as it's one of the varieties that's most easily available throughout the year. If you want to experiment, try a few different varieties in the autumn, when there are lots around, and see which is your favorite.

- The skins of squash are usually delicious to eat, though in winter they can get a bit thick, so it's best to peel them then, either before or after cooking.

- When you're deseeding a squash, keep all the seeds, toss them in oil and salt and roast until crispy – great eaten as a snack or sprinkled over your squash risotto or soup.

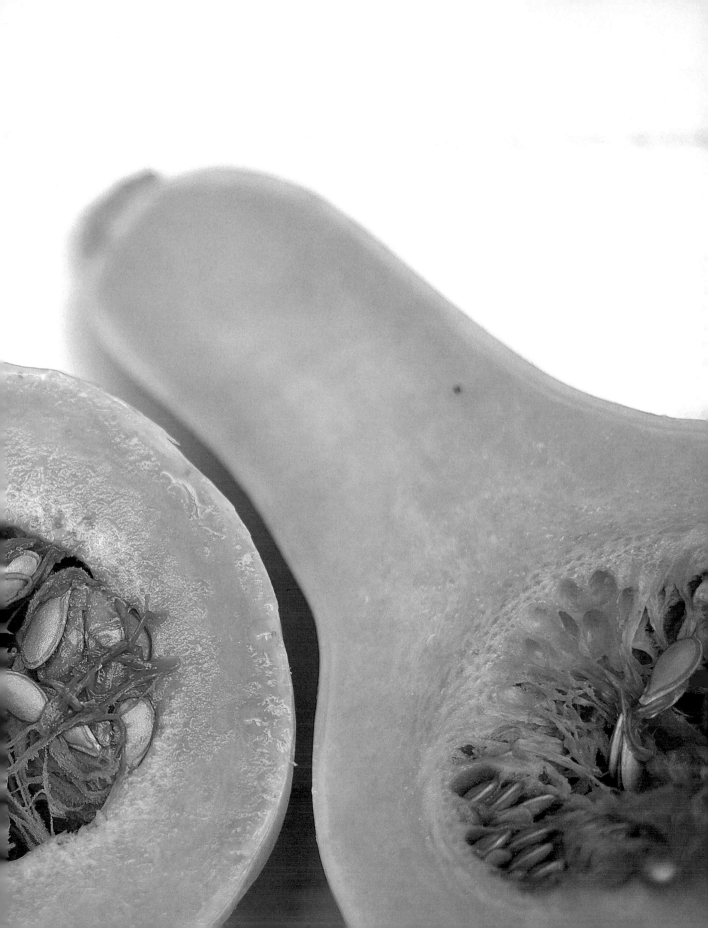

Incredible boiled butternut squash with squash seed and Parmesan pangrattato

This is a really unusual dish that can be served as a lovely lunchtime snack with bread and salad. It champions the true flavor of butternut squash and is also really good as a starter in the middle of the table with a large bowl of buffalo mozzarella and a bottle of balsamic vinegar. It can even be a vegetable side dish served alongside meat or fish.

Put your butternut squash, whole, into a large pot of boiling salted water with a lid or plate on top to keep it submerged. Simmer for 1 hour and 15 minutes, topping up with water if and when needed. While this is cooking, make your pangrattato – fry the breadcrumbs off with a glug of olive oil, a good pinch of salt and pepper, the thyme and the crumbled chilli, until lightly golden and crisp, then put to one side on some paper towels.

You can test to see if the squash is cooked by using a knife – if the inside is soft and the knife goes all the way through then it's done. Drain using a colander and then allow the squash to sit and steam for a while. When cool enough to handle, remove the two ends (the flesh should cut like soft butter), leaving the skin on as it will be soft and sweet. Cut in half lengthways and remove the seeds. Put them in the colander and rinse under the cold tap, then place them into the pan that you used for frying the breadcrumbs. Slowly fry in a little oil for a minute or so while you cut up your squash in big chunks and move it, and all the juices, to a nice big platter.

When the seeds have been frying for a couple of minutes, turn the heat right down and add the pangrattato to the pan. Tossing the pan, slowly sprinkle the Parmesan over the breadcrumbs and pumpkin seeds and mix in gently. Keeping your eye on the pan to make sure it doesn't burn, from a height drizzle the hot squash with good extra virgin olive oil and thick balsamic vinegar, and add a large pinch of salt and pepper. If you have some, a little chopped parsley or basil would also be good. When the breadcrumbs are golden, crunchy and perfect, transfer them to a little bowl and serve next to your squash platter for everyone to sprinkle over – absolutely delicious.

serves 4–6

1 large butternut squash
a big handful of breadcrumbs
olive oil
sea salt and freshly ground black pepper
a small bunch of fresh thyme, leaves picked
1–2 dried red chillies, crumbled
a handful of freshly grated Parmesan cheese
good-quality extra virgin olive oil
good-quality balsamic vinegar

Creamy butternut squash

This is a great combo and a real crowd-pleaser – what more can I say?

Preheat the oven to 400°F. Carefully cut the butternut squash in half lengthways, remove the seeds with a spoon, then cut into 1 inch slices and toss in a bowl with the smashed coriander seeds and chilli, the thyme leaves, salt and pepper, and a good glug of olive oil to coat everything. Mix around then place the squash slices in a roasting pan or earthenware dish, standing up on their sides. You don't want to have too many gaps in between the slices; ideally you want the squash to be squashed in – excuse the pun!

Cut some wax paper to the size of the pan or dish, dampen it under the tap and scrunch it up, then drape it over the squash, tucking it in at the sides. Place the pan in the preheated oven for about 30 minutes or until the squash starts to soften. Then remove the wax paper and pop the pan back in the oven while you grate the nutmeg into the cream and mix it with the wine, half the Parmesan and a good pinch of salt and pepper.

Take the butternut squash out of the oven, pour over the creamy sauce and sprinkle with the rest of the Parmesan. Place the squash back in the oven for another 10 minutes until golden, bubbling and delicious.

serves 4

1 medium butternut
   squash, peeled
1 heaped teaspoon
   coriander seeds, smashed
1–2 dried red chillies,
   crumbled
6 sprigs of fresh thyme,
   leaves picked
sea salt and freshly ground
   black pepper
olive oil
1 cup plus 2 tablespoons
   light cream
½ a nutmeg
a wineglass of Chardonnay
2 handfuls of freshly grated
   Parmesan cheese

Superb sweet and sour squash

The squash and raisins are the sweet bit and the vinegar the sour bit. This incredible vegetable dish can double up as a topping for crostini, as a starter with mozzarella, with salads, beside simply roasted or grilled fish or white meat ... As you can see, it's a really good all-rounder and can be served either hot, or cold the next day.

Cut the squash into finger-sized pieces. Add a good glug of olive oil to a nice big casserole-type pan and heat it up, then add the coriander seeds, chilli, squash, onion and a wineglass of water and put the lid on the pan. Cook for around 10 minutes, then remove the lid. The water will cook away and everything in the pan will soften.

You can now begin to fry again. Add a good pinch of salt and pepper, the garlic and thyme. Fry on a medium to low heat, slowly but surely cooking the veg through until it begins to turn a light golden color. At this point add the raisins, parsley stalks and pinenuts. Fry for another minute or so then add the two types of vinegar and the sugar. Fry for a final 3 or 4 minutes – this is enough time to cook the harshness of the vinegar away and the sugar will give it a sweet glaze. Check the seasoning one more time and adjust if need be. Stir through the parsley leaves and serve immediately.

serves 4

1 medium butternut squash, peeled, halved and deseeded
olive oil
1 tablespoon coriander seeds, smashed
1 dried red chilli
2 red onions, peeled and finely sliced
sea salt and freshly ground black pepper
4 cloves of garlic, peeled and roughly chopped
6 sprigs of fresh thyme, leaves picked
a handful of raisins
a small bunch of fresh flat-leaf parsley, leaves picked and chopped, stalks finely chopped
a handful of pinenuts
1 tablespoon white wine vinegar
2 tablespoons balsamic vinegar
1 tablespoon sugar

CABBAGE

Cabbage is another veg that has been cultivated and eaten all round the world since Adam and Eve got their veggie patch going. They come in all sorts of shapes, sizes and colors, and there are varieties that grow in every season.

The lowly cabbage isn't the coolest of vegetables. It has a bit of a bad rep because most people tend to have nasty memories of old boiled cabbage at school and therefore think they don't like it. If this is you, prepare to change your mind, because cabbage can be absolutely delicious when prepared and cooked properly.

How about these ideas for starters: tender spinachy spring greens are excellent when steamed and buttered; hard white cabbage is brilliant shaved raw to make coleslaw; Chinese cabbage is great in stir-fries; the good old crinkly Savoy is wonderful when braised with garlic and fennel seeds; Brussels sprouts go so well with bacon and chestnuts; Italian cavolo nero is the only thing to eat with new-season extra virgin olive oil; and dark purple cabbage braised with apples and balsamic vinegar is a very special thing (see page 358). Try a few recipes from this section – there's bound to be one that does it for you. And remember, any cold leftover cabbage can be turned into an awesome bubble and squeak!

Like its cousins broccoli and cauliflower, cabbage is very good for you as it contains vitamin C, vitamin K, folic acid and various other nutrients, including sulphur, which is good for your liver, hair and skin. To get the most out of cabbage, both for flavor and nutrients, remember not to cook it for too long.

- If your cabbage looks a bit scruffy and weather-beaten, remove the first few outer layers – the leaves underneath will be crisp and beautiful.

- If you are putting cabbage in a salad, make sure you slice it as thin as possible or it can be hard work to eat.

- Don't boil your cabbage for too long or you will lose all the flavor and goodness in the water. However, if you are braising cabbage in a pot you can't really overcook it, it just gets softer and tastier the longer you braise it and the goodness can't go anywhere.

- Cabbage is great friends with bacon, dried fruit, vinegar, rosemary, butter and soy sauce.

Savoy cabbage with Worcestershire sauce

This is one of the simplest yet most delicious Savoy cabbage recipes I've ever come across. I prefer using Savoy rather than any other type of cabbage because it has structure to it, but do feel free to mix it up with other cabbages, or try using Chinese cabbage instead. It's an absolutely fantastic vegetable dish to have alongside steak, shepherd's pie or other pies. I think of it as classic pub food – proper cabbage with attitude!

serves 4–6

1 large Savoy cabbage
olive oil
½ cup Worcestershire
  sauce
sea salt and freshly ground
  black pepper
2 knobs of butter

Remove and wash the outer green leaves of the cabbage, then roll them up like a cigar and finely slice them – this is called 'chiffonade' (see page 430). Put a large frying pan on a high heat and add a good glug of olive oil. Add the sliced cabbage to the pan and move it around, giving it a shake. Cook for about 4 minutes. Halve the rest of the cabbage, remove and discard the core and finely slice it. Add to the pan, keep stir-frying for another minute, then add the Worcestershire sauce and some salt and pepper. Keep moving the cabbage around so it all gets nicely coated and cook for another 4 minutes until it has softened. Keep an eye on it, moving and tossing it around so it doesn't catch on the bottom of the pan. Remove the pan from the heat and add the butter – this will give it a nice sweetness.

Must-try red cabbage braised with apple, bacon and balsamic vinegar

This recipe is based on a classic red cabbage and apple dish I used to make when I was younger, but I've given it a twist by adding the balsamic vinegar, which my mate Pete added to his version a few weekends ago. It's so bloody good you could eat the whole thing on its own without anything else, but it's also great with roast pork.

Pour a good glug of olive oil into a saucepan, get it hot and add the bacon and fennel seeds. Cook until golden then add the onion and continue to cook, with the lid on, for a few more minutes until golden and sticky. Add the apple, followed by the cabbage chunks, salt and pepper and the vinegar, and stir everything together well. Put the lid back on and continue to cook on a low heat for an hour, checking and stirring every so often. You will end up with a gorgeously sticky-sweet cabbage dish that you'll want to eat immediately, straight out of the pan! Or, if you can wait long enough, scoop it into a serving dish, pop the butter on top and sprinkle over the parsley.

serves 4

olive oil
½lb bacon, finely sliced
1 tablespoon fennel seeds, bashed
1 onion, peeled and sliced
2 good eating apples, peeled and chopped into 1 inch pieces
1 red cabbage, outer leaves and core removed, chopped into irregular chunks
sea salt and freshly ground black pepper
¾ cup balsamic vinegar
a knob of butter
a handful of chopped fresh flat-leaf parsley leaves

Braised white cabbage with bacon and thyme

I love cooking my white cabbage like this – not only does it cook extremely quickly (which is good, considering most people think it has to cook for hours) but it's delicious. The key is to slice the cabbage nice and fine. This is the kind of thing I'll have next to chicken or ham.

An extremely simple method: place your stock, bacon and thyme in a pan on the stove, bring to the boil and then sprinkle in your finely sliced cabbage. Mix up, put the lid on and boil furiously for 5 minutes. Turn the heat down to a simmer and continue to cook until the cabbage is a pleasure to eat. Top up the stock a little bit if you feel it's reducing too much. Add the butter, a good glug of extra virgin olive oil, season to taste and serve immediately.

serves 4–6

1 pint chicken or vegetable stock
6 slices bacon
½ a handful of fresh thyme leaves
1 white cabbage, outer leaves discarded, halved and very finely sliced
2 knobs of butter
extra virgin olive oil
sea salt and freshly ground black pepper

ZUCCHINI

Zucchini are small and sweet and gardeners are fond of growing them. They are versatile in cooking, too.

Zucchini plants flower in the summer and the Italians love to pick the male flowers, dip them in batter and deep-fry them as a starter. The female flowers develop into zucchini and, while they're still small, they're fantastic used raw in salads. As the summer progresses and they grow bigger, zucchini can be cooked in lots of different ways: boiled, stewed, fried, roasted, even sliced into slabs and grilled. They go well with just about anything and love to be cooked or dressed in olive oil.

Zucchini aren't as full to bursting with vitamins and nutrients as some other vegetables, but they do contain vitamin C and fiber, which we all need in our diets. One of the best things about zucchini, though, is that they are soft in texture and mild in flavor, meaning they are an excellent vegetable to feed to children who are not sure about trying new things.

- Zucchini flowers are great torn up in salads or stirred into pasta sauces, risottos, light stews or soups for the last 30 seconds of cooking.

- If you cook male flowers, make sure you pull the stem with the pollen on out of the flower first.

- If you are using zucchini raw in a salad, use the smallest and firmest ones you can find – they're sweeter and crunchier than the bigger ones, which can be floury and bitter if not cooked.

- Thinly sliced fried zucchini are great instead of bacon in a veggie spaghetti carbonara.

- Zucchini are best friends with mint, garlic and chilli.

Simple sautéed zucchini with chilli and lemon

This recipe was inspired by the trip the Fifteen Amsterdam students made to Italy. The trick is to slice the zucchini consistently just under ¼ inch thick. A mandolin slicer would be good for this – I've bought myself one and use it all the time to make this recipe at home. You can slice other veg like asparagus and leeks and cook them in the same way. Absolutely delicious and very quick.

Slice your zucchini with a mandolin slicer or sharp knife so they're just under ¼ inch thick. Heat a large frying pan over a high heat and pour in a good splash of olive oil.

Drop the zucchini slices into the pan and fry for 2 minutes with the chilli and garlic until the zucchini begin to brown. Season well with salt and pepper and add the lemon juice and butter and cook for another 2 minutes. When the lemon juice has evaporated, take the pan off the heat, divide the zucchini over the plates and serve.

serves 4

4 small zucchini
olive oil
1 dried red chilli, crumbled
2 cloves of garlic, peeled
  and sliced
sea salt and freshly ground
  black pepper
juice of ½ a lemon
a knob of butter

Baked and dressed zucchini

This is an ultra-simple zucchini recipe, best made with the small zucchini that are readily available in summer. I like to get both the green and yellow ones for a bit of excitement, and perhaps patty pan squash for a bit of variety – they're small and round and look like spaceships, so kids seem to like them too!

Preheat your oven to 400°F. Give the zucchini a good wash and pat them dry with paper towels. In a ceramic baking dish, toss the zucchini in a glug of olive oil and a generous amount of sea salt and freshly ground black pepper. Bake the zucchini in your preheated oven for 15 minutes until soft and the skin has blistered. Once out of the oven, dress the zucchini with a couple of splashes of red wine vinegar and the chopped parsley and mint. Loosen and balance the dressing with a splash of the extra virgin olive oil and a sprinkle of salt and pepper.

serves 4

8 small zucchini
olive oil
sea salt and freshly ground
  black pepper
red wine vinegar
a small handful each of
  chopped fresh parsley
  and mint leaves
peppery extra virgin
  olive oil

Zucchini fritters

This is a little recipe I made up recently. I wasn't sure if it would work but it did and I was really pleased with the results. If you cook them correctly, you'll be rewarded with a lovely mixture of golden, crunchy zucchini on the outside and soft, fresh zucchini in the middle. I love to eat them on their own as nibbles, or as part of an antipasti selection with some feta cheese and a plate of nice ripe tomatoes, or next to some grilled pork, chicken or fish. Delicious summertime cooking!

Remove the ends from the zucchini and cut them lengthways into quarters. Remove and discard the fluffy white center from each one with your knife. Then, in no particular way, slice the zucchini up into matchsticks – don't worry about being precise and perfect, just do the best you can.

Separate the egg and put the white into one bowl and the yolk into another. Add the zucchini matchsticks, white pepper, flour, chilli, mint, lemon zest and Parmesan to the yolk and mix up with your hands. You can be rough and scrunch the mixture together quite hard. Whip the egg white up with a pinch of salt until stiff (if you have someone else in the kitchen with you looking for something to do, ask them to do this job!), then carefully fold it into the zucchini mixture.

When it comes to shaping the fritters, feel free to make one large one (½ inch thick) or get two non-stick pans on the heat to do a batch of smaller ones. Put a good couple of glugs of olive oil into each pan and put 5 or 6 little bundles of the mixture into each pan (they'll resemble mini onion bhajis). Sprinkle over some cumin and cook the fritters on a medium heat. They should need about 2½ minutes on each side to go golden.

While they're frying is a good time to get your guests around the table with the white wine flowing! As soon as the fritters are golden on both sides, take them to the table on a platter with the lemon quarters – they won't hang around for long, that's for sure!

serves 4

4 large zucchini
1 large free-range or
  organic egg
1 teaspoon white pepper
1 heaped tablespoon
  flour, sifted
1 fresh red chilli, deseeded
  and finely chopped
a bunch of fresh mint,
  leaves picked and
  chopped
1 lemon, zested and
  quartered
a good handful of freshly
  grated Parmesan cheese
sea salt
olive oil
½ teaspoon cumin

desserts

DELICIOUS DESSERTS

Making desserts, pastries and cakes is a very important part of a chef's training. Often chefs are started off on the pastry section because it requires a lot of attention to detail, accuracy and self-control. Once they've learned this, they can then train in other parts of the kitchen. Now, don't be put off by this. Desserts are not necessarily difficult to make, but there are a few things to bear in mind if you want to make them well.

For instance, if you're making a salad you can more or less make up your own mind what you want to put in it: lettuce, croutons if you feel like it, lemon in the dressing instead of vinegar, or maybe some creamy goat's cheese. Or, if you're following a recipe and don't have one of the ingredients, you can very often substitute something else and it'll still turn out pretty nice if you use your common sense. However, desserts rarely work like this. I was never brilliant at math at school but desserts are kind of like an equation – if you combine the right things in the right proportions then you will get the same answer every time. So, when you're following a recipe for a cake, pastry or cookies, you have to follow it strictly – otherwise what you end up taking out of the oven will probably not be quite what you wanted to make!

I want to start at the beginning with this chapter by taking you back to basics. Let's consider all those things you think you know already – cakes, meringues, custards – and let's start really getting to know them and understand the techniques involved. I could try getting you to brandish your palette knife, shaping posh chocolate boxes with pretty dribbles or coulis and brandy biscuits – don't get me wrong, it's nice to have things like that sometimes when you go out to eat. Personally, though, I think the important thing is to have pride in your ingredients and simple, solid techniques, and then your desserts can be as fancy or as simple as you like. I think it's humble, true and brave to make something like a beautiful Bakewell tart and big it up with homemade jam and a blob of crème fraîche. It's when you don't really understand what you are doing, and then you try to get clever (and that goes for all cooking, really), that you end up doing the kind of things you see in far too many 'try-hard' restaurants.

Once you've learned the fundamentals of desserts you understand what can and can't be changed, so you can start to stretch and change recipes in different ways. A bit of inspiration on top of sound technique and common sense is when you become a real cook.

Don't be scared, guys, just follow the recipes and you'll be making some beautiful desserts to be really proud of!

Top tips for making desserts

- Remember to follow all recipes exactly, using the correct ingredients and quantities. If you substitute ingredients with others, the recipes might not work.

- Accurate scales are a very important piece of equipment. Buy see-saw weights that you balance, or a spring balance with a clock face, or an electronic set. Always make sure the scales are set at zero before you start!

- Having the correct oven temperature is crucial when baking. Ovens are different, that's a fact of life – some are old and not terribly accurate, and some of the new fan-assisted ones can be very hot – so I'd buy a small oven thermometer and put it in your oven to check that it's doing what it's supposed to do.

- Every time you open your oven door to check whatever you're baking, the heat rushes out, cooling the oven down. This can destroy many cakes and desserts. Please resist the temptation to open the oven door unless you really need to!

- Make sure your hands, equipment and work surfaces are clean. Clear your work surfaces of unnecessary clutter before you start – you can always put things back when you've finished.

SPONGES AND CAKES

Sponges and cakes are mostly made from a basic mixture of fat, sugar, eggs and flour, which sometimes has a rising agent added. This creates bubbles in the cake as it cooks, making it spongy and light. Baking powder is the most commonly used rising agent, and is what's added to plain flour to turn it into self-rising flour. The proportions and quality of these ingredients in a recipe, and the way they're combined, is what determines the kind of cake you'll end up with. Pretty much all cakes are made using one or more of the following methods: whisking, creaming and melting. In this chapter I'm going to give you some fantastic examples of cakes that can be made using these methods, and below you'll find an explanation of each one so you really get an idea of what it is you're actually trying to do.

Whisking gives you a very light, delicate sponge which contains a low amount of fat, and can actually be made with no fat at all. A whisked sponge is quite airy and dry, and is the cake mixture to use if you're making a cake with lots of layers and a rich filling. Cakes made by the whisking method include Genoise sponge, Swiss rolls (see page 381 for a great recipe) and lady fingers.

Eggs and sugar are whisked together until they treble in size and turn into a foam. If butter is added to the recipe, it's melted first and then mixed carefully into the foam at this stage, then plain flour is folded in very lightly and carefully (or all the bubbles of air will burst and you'll end up with a pancake!).

Creaming is used for the good old Victoria sponge (see page 376), carrot cake (see page 387), steamed puddings and Christmas cake.

The butter is beaten with the sugar until it's very light and fluffy and all the sugar granules have dissolved. Then eggs are added one at a time, each one being beaten into the creamed butter and sugar really well before the next is added. Self-rising flour is then folded in with any fruit, nuts or other ingredients, making a dense, smooth, sticky batter which will rise in the oven. You can be slightly less delicate, but don't beat the flour too much as it might start to develop gluten, which will make the texture of the cake tough.

Melting is the easiest of all the methods and makes for dense, rich cakes and biscuits with the highest amount of fat and sugar. The melting method is used for chocolate brownies (see page 384) and gingerbread (see page 414). With these, the fat and sugar are basically just melted together and the rest of the ingredients – flour, eggs, perhaps nuts or chocolate – are stirred in afterwards.

Because these cakes don't need to rise that much, raw, brown sugar and even molasses and golden syrup can be used, giving you loads of scope for different flavors and textures. Rising agents are sometimes added, either in the form of baking powder or self-rising flour, depending on the desired texture of the end product. For example, cookies are softer with baking powder and crisper without it.

Top tips for making cakes

- Sieve your flour, sugar and other dry ingredients before you start, making sure there are no lumps anywhere.

- Ingredients seem to combine better if they're the same temperature, so get your eggs and butter out of the fridge well before you start using them. It's much easier to cream butter and sugar if the butter's soft to begin with!

- When you add eggs or egg yolks to creamed butter and sugar, don't be tempted to add them all at once. Butter needs a bit of gentle persuasion to blend with egg, or it will curdle.

- If adding fruit or nuts to a melted cake or a rich fruit cake, tossing them in a little flour before you stir them into the batter will help them hold their position in the cake without sinking to the bottom.

- If you're making a whisked sponge, remember that the bubbles are very delicate until the cake's cooked. Don't tap your spoon on the edge of the pan, thump the mixing bowl on the table or slam the oven door, or your bubbles will suffer and so will the lightness of your cake!

- It's important to prepare your cake pan carefully before you put the batter into it. For whisked and creamed cakes, grease the inside of the pan with butter, add a tablespoon or two of flour, shake it so a thin layer of flour sticks to the butter and then tip out the excess. You should end up with an even floury coating all over the inside of the pan which will stop your cake sticking to the sides, letting it rise properly.

- Melted cakes and large fruit cakes that are going to be in the oven longer need a little more protection from the heat of the oven and are best baked in pans that are lined with one or two layers of wax paper. Make sure you line both the sides and the base of your pan.

- Bake your cakes on a shelf in the middle of the oven unless otherwise instructed.

- If you're baking your cake in a low, flat pan or on a baking sheet, make sure you use one that won't buckle too much in the heat of the oven. Cheap pans buckle badly and you might end up with a cake that's deep in some places and shallow in others!

- Cooling racks might seem like a fussy extra you don't really need but they're great, as they allow steam to evaporate from the surface of the cake, cooling it down quickly.

Classic Victoria sponge with all the trimmings

This sponge was named after Victoria Beckham – oh no, sorry, I mean Queen Victoria! Whether you want to make a big one (as in the picture), or little cupcakes (see page 378), this is a classic cake recipe that is perfect for birthdays, special occasions or simply for afternoon tea. I've used strawberry jam and fresh strawberries because I love the taste, but feel free to use raspberries or blackberries instead, or a mixture of all three.

Preheat the oven to 350°F. Grease the bottom and sides of two 8 inch sandwich cake pans with butter, line the base of each pan with wax paper, then dust the sides lightly with flour. To make your sponge batter, beat the butter and sugar together, either using an electric mixer or by hand with a wooden spoon, until very light and fluffy. Add the eggs one at a time, beating each one in well before you add the next, then fold in the flour and lemon zest.

Divide the cake batter into the prepared pans, spread it out using a spatula and bake in the preheated oven for around 20 minutes until lightly golden brown and risen. You can check to see if the cake is cooked by sticking a toothpick right into the middle of the cake. Remove it after 5 seconds and if it comes out clean the cake's cooked; if slightly sticky it needs a bit longer, so put it back into the oven. Allow the cakes to cool slightly, then carefully turn them out on to a rack to cool completely.

Meanwhile, gently warm the jam in a pan, then remove from the heat and stir in your strawberries. Whip the cream with the sugar, lemon juice and vanilla seeds until you have nice soft peaks. Pick the least attractive sponge layer to go on the bottom and put it in the middle of your serving platter or cake plate. If it's a little rounded on top, simply trim and flatten it off by using a sharp knife and rotating the plate and sponge as you cut. Smear over the jam and strawberries, then spread the sweetened cream over the top. Place your second cake, with the pretty side facing up, on top and dust it with powdered sugar.

serves 6–8

for the sponge
1 cup unsalted butter, softened, plus extra for greasing
2 cups self-rising flour, sifted, plus extra for dusting
¾ cup & 2 tablespoons superfine sugar
4 large free-range or organic eggs
zest of 1 lemon

5½oz good-quality strawberry jam
9oz fresh strawberries, hulled and sliced
1 cup heavy cream
2 heaped tablespoons superfine sugar
juice of 1 lemon
1 vanilla bean, scored lengthways and seeds removed
powdered sugar, for dusting

Tea-party cupcakes

These are great cupcakes to serve at tea parties. They are made using the sponge recipe for the Victoria sponge, but then you can take the basic cakes in so many different ways by making a variety of icings and toppings – far too many to mention here! So I'm going to give you my two favorites. See what you think and then have a go at making up some of your own toppings. As you can see in the photo, the cakes are pretty and a little bit camp, but that's what cupcakes are all about!

PS The fresh fruit icing won't keep for long, so eat these cakes up quickly. You'll need two 12-cup muffin tins or, without wanting to sound too hard-sell, I came up with my own version with Tefal – they're flexible and the cakes simply pop out of them (no need for greasing or paper liners). My mum loves using them.

Preheat the oven to 375°F. Make your sponge recipe, then place 18 paper liners into your muffin tins. Evenly spoon the mixture into your paper liners. Put the muffin tins into the oven and bake for 15 minutes. You can check to see if the cakes are cooked by sticking a toothpick right into one of them. Remove it after 5 seconds and if it comes out clean they're cooked; if slightly sticky they'll need a bit longer, so put them back in the oven for another 5 minutes, or until cooked through and golden on top. If you cook them for too long, though, they will just go dry so keep an eye on them. Remove the cakes from the tins and let them cool on a rack.

Now's the time to make your icing. The ingredients given for each icing make enough to cover all the cupcakes, so you only need to make one – or do what I did for the picture and make half quantities of each.

To make the fresh fruit icing, mash up your chosen berries with a fork or whiz them in a food processor. If the fruit has seeds you may want to pass it through a sieve. Mix in the sifted powdered sugar until you have a smooth paste.

To make the chocolate icing, mix together the powdered sugar, cocoa powder and ¼ cup water until you have a smooth paste.

When the cakes have cooled, drizzle a teaspoon of your chosen icing over each one and top with the extra fruit or crystallized fruit petals.

makes 18 cakes

1 x sponge recipe
(see page 376)

for the fresh fruit icing
1¾oz fresh berries
(raspberries, strawberries
or blackberries), plus
extra fruit or crystallized
flower petals for
decoration
1½ cups powdered sugar,
sifted

for the chocolate icing
1½ cups powdered sugar,
sifted
4 tablespoons cocoa
powder, sifted

1980s-style Black Forest Swiss roll

This is a recipe for a Swiss roll that I decided to take down the Black Forest route, bringing back lots of memories of working in my dad's pub. I know it's a bit retro, but sponge, cherries and booze are a match made in heaven, and as long as you don't go crazy with the cream, this recipe is really delicate.

Preheat the oven to 350°F and line a jelly roll pan (about 10x14½ inches) with wax paper.

To make your sponge, whisk the eggs and sugar for 2 or 3 minutes until tripled in size (an electric mixer is brilliant for this job). Stop the mixer and lift the beaters up so any eggy foam sticking to them will drip back down into the bowl. Count to ten and if you can still clearly see the ribbon of foam that has dripped off the beaters, then the mixture has passed the 'ribbon test' and you can stop beating it. Otherwise, continue beating for another 30 seconds and try again.

Very slowly whisk your melted butter into the foam. Fold in the sifted flour and cocoa powder bit by bit – do this as lightly and gently as you can. Scoop the mixture on to the prepared baking pan, carefully smoothing it out into the corners. Gently place the pan into the preheated oven. Bake for about 15 minutes, then check the sponge by pressing down lightly on the surface with your finger. If the cake springs back, you're in business. Remove it from the oven and, leaving it on the wax paper, put on a rack to cool slightly.

To make your filling, heat the orange zest, juice and sugar in a saucepan until the sugar has dissolved. Add all the cherries and cook for about 5 minutes until they have softened. Turn off the heat and add 2 good splashes of kirsch or brandy. Allow to cool, then strain through a sieve, reserving the syrup.

Heat a quarter of the cream in the empty cherry saucepan. As soon as it starts to bubble, take it off the heat and mix in the chocolate. Stir gently so the chocolate melts, then put to one side. Whip the rest of the cream until it forms stiff peaks.

Keeping it on the wax paper, lay the cooled cake on a clean work surface and brush it with the cherry syrup. Spread the cake evenly with a layer of chocolate cream, making sure you leave a 2 inch gap all around the edges. Follow with a layer of the fresh cream, then sprinkle the cherries over the top. Now take hold of one end of the wax paper and roll the cake over, peeling back the wax paper as you go. When you have a tight roll, wrap it in the wax paper and place it in the fridge for an hour to chill and set.

To serve, carefully unwrap the Swiss roll, trim the ends and then dust it with powdered sugar. Sprinkle with chocolate shavings, cut into big chunks and tuck in!

serves 8

for the sponge
4 large free-range or
   organic eggs
½ cup plus 2 tablespoons
   superfine sugar, sieved
4½ tablespoons unsalted
   butter, melted
10 tablespoons flour, sifted
½ cup cocoa powder,
   sifted

for the filling
zest and juice of 2 oranges
3 tablespoons superfine
   sugar
1lb 2oz fresh cherries,
   pitted, or 1 x 14oz can
   pitted black cherries in
   syrup
3½oz dried sour cherries
kirsch or brandy
1½ cups heavy cream
3½oz good quality dark
   chocolate (minimum 70%
   cocoa solids), or other
   cherry chocolate broken
   into small pieces

powdered sugar, for
   dusting
extra chocolate, for
   shaving

My nan's lemon drizzle cake

This is a great old-fashioned tea cake – and perfectly presentable as a dessert with a big serving of ice cream. The trick is to make the lemon icing as fresh and zingy as possible, so try and buy nice thick-skinned organic leafy lemons instead of the waxed and sprayed everyday ones. I used to make this cake for my nan and she would serve it to her card game friends – one of them liked it so much they choked on their false teeth and my nan's boyfriend had to perform the Heimlich maneuver!

Preheat the oven to 350°F. Grease and line the bottom and sides of an 8 inch springform cake pan with wax paper.

Using an electric mixer, beat the butter with the sugar until light and creamy. Add the eggs one by one, beating each in well. Fold in your ground almonds, poppy seeds, the lemon zest and juice and the sifted flour. Spoon the mix into the prepared cake pan and bake in the preheated oven for 40 minutes or until lightly golden. You can check to see if the cake is cooked by poking a toothpick right into the sponge. Remove it after 5 seconds and if it comes out clean the cake is cooked; if slightly sticky it needs a little longer, so put it back in the oven. Allow the cake to cool on a rack.

Make your lemon syrup by heating the sugar and lemon juice in a pan until the sugar has dissolved. While your cake is still warm, make lots of little holes in the top with a toothpick and pour your syrup over.

To make your icing, sift the powdered sugar into a bowl and add the lemon zest and juice, stirring until smooth. When your cake is almost cool, put it on a serving plate and pour the icing carefully over the top. If you pour it on to the middle of the cake, then let gravity disperse the icing down the sides, you get the 'drizzle' effect! Give it a helping hand with a spoon if you want.

serves 8–10

½ cup unsalted butter, softened
⅓ cup plus 1 tablespoon sugar
4 large free-range or organic eggs
1½ cups ground almonds
1½ tablespoons poppy seeds
zest and juice of 2 lemons
1 scant cup self-rising flour, sifted

for the lemon syrup
¼ cup superfine sugar
7 tablespoons lemon juice

for the lemon icing
1¼ cup powdered sugar
zest and juice of 1 lemon

Fifteen chocolate brownies

These are the classic Fifteen chocolate brownies that have been on the Trattoria menu in London since day one as everyone loves them! It's a great recipe, but the real trick is to make sure you don't overcook them – otherwise they will go hard all the way through. As all ovens are different, you'll need to keep your eye on them – and remember that chocolate always firms up at room temperature, so if you take them out of the oven when they're a little bit gooey, they'll be perfect. They work really well on their own, but adding a handful of nuts is great too, like crushed macadamias, pecans, even walnuts or Brazils. And I really love to put dried sour cherries in mine (they go so well with chocolate). Make an effort to get some really good-quality chocolate as it will make all the difference.

Preheat your oven to 350°F. Line a 12 inch rectangular baking pan with wax paper. In a large bowl over some simmering water, melt the butter and the chocolate and mix until smooth. Add the cherries and nuts, if you're using them, and stir together. In a separate bowl, mix together the cocoa powder, flour, baking powder and sugar, then add this to the chocolate, cherry and nut mixture. Stir together well. Beat the eggs and mix in until you have a silky consistency.

Pour your brownie batter into the baking pan, and place in the oven for around 25 minutes. You don't want to overcook them so, unlike cakes, you don't want a skewer to come out all clean. The brownies should be slightly springy on the outside but still gooey in the middle. Allow to cool in the pan, then carefully transfer to a large chopping board and cut into chunky squares. These make a fantastic dessert served with a dollop of crème fraîche mixed with some orange zest.

makes 8–10

1 cup plus 2 tablespoons unsalted butter

7oz best-quality dark chocolate (70% cocoa solids), broken up

optional: 2½oz dried sour cherries

optional: 1⅓oz chopped nuts

¾ cup cocoa powder, sifted

½ cup all purpose flour, sifted

1 teaspoon baking powder

1¾ cup superfine sugar

4 large free-range or organic eggs

optional: zest of 1 orange

optional: 9fl oz crème fraîche

A rather pleasing carrot cake with lime mascarpone icing

This carrot cake is an exceedingly good cake made all the more pleasing by the twist of lime mascarpone icing. It's delicious, it works and it's better than any other carrot cake I've tried. I would normally bake this in a square or round cake pan, but for the picture I used a lovely old loaf pan and it came out looking gorgeous.

Preheat the oven to 350°F. Grease and line a 9 inch square cake pan or a round equivalent with wax paper. Beat the butter and sugar together by hand or in a food processor until pale and fluffy. Beat in the egg yolks one by one, and add the orange zest and juice. Stir in the sifted flour and baking powder, and add the ground almonds, walnuts, spices and grated carrot and mix together well.

In a separate bowl, whisk the egg whites with a pinch of salt until stiff, then gently fold them into the cake mix. Scoop the batter into the prepared cake and cook in the preheated oven for about 50 minutes until golden and risen. You can check to see if the cake is cooked by poking a toothpick into it. Remove it after 5 seconds and if it comes out clean the cake is cooked; if slightly sticky it needs a bit longer, so put it back in the oven. Leave the cake to cool in the pan for 10 minutes, then turn it out on to a rack and leave for at least an hour.

Mix all the icing ingredients together and spread generously over the top of the cake. Finish off with a sprinkling of chopped walnuts.

serves 8–10

1¼ cups unsalted butter, softened
2 cups light brown soft sugar
5 large free-range or organic eggs, separated
zest and juice of 1 orange
1½ cups self-rising flour, sifted
1 slightly heaped teaspoon baking powder
1 cup ground almonds
4oz shelled walnuts, chopped, plus a handful for serving
1 heaped teaspoon ground cinnamon
a pinch of ground cloves
a pinch of ground nutmeg
½ teaspoon ground ginger
10oz carrots, peeled and coarsely grated
sea salt

for the lime mascarpone icing
4oz mascarpone cheese
8oz full-fat cream cheese
1 scant cup powdered sugar, sifted
zest and juice of 2 limes

MERINGUES

Meringues are a brilliant thing to learn how to make. They aren't difficult, they aren't expensive, you can make them way ahead of time if you're having a dinner party, they always look impressive and everyone LOVES them! They are generally made from just two ingredients – whisked-up egg whites and sugar. But even with just two ingredients there are three different ways of making them:

Italian meringue is made by slowly heating the sugar in a pan until it gets to 250°F, and then pouring this sugar syrup slowly into the stiff egg whites as they're being continuously whisked. It's a very stable meringue which you don't need to cook immediately. This is good news for pastry chefs because they can make it at the beginning of the night rather than having to make it every time they need some. It's best to make this type of meringue using an electric mixer or a free-standing KitchenAid. Don't try doing it by hand unless you have someone who can do the pouring for you while you keep whisking!

Cooked meringue is made by whisking your egg whites and sugar over a pan of simmering water so the mixture heats up and cooks as it's whisked. This is even more stable than Italian meringue, but is hard work to make!

Simple French meringue is the easiest meringue to make and the one I'm going to concentrate on in this chapter. You need to cook it as soon as you've made it or it starts to break down, but unless you're a chef with a busy service ahead of you this won't be a problem.

Top tips for making meringues

- Always start with clean, dry equipment, as grease, water or oil in bowls or on whisks will stop your whites from whipping and all your efforts and ingredients will be wasted! To be absolutely sure, pour boiling water over your equipment as well, then wipe dry with paper towels and you're in business.

- Always use superfine sugar for your meringues. Granulated and brown sugar are too coarse and will give you a grainy and flat meringue.

- Sift your sugar as you weigh it out, to make sure there are no lumps in it.

- Make sure your egg whites have no bits of shell or yolks in them. Egg yolks contain fat and fat is the enemy of meringues!

- If your egg whites are in a jug or have been frozen together and you can't work out how many you've got, remember that a large egg white should weigh about 1½oz and you will be able to work it out. Allow 1¾oz of sugar per large egg white.

- If you're going to bake your meringues, cut a piece of wax paper the same size as your baking tray and 'glue' it to the tray by putting a little blob of the meringue mixture underneath each corner. Spoon or pipe your meringues on to the paper, making sure you leave a bit of room between them as they'll swell a bit when they cook.

- When cooking meringues there are two textures you can try to achieve. Some people like their meringues white and crunchy all the way through. If you're one of these people, cook your meringues at 300°F for 2 hours, then turn the oven off and leave the door ajar as it cools. This will dry them out nicely. On the other hand, if, like me, you want your meringues beigey white on the outside and slightly soft and chewy on the inside, bake them at 300°F for an hour or so, then take the tray out of the oven to cool them down a little more quickly. This will keep the insides nice and soft.

Basic meringue

Meringues can be tricky buggers – make sure you read my top tips for making meringues first (see page 389).

Preheat your oven to 300°F. Line a baking sheet with wax paper. Put your egg whites into a bowl, making sure there are absolutely no little pieces of egg shell or egg yolk in them. Whisk on medium until the whites form firm peaks. You'll know that it's thick enough if you can hold the bowl upside down over your head – in 15 years of cooking it's only fallen on my head once!

With your mixer still running, gradually add the sugar and the pinch of salt. Turn the mixer up to the highest setting and whisk for about 7 or 8 minutes until the meringue mixture is deliciously white and glossy. Dip your finger in the meringue and rub the mixture between your thumb and index finger. It should feel perfectly smooth. If it feels at all grainy, whisk for a little bit longer. Keep a close eye on the meringue, because if you whisk it for too long, it will collapse.

It's at this point that you can gently fold in one of the flavors from the list below if you fancy. Personally, I quite like to eat a meringue that has a secret extra flavor added to it, especially when it's so subtle that you end up kicking yourself trying to work out what it is! Choose one of the following:

- a good pinch of saffron
- zest of 2 oranges
- a handful of pistachio nuts, bashed
- 1 teaspoon mixed spice
- zest of 3 lemons
- 2 tablespoons cocoa powder, sifted
- 2 tablespoons crystallized ginger, finely chopped
- 1 teaspoon fennel seeds, lightly toasted and crushed

Spoon your plain or flavored meringue mixture on to the prepared baking sheet, either in one big blob or several smaller ones, leaving a bit of space between them. Dab them with the bottom of your spoon so you get wispy bits coming up from the surface of the meringue. Pop the baking sheet into the oven for around an hour, until the meringues are crisp on the outside and chewy and a little gooey in the middle.

serves 6–8

6 large free-range or
   organic egg whites
1 cup plus 5 tablespoons
   superfine sugar
a pinch of salt

Eton mess

Eton mess is such a classic old-school dessert. I've kept this one pretty simple, using bashed-up meringues with raspberries and strawberries. I like to keep half the fruit whole and mush up the rest; this gives you beautiful flavor and lovely chunks of fruit. Eton mess is always a treat to eat, but if you want to make it look extra special then you can serve it in pretty individual glasses. And a lovely addition is a few drops of rose water ... perfect for a summer's day!

First of all, make your basic meringue recipe – you should end up with 6 to 8 meringues. Whip the cream with the vanilla seeds and 1 tablespoon of your sugar until you have soft peaks. Don't over-whip it or the cream will go thick and cloddy – you want it to stay light and delicate. Take half the strawberries and half the raspberries and put them into a bowl with the rest of the sugar and the balsamic vinegar. Mash up with a fork. Put your flavored cream and the mashed-up fruit into the fridge until your meringues are ready and have cooled down.

You can serve Eton mess on a large platter or in individual glasses. To assemble, break up your meringues into a bowl – you can crush some of the bits into powder, leaving other bits chunky. Fold the vanilla cream and mushed-up fruit together till well mixed, then sprinkle in the rest of the fruit and fold again. Layer your crushed meringues and fruity cream into your serving dish or glasses, then sprinkle with the toasted almonds (if using) just before serving. Put everything together right at the last minute so that the meringue won't go all soft.

serves 8

1 x basic meringue recipe
    (see page 390)
2 cups heavy cream
1 vanilla bean, scored
    lengthways and seeds
    removed
2 heaped tablespoons
    superfine sugar
9oz strawberries, hulled
    and sliced
9oz raspberries
1 teaspoon good-quality
    balsamic vinegar
optional: a handful of
    flaked almonds, toasted

The ultimate fruit meringue with vanilla cream, hazelnuts and caramel

This recipe is a little less involved than a normal pavlova because it is just one layer and it's so easy to make. Meringue and sweetened vanilla cream are a joy when eaten together on their own, but once sprinkled with lovely seasonal fruit it becomes a totally perfect combination! Feel free to change the fruit to wild strawberries or blueberries, or any mixture of soft fruit that you fancy. With a sprinkling of hazelnuts and a caramel that sets hard on top, this is definitely naughty but nice! But as far as kids are concerned, you could probably up the fruit to get the good stuff into them if you want to.

Preheat your oven to 300°F and line a 12x4 inch baking pan with a sheet of wax paper. Then make your basic meringue mixture. Using a spatula, spread the meringue mixture on to the wax paper so that it covers the whole baking pan. Carefully place the tray into the preheated oven and bake the meringue for an hour until crisp on the outside, but chewy and soft inside. Take the meringue out of the oven and leave to cool.

Put the hazelnuts in a baking pan and pop them into the oven until they're light brown – don't turn your back on them because they burn easily. Crush them lightly in a pestle and mortar and put to one side. Whip the cream with the sifted powdered sugar and vanilla seeds until it forms soft peaks. Using your fingers, gently press down on the center of the cooled meringue to create a hollow in the middle of it. Sprinkle in some of the crushed hazelnuts, then some berries and some vanilla cream. Repeat these layers until you have used up all the ingredients.

Put the superfine sugar into a saucepan, add 1 cup of water and bring to the boil, then reduce until the liquid turns into caramel. Carefully drizzle this over the top of the meringue and finish with a scattering of mint leaves.

serves 8–10

1 x basic meringue recipe
  (see page 390)
1¾oz peeled hazelnuts
1⅔ cups heavy cream
2 tablespoons powdered
  sugar, sifted
1 vanilla bean, scored
  lengthways and seeds
  removed
1 container of raspberries
1 container of blackberries
sugar
a small bunch of fresh mint,
  smallest leaves picked

Coconut, banana and passion fruit pavlova

Throughout history a lot of famous chefs seem to have been a bit flirtatious and named their special desserts after film stars, dancers and beautiful women. Escoffier did it with his Peach Melba, after the Australian singer Dame Nellie Melba, and Pavlova was named after the ballerina Anna Pavlova – the meringue and cream layers are supposed to resemble her delicate, floaty layers of skirts. (Thinking about it, there aren't many desserts named after blokes, are there?!) There seems to be an ongoing debate between the Australians and the New Zealanders as to who invented this dessert. I'm not going to get involved – whoever it was, they did a bloody good job, as it's a top combination!

Preheat the oven to 300°F. Whip up your basic meringue recipe and delicately fold in your lime juice and coconut.

Line two baking sheets with parchment paper. Divide the meringue mixture between them and shape each blob into a circle about 8 inches in diameter. Put both sheets into the preheated oven and bake for 45 minutes, by which time the two pavlova halves will be creamy white on the outside and fluffy in the middle.

Whip your cream with the sugar till it forms soft peaks and fold in most of the lime zest. Spoon the cream on top of one pavlova half, smooth it out and top with the sliced bananas and the passion fruit seeds. Carefully place the other pavlova half on top and press down very very gently to stick them together. Sprinkle the top layer of pavlova with the shavings of coconut and the remaining lime zest and serve.

serves 10–12

1 x basic meringue recipe
  (see page 390)
juice of ½ a lime
5 tablespoons coconut
1 cup heavy cream
1 tablespoon superfine
  sugar
zest of 1 lime
2 bananas, peeled and
  sliced at an angle
2 passion fruit, halved and
  insides scooped out
flesh of ¼ a fresh coconut,
  shaved with a speed
  peeler

Floating islands

In all other recipes in this section, the meringues are baked. Here they are poached in hot milk instead and served floating on a sea of custard. Floating islands are quite time-consuming to make but not very difficult at all. Restaurant critic Fay Maschler made a knockout version for me one Sunday lunch. Since that Sunday I've cooked them a whole bunch of times, especially last summer.

Make your custard, reserving 6 egg whites for your meringues.

Now make the spun sugar, but please remember that the caramel will be roasting hot. Whatever you do, don't put your fingers in the caramel as you'll give yourself a nasty burn! Fill your sink with cold water, then lay out a large sheet of oiled wax paper with an oiled rolling pin on top of it. In a saucepan, gently heat the sugar with 1 cup water, stirring until the sugar has completely dissolved. Bring to the boil and cook down until you have a golden caramel. The sugary syrup will turn into caramel at 325°F – you can check with a kitchen thermometer if you like. Then carefully dip just the base of the pan into your sink of cold water to prevent the caramel cooking any further. Put the pan out of the way, somewhere safe, to cool.

To see whether it's ready to be spun, dip a fork into the caramel and let the excess drip off, then shake it vigorously. You want the caramel to turn into fine shreds – if it's too hot it will just drip and if it's too cool it won't even flick off the fork. If the caramel gets too hard you can heat it up again and try once more. You may be thinking this all sounds like a fuss, but once you get the temperature right it works a treat. So, when it's the right consistency, dip your fork in and shake it vigorously over your oiled rolling pin and paper. Keep going until you have a big pile of spun sugar over the rolling pin – it will look like a fuzzy nest of caramel. Place in a cool, dry place until needed.

Make your basic meringue mixture. Instead of dividing the mixture into blobs on a baking tray, you're going to poach them. Heat the milk in a wide, shallow saucepan and, when simmering, drop in 3 heaped tablespoons of the meringue, spaced well apart as they expand when cooking. Cook for about 30 seconds on each side. Remove these 'floating islands' with a slotted spoon and let them drain on some paper towels. Repeat until all the meringue mixture has been used up, then discard the milk.

Spoon the custard into your serving bowls, then divide the floating islands between them. Sprinkle with the toasted almonds and lay over a whole load of your spun sugar. Great with fresh strawberries or raspberries, lightly crushed with a fork.

serves 6–8

1 x proper custard recipe
  (see page 402)
¾ cup flaked and toasted
  almonds, to serve

for the spun sugar
olive or vegetable oil,
  for greasing
1 cup superfine sugar

for the meringues
1 x basic meringue recipe
  (see page 390)
5 cups whole milk

CUSTARD

European chefs have been using custard as a filling for sweet pies and tarts for hundreds of years. The fact that people are still doing exactly the same thing 500 years later proves what a brilliant crowd-pleaser it is.

Real custard, or crème anglaise as the French call it, is lovely as a sauce for cakes and puddings of all kinds, and is the backbone of desserts like trifles, fools, ice cream (see page 407) and floating islands (page 398). It's also an essential accompaniment to British classics like steamed puddings and stewed rhubarb (see page 404), so is well worth learning how to make.

Top tips for making custard

- To flavor custard, infuse the milk with the flavoring of your choice as you warm it up, then sieve the milk as you pour it on to the eggs.

- Vanilla, cinnamon sticks, lemon or orange zest and even saffron are great flavors to try out.

- Use whole milk and the best quality eggs you can find for maximum flavor and the loveliest color.

- Don't make custard in huge batches – you have more control over the cooking if you make a little at a time.

- To prevent a skin from forming on your custard, put a piece of plastic wrap directly on to the surface.

Proper custard

Custard is a basic sauce made in most restaurant kitchens around the world. No matter how bad the reputation for British food has been over the last fifty or more years, custard remains one of our great legacies. Here's the basic recipe, and on the next few pages you'll find a few different ways of serving it.

Mix the milk, cream, 4 tablespoons of the superfine sugar, the vanilla bean and seeds together in a saucepan. Bring to the point of boiling, then remove from the heat and leave for a couple of minutes to cool slightly – this will also allow the vanilla flavor to infuse.

In a large mixing bowl, whisk the egg yolks with the remaining 2 tablespoons of sugar until pale. Remove the vanilla bean from the milk mixture, then ladle a little of it on to the egg yolks and whisk immediately. Add the remaining milk a ladleful at a time, whisking in well before adding the next. Pour the egg mixture back into the warm saucepan and cook very gently for a few minutes, stirring all the time using a rubber spatula or a wooden spoon. After a matter of minutes the yolks should cook just enough to thicken the custard and make it shiny – you should be able to coat the back of a spoon with it.

Once you've reached this point, take it off the heat immediately. If you cook it too fast, for too long or on too high a heat, the mixture will probably scramble. But don't worry; if you start to see flecks or lumps of egg in your custard, pull it off the heat right away and pour it into a cold saucepan to cool it down a little, then strain the custard through a sieve into a clean pitcher. Served hot or cold, it's delicious.

PS If you want to warm up cold custard, it's best to place it in a bowl over a pan of boiling water – this way it won't curdle.

serves 4–6

2 cups plus 3 tablespoons whole milk
2 cups heavy cream
6 tablespoons superfine sugar
1 vanilla bean, scored lengthways and seeds removed
8 large free-range or organic egg yolks

Rhubarb and custard

It's quite sad that today most kids think that rhubarb and custard is just an old-fashioned flavor of boiled sweet instead of the original recipe for one of the most delicious but simple desserts you can make – with proper custard and stewed rhubarb. Feel free to vary the flavors you add to the rhubarb – ginger, orange, a swig of white wine or champagne, a couple of star anise, a couple of drips of rose water, or some vanilla beans will all give your rhubarb the edge. Just make sure that when you serve it, you pour the custard over the rhubarb in front of everyone so that they can see the beautiful marbling effect as it happens. Genius!

Preheat the oven to 400°F. Put the rhubarb pieces in an ovenproof dish or pan, with the sugar, orange zest and juice and the grated ginger sprinkled over the top. Cover with foil and cook in the preheated oven for 15 to 20 minutes until the rhubarb has softened. The cooking time will depend on the variety and thickness of your rhubarb, so trust your instincts and keep checking it. Meanwhile, make your custard. Once your rhubarb is cooked, taste it to see whether you think it's a little tart – it may need a bit more sugar.

Serve the rhubarb either in a big serving bowl or in individual bowls, with a generous amount of your delicious homemade custard.

serves 4

1¾lb rhubarb, washed and
    cut into 3 inch pieces
4 tablespoons superfine
    sugar
zest and juice of 2 oranges
a thumb-sized piece of
    fresh ginger, peeled and
    finely grated
1 x proper custard recipe
    (see page 402)

Homemade ice cream

If you can make good custard (which, of course, by now you've established is really easy!) you can make really good ice cream as well. There are basically two ways in which you can do this and I think that both are generally much better for you than buying ice cream.

The first method involves putting your chilled custard into a big bowl or dish in the freezer, then every 20 minutes taking it out and either whisking or beating it with a spoon until it forms into ice cream. The reason you have to go back to it every 20 minutes is because you need to aerate it as it freezes. Not only does this make it light and delicate but it also makes sure that the ice crystals are kept as small as possible so that you get the silky texture that you want, rather than icy granules. This method is a little bit manual and a bit of a pain because you have to keep going back to it over the two hours it takes to set. However, the results are very good.

The second method involves you going down to a shop – somewhere like a good department store or kitchen shop – and dipping your hands in your wallet and buying an ice cream machine! The beauty of them is that they churn the ice cream at the same time as freezing it. This makes the whole process easy-peasy. When your ice cream has been churned into what looks like thickly whipped cream, you can just turn the ice cream maker off and spoon the ice cream into little freezer-safe dishes, bowls or Tupperware pots. These can be kept in the freezer until you need them. If you've got kids or a large family that enjoys ice cream, investing in an ice cream maker is definitely worthwhile.

Ice cream flavors

As someone who might be making ice cream for the first time, I want you to start out with some really basic flavors, like adding a little cinnamon or cocoa powder to the custard mix, or some honey. Taking it up a step, you can mix the finished custard with fruit compotes, or add a caramel or toffee sauce. Even chocolate bits or smashed cookies can be folded in once you've started to churn the ice cream. And soaked cherries or fruit will give you a ripply effect, which is great. One of the nicest flavors of ice cream I've ever made was vin santo and orange zest, served with a hot almond tart. But be careful using alcohol . . . swigs of various liqueurs or things like raisins soaked in brandy can all work fantastically well, but if you add too much alcohol it will stop the ice cream from setting as it should.

Once you've mastered how to make ice cream, and come up with a combination of flavors that you're happy with, you can keep it quite happily in the freezer for a month. Do a number of different flavors and let your guests choose the winner!

Family Favorites

This section is full of recipes we all reminisce about. From classics like shortbread and gingerbread, the mighty tarte tatin and the delicious Fifteen chocolate tart to that old favorite, bread and butter pudding. Have a flick through and I'm sure you'll find a handful of recipes that are a real blast from the past, as well as some you'll end up making for ever. Enjoy!

Bloomin' easy vanilla cheesecake

This recipe somehow made its way on to the menu in the Fifteen Trattoria (I don't know of many Italian trattorias that have American cheesecake on their menus!) and I'm glad that it did because it's absolutely delicious.

As you can see, the ingredients are all pretty everyday things. However, my tip for getting the very best out of this recipe is to make sure that you try and get the best ingredients that you possibly can.

Preheat the oven to 350°F, and grease and line the bottom and sides of a 9½ inch springform cake pan. Mix the biscuits and butter in a bowl, press into the base of the prepared pan and cook for 10 minutes. Then remove from the oven and allow to cool.

Turn the oven up to 400°F. Combine the sugar and cornstarch in a bowl. Add the cream cheese and beat, ideally with an electric mixer, until creamy. Add the eggs and beat well. Gradually add the cream, beating until smooth, then beat in the vanilla seeds or extract and lemon and orange zest.

Scrape the mixture on to the biscuit base, and gently shake it to level out the surface. Put the cheesecake in the center of the oven and bake for 40 to 45 minutes until the top is golden brown and the filling has set around the edges. (A piece of foil over the top will stop it browning too much.) Let it cool at room temperature and serve after 2 or 3 hours, or, for a slightly firmer texture, put it in the fridge until it's nice and cold.

Before serving, put the cherries in a pan, sprinkle over the sugar and add a splash of water. Put on a low to medium heat and simmer gently for 10 minutes. If you've got some port or whisky handy, feel free to add some. When the compote has reduced down it may be a little dry, so add a splash of water to loosen it. Remove from the heat and let it cool down, then serve spooned over the cheesecake with a dusting of powdered sugar.

serves 8–10

11 tablespoons unsalted butter, melted, plus extra for greasing
9oz digestive biscuits, crushed
½ cup superfine sugar
3 tablespoons cornstarch
2lb full-fat cream cheese, at room temperature
2 large free-range or organic eggs
½ cup heavy cream
1 vanilla bean, scored lengthways and seeds removed, or ½ teaspoon vanilla extract
zest of 1 lemon
zest of 1 orange

for the cherry compote
14oz pitted cherries
3 heaped tablespoons superfine sugar
optional: a swig of port or whisky
powdered sugar, for dusting

The best shortbread in the world

Shortbread is a great recipe to start with if you are not too confident with desserts. It is a staple in most restaurant kitchens, where it's used next to a pannacotta or a tart, but it's just as good dunked in a nice cup of tea! This recipe will make buttery, crumbly, delicious fingers of shortbread, but, if you're feeling adventurous, why not try adding some orange or lemon zest, or, my favorite, a bit of lavender to your dough.

Preheat the oven to 300°F. Butter a 9 inch square pan. Cream your butter and sugar together with a whisk or wooden spoon until pale, light and fluffy. Add the flour and semolina or cornstarch. Mix very lightly with a wooden spoon and then your hands until you have a smooth dough.

Transfer your dough to a floured surface and roll it out until it's an even 1 inch thick all over. Press the rolled-out dough into your pan, poking it into the corners with your fingers – don't worry about it having to look perfect. Prick the dough all over with a fork, then pop it in the preheated oven for 50 minutes until lightly golden.

While it's still warm, sprinkle with a generous dusting of sugar. Allow the shortbread to cool slightly, then cut into 12 chunky finger-sized pieces.

makes 12 chunky fingers

1 cup plus 2 tablespoons unsalted butter, at room temperature, plus extra for greasing

½ cup plus 1 tablespoon superfine sugar, plus extra for sprinkling

2 scant cups all-purpose flour, sifted, plus extra for dusting

⅔ cup semolina or 1 scant cup cornstarch

Ultimate gingerbread

The best gingerbread I've ever eaten in my life is from a shop in Grasmere, in England's Lake District, that I visited some years ago. They use a secret recipe which is about 150 years old and, of course, they wouldn't let me in on it, so I decided to have a go at my own ... and it's not half bad – in fact, this will be some of the best gingerbread you'll ever eat! So, here we go. Don't forget, you can eat this simply as a cookie, but it also works well sprinkled over ice cream or dipped into warm compote and cream for afternoon tea. And it's especially nice when used as a cheesecake base.

If you're making your own shortbread, make it first. Then preheat the oven to 325°F and find a baking pan about 8x14 inches. Put the shortbread, sugar and 2 teaspoons of the ground ginger in a food processor and whiz until you have crumbs. Remove 3½oz of the mix and keep this to one side. Add the remaining teaspoon of ginger to the processor, along with the mixed peel, crystallized ginger, flour and baking powder, and pulse until well mixed.

Melt the syrup, molasses and butter together in a saucepan big enough to hold all the ingredients. When melted, add the mixture from the food processor and stir with a wooden spoon until everything is thoroughly mixed together. Tip into the baking pan and spread out evenly. Press the mixture down into the tray, using your fingers or something flat and clean like a potato masher or a spatula. When the mix is a flat, dense and even layer, pop the tray in the preheated oven for 10 minutes.

Take the tray out of the oven and sprinkle the hot gingerbread with the reserved crumbs, pressing them down really well with a potato masher or spatula. Carefully cut into good-sized pieces with a sharp knife, and leave to cool in the pan before eating.

makes 8–10 pieces

1 x shortbread recipe (see page 412) or 14oz shop-bought shortbread

6oz plantation or raw sugar

3 level teaspoons ground ginger

1½oz mixed peel, chopped (⅓ cup)

1½oz crystallized ginger, chopped

7 tablespoons all-purpose flour

a pinch of baking powder

2 tablespoons golden syrup

2 tablespoons treacle

5 tablespoons unsalted butter

Good old bread and butter pudding
with a marmalade glaze and cinnamon and orange butter

Bread and butter pudding is one of those classic old English recipes that everyone loves. The addition of marmalade brushed over the bread makes it fantastically crisp, with a zingy orangey bitterness that just makes the whole thing superb. This is another dessert that you don't want to overcook because you want to have the soft insides contrasting with the crispiness on top.

Preheat the oven to 350°F. First make your flavored butter by mixing the butter with the nutmeg, cinnamon and orange zest. Use a little of it to butter a medium-sized shallow, ovenproof dish.

Butter the bread using the flavored butter, then cut each slice in half diagonally. Put the slices in your buttered dish. Now separate the eggs, reserving all 9 yolks but just 1 egg white. Whisk together the egg yolks and egg white with the sugar, then gently heat the milk and cream in a saucepan with the vanilla seeds and bean. Pour into the eggs, stirring all the time. Remove the vanilla bean then pour the mixture over the bread and leave to soak for at least 20 minutes. Put the dish in a roasting pan and pour in enough boiling water to come halfway up the side of the dish. Then put it in the preheated oven for about 45 minutes until the custard has just set. Meanwhile, gently warm the marmalade in a saucepan, then remove the dish from the oven and brush the marmalade over the top of the bread. Pop the dish back into the oven for another 5 to 10 minutes. Allow it to cool and firm up slightly before serving.

serves 6

for the flavored butter
7 tablespoons unsalted butter, softened
a large pinch of ground nutmeg
a large pinch of ground cinnamon
zest of 1 large orange

8 x ½ inch slices of good-quality bread
9 large free-range or organic eggs
¾ cup superfine sugar
2 cups whole milk
2 cups heavy cream
1 vanilla bean, scored lengthways and seeds removed
4 tablespoons good-quality fine-cut marmalade

Doughnuts with Old English spiced sugar

Doughnuts are a fantastic naughty snack or dessert, and everyone has got a soft spot for them. The important thing is they must be served warm and tossed in spice and citrus-flavored sugars. Little doughnuts are great to dip into a rhubarb, cherry or apple compote – the contrast between the fresh and sour fruit and the hot, crisp, bun-like doughnuts is delicious!

Put the yeast in a bowl with a tablespoon of the sugar and a tablespoon of the flour and mix in the warm milk. Put in a warm place for about 15 minutes until the mixture becomes frothy.

Next, put the rest of the sugar and flour, lemon zest, orange zest and butter in a bowl. Add the yeast mixture and use a spoon to start bringing it all together, then get stuck in with your clean hands to mix it into a ball. Don't worry if it's too sticky, just add a bit more flour. Knead the dough for 5 minutes or so until it's smooth and silky, then pop it into a bowl, cover with a clean damp cloth and leave to rise for about an hour or until doubled in size. Meanwhile, make your flavored sugar by mixing the sugar, spices, zest and vanilla seeds together in a bowl or smashing them up in a Flavor Shaker. Put to one side for later.

When the dough has doubled in size, you can knock it back – this means you give it a bit of a punch to knock out some of the air so it can rise again later. This way your doughnuts will be light and fluffy. On a floured surface roll the dough out until it's an even ½ inch thickness. Using a little cutter or a small glass (approximately 2 inches diameter) cut out about 25 little circles and pop them on to a greased baking pan to rise again, making sure there is a sufficient gap between each one to allow them to spread. Cover with your damp tea towel and allow to rise for 45 minutes.

When the blobs of dough have almost doubled in size again, use a chopstick to make a little hole in the centre of each doughnut. Now they are ready to be fried. Carefully heat the vegetable oil in a large deep saucepan, keeping an eye out for anyone who may accidentally bump into you or the pan! You can test the temperature by putting a leftover pea-sized piece of dough into the oil – if it sizzles and turns golden brown after about a minute your oil is at the right temperature. Fry your doughnuts in batches. After about 2 minutes, when they are golden brown, carefully remove them with a slotted spoon, and place them on some paper towels to drain. While your doughnuts are still piping hot, sprinkle over your flavored sugar. Lovely eaten warm – feel free to pig out and eat them all in one go because they don't keep very long.

makes about 25

1 x ¼oz package active dried yeast
⅓ cup superfine sugar
3½ cups all-purpose flour
1½ cups plus 2 tablespoons whole milk, warmed until tepid
zest of 2 lemons
zest of 1 orange
5½ tablespoons unsalted butter, softened and cubed
1¾ pints vegetable oil

for the flavored sugar
½ cup superfine sugar
1 teaspoon ground cinnamon
½ teaspoon freshly grated nutmeg
½ teaspoon ground allspice
zest of 1 lemon
zest of 1 orange
1 vanilla bean, scored lengthways and seeds removed

Fifteen chocolate tart

This chocolate tart has been on the menu at Fifteen since the restaurant opened, and it has slowly evolved into the perfect chocolate indulgence where the pastry is also made with chocolate. The recipe is really reliable, but the thing to remember is not to overcook the chocolate filling as you want it to retain a little ooziness in the middle.

First you will need to grease an 11 inch tart tin with a removeable bottom with a little of your butter. To make your pastry, cream together the butter, sugar and salt, then fold in the flour, orange zest (if using), eggs and cocoa powder – you can do all this by hand or in a food processor. When the mixture looks like coarse breadcrumbs, gently work it together until you have a ball of dough, then flour it lightly. Don't work the pastry too much, otherwise it will become elastic and chewy, not crumbly and short as you want it to be. Wrap the dough in plastic wrap and put it in the fridge for at least an hour. Remove it from the fridge, roll it out, line your tart tin with it and put it in the freezer for half an hour.

Preheat the oven to 350°F and bake the pastry case 'blind' for around 12 to 15 minutes or until it's firm and almost cookie-like. Remove from the oven and turn the heat down to 325°F.

Meanwhile, to make the chocolate filling, put the milk, cream and sugar into a saucepan and slowly bring to the boil, stirring gently. Take off the heat and add the broken chocolate, whisking until smooth, then add the eggs and whisk again. Pour the filling into a pitcher. Put the baked tart case back in the oven, carefully pull out the oven rack and pour in the filling. Push the oven shelf back in and bake for 15 minutes. It is cooked when the filling still has a slight wobble to it – remember, it will keep firming up a little as it cools down. Lovely served with a big dollop of crème fraîche.

serves 8-10

for the pastry
1¼ cups plus 3 tablespoons unsalted butter
1 cup superfine sugar
a pinch of salt
4 cups all-purpose flour, sifted, plus extra for dusting
optional: zest of 1 orange
3 large free-range or organic eggs
1 cup plus 2 tablespoons cocoa powder

for the filling
¾ cups plus 2 tablespoons whole milk
2 cups heavy cream
3½ tablespoons superfine sugar
12½oz best-quality dark chocolate (70% cocoa solids), broken up
2 large free-range or organic eggs

Pear tarte tatin

This is an absolute classic tart that is more usually made with apples. Once you've made it a few times you'll find that it's really easy. A little butter, fruit and puff pastry and you're done! Instead of using the more traditional apples, I've swapped them for pears and it can also be very nice to sprinkle some ginger over the top. A little bit of thyme is a great addition to pear as well. The beauty of these tarts is that you can assemble them in advance and then keep them in the fridge until you're ready to cook them.

Preheat the oven to 375°F. Put your sugar, vanilla bean and ½ cup water into a 8 inch ovenproof, heavy-bottomed frying pan and bring to the boil. Simmer this syrup until it thickens to become a lovely deep brown caramel. (When making caramel it's important that you don't stir it at all as this can affect the way the sugar behaves, so don't be tempted!)

Cut each of your pears into 6 wedges. Put the pears in with the caramel and gently toss them around so they get nicely coated. Stir in the butter and reduce for a further 5 minutes until you've got a thick, buttery caramel sauce. Carefully take off the heat and sprinkle over the ginger and then the almonds.

Next, roll out your puff pastry until it's about the thickness of a silver dollar and cut it into a circle about the same size as your frying pan, so it will fit snugly inside it. Mix the egg with the milk, then lay the pastry on top of the pears, tucking it in around the edges, and brush the pastry top with a little of the egg mixture. Put the pan in the preheated oven for about 20 minutes until the pastry is golden brown on top, then remove from the oven and put to one side to cool down. To turn out your tatin, carefully place a plate on top of your frying pan and, using an oven mitt or potholder, put your hand on top. Being very careful, as there will be hot liquid caramel around, quickly flip the tart over on to the plate.

Serve straight away, sprinkling with some thyme tips. Really lovely with thick clotted cream. Yum!

serves 4

½ cup superfine sugar
1 vanilla bean, scored lengthways, seeds removed and reserved
3 firm, slightly underripe pears, peeled, cored and rubbed with lemon juice
1½ tablespoons unsalted butter
½ teaspoon ground ginger
a handful of flaked almonds, toasted
9oz frozen puff pastry, defrosted
1 large free-range or organic egg
1 teaspoon milk
a few sprigs of fresh thyme, leaves picked

SOME BITS AND BOBS

How to cook safely

You probably know most of this already as it's basically common sense, but if there's something here you hadn't thought of, and it prevents an accident, it'll have been worth reading!

- Aprons aren't just to keep your clothes clean; chefs wear them so that if they're splashed with hot oil or water they can quickly pull the apron away from themselves before the liquid soaks through to their skin.

- If you spill a little water or oil on the floor while you're working, tell anyone else in the room to watch out for it, then stop and clean it up right away. It's not a good idea to have people going head over heels with pots of boiling water and sharp knives about.

- When cooking on the stove top, try not to leave pan handles sticking out over the edge. It's easier than you think to knock them and you don't want to spill what you're cooking, especially if you don't have an apron on or there are kids around.

- If you're moving a hot pan or a pot full of hot oil or water to the sink or to another part of the kitchen, make sure people around you know about it – don't wait for them to bump into you.

- Unless you're sure that a metal handle is cool, always pick it up using an oven mitt or a folded tea towel. Make sure your tea towel is dry – the heat will penetrate through a wet one.

- If you're making caramel, always wear an apron and oven mitts, and clear the room of inquisitive children and pets. Boiling caramel is much hotter than boiling water and can seriously burn you.

- When you're using a chopping board, always lay a damp cloth, tea towel or piece of paper towel underneath it. This will stop the board slipping as you chop things.

- Keep your knife handle clean. If you get grease or oil on it, stop what you're doing and wash it off so your grip on the knife is good at all times.

- When you've finished with a knife, either clean it and put it away immediately, or put it somewhere where others can see it. The worst place you can leave a knife is in a sink under a whole lot of other stuff or in soapy water. If anyone puts their hand into the sink to wash something up, they stand a good chance of cutting themselves.

- If you don't have a knife block for your knives, lay them flat in an uncluttered drawer where everyone can see them. If you keep your knives jumbled up with wooden spoons, whisks and tongs, the next time you rummage around for something, you'll wish you hadn't.

- Every professional kitchen has a first-aid kit and so should yours. Make sure you have a good range of bandages in it. Chefs use blue bandages so if they fall off into food, they are easily spotted. Fire extinguishers are a good idea too.

Sharpening a knife

Knives get blunt when you use them: their sharp edges wear down when they thump against a chopping board or cut through tough things like root vegetables. Every chef, every fishmonger and every butcher knows it makes sense to keep knives sharp, because if your knives are blunt you have to use more force and that's when things start to slip and you're in danger of hurting yourself.

Keeping knives sharp isn't hard, and the best way to do it is to buy yourself a steel. A steel is a metal rod 8 to 12 inches long with a handle at one end. The metal of the rod is grooved – a bit like a file – and when you rub your knife along the steel, it grinds it finely. Knives don't need to be razor sharp, just make sure you sharpen them a little every time you use them and again before you put them away.

- Start with your knife in your right hand (if you're right-handed that is; use your left hand if you're left-handed) and the steel in the other.

- Cross them over each other – the steel under the knife – and lay the blade of your knife flat against the steel, the sharp edge facing away from you.

- Rotate your knife very slightly so it's angled at about 20 degrees to the steel and just the side of the blade is touching it.

- Move your hands apart, keeping the steel and the knife in contact, so the blade of the knife runs down the length of the steel, scraping against it, as if it's a piece of wood and you're trying to whittle it to a point.

- Replace the knife where it started, but this time underneath the steel angled the opposite way.

- Move your hands apart again so the blade of the knife 'whittles' the underside of the steel.

- Keep grinding your knife against the steel on alternate sides until you can feel the blade sharpened to the point where you're happy with it. Test the sharpness by cutting a tomato: when it cuts into it like it's butter, then your knife is sharp. If there's any resistance, keep on sharpening.

- Carefully wipe your knife with a piece of kitchen paper before you use it as it'll have a fine metal dust on it that you don't want to get in your food.

How to handle food safely

Every year, tens of thousands of people get some sort of food poisoning, and they're just the ones who see their doctor – the real figure is probably much higher. We all know what it's like: stomach cramps, sickness and the runs if you're lucky; if you're unlucky, you could land up in the hospital. So when you're cooking at home for your friends or family, here are a few pointers to help you avoid it:

- Bacteria are everywhere. Some of them are good, like the bacteria that turn cheese blue or milk into yogurt, or the bacteria that we have in our gut that help us digest our food. Some of them are bad, and they're the ones that give us food poisoning. The more of them there are around, the more likely we are to get sick. There's very little we can do to eliminate bacteria completely from our kitchens, but what we can do is control the amount of bacteria around by denying them what they need to grow and multiply – that is, food, moisture, warmth and time.

- Foodstuffs that bacteria particularly like to grow on are raw fish, raw meat, dairy products and cooked food of any sort – including soups, stocks and stews, and especially starchy things like rice, pasta and beans. By covering food up, you can stop bacteria in the air landing on it and finding the food they need to grow, so anything from the fishmonger's or butcher's should be well wrapped, and cooked food should be covered as soon as it's cool.

- Bacteria need a certain level of heat to multiply, so don't leave meat or fish lying around for too long at room temperature. Remember, the more time bacteria have to multiply, the more of them there will be. The time it takes you to drive home from the store is fine, but make sure you put your food in the fridge afterwards asap.

- Bacteria prefer to grow between 46°F and 167°F, so it's OK to keep cooked food hot, as long as you keep it above 167°F, and if you're cooling something down, make sure it doesn't hang around in the bacteria-friendly temperature zone for too long. On the other hand, make sure it has completely cooled before you put it in the fridge. as otherwise you'll be making everything else in there vulnerable to bacteria.

Cross-contamination

Imagine for a minute that you're making chicken and salad for dinner. If you chop your chicken up on a board before cooking it, and then use the same knife and board to prepare your salad, the salad will be contaminated with bacteria from the uncooked chicken. This is called 'cross-contamination' and here are the golden rules for avoiding it:

- After preparing raw meat or fish on a chopping board, give the board a good scrub in really hot water to kill the bacteria, with a little dish liquid to get rid of any grease. Wash the knife and your hands thoroughly so that the bacteria don't spread on to food that is cooked or that is ready to eat. Some restaurants have color-coded chopping boards for raw and cooked foods to minimize the chances of this happening.

- Be careful too with dirty, muddy vegetables. Peel them in the sink, rinse them before you use them and remember to clean the sink and your hands before you do anything else.

- Store raw meat and fish on the bottom shelf of your fridge, and food that is ready to be eaten, whether it's salad, cheese, dairy or cooked food, on the shelves above. This means that raw foods can't drip on to cooked foods and cross-contaminate them.

- When you've cooked your food, serve it with clean implements that haven't touched anything raw or dirty. It's a scary thing to see the same tongs put raw chicken on the barbecue one minute and then lift cooked chicken off it a few seconds later . . . see what I mean?

- Wash your hands after touching anything that might have bacteria on it, like the dustbin or the dog, and never forget to wash your hands after going to the loo! Keep the work surfaces in your kitchen clean. Wipe them regularly with antibacterial kitchen spray, and don't forget to wash your kitchen cloth or spongy scourer itself in hot soapy water, as it can harbor germs too.

Freezing

If you looked round the average supermarket you'd think that all freezers were suitable for was storing oven fries, economy burgers and frozen dinners, but they're miles more useful than that, an incredible help to the modern-day cook, preserving things for much longer than fridges. There is sometimes a price to pay, though. When you freeze vegetables, for instance, the tiny cells inside freeze, the water within the cells expands as it turns into ice and sometimes the cell walls break – a bit like your pipes freezing and bursting in winter! – and this can give you food that's limp and soggy.

So what can or can't you freeze? Peas freeze brilliantly, and most people have a bag or two in their freezer any day of the year. Sweet corn is fantastic frozen, and it's much sweeter than the canned stuff; and fava beans and pearl onions freeze well too. But root vegetables like carrots, turnips and beetroot don't freeze very well at all. They lose their texture completely, as do more delicate vegetables like green beans, cauliflower, broccoli and spinach. Spinach freezes very well, though, after it's been cooked.

Meat is a bit tougher than vegetables and handles freezing much better. Just about any cut of any animal can be frozen pretty successfully, especially stewing cuts that need to be broken down and tenderized by long slow cooking anyway.

Fish isn't quite as tough as meat and freezing it can break it down a little too much for some people's liking. Frozen fish can end up leaking water in the pan when it's fried, which isn't ideal, but if you're adding it to a soup, a stew or a pasta sauce it'll be fine.

Pasta dough and pastry freeze very well, so if you've made a batch and have a bit left over, freeze it for next time.

Stock freezes well too, as do all the little bones you need to make it. It's only a bit more expensive to buy a whole chicken than it is to buy two skinned chicken breasts. Next time, why not buy a whole one, cut the breasts off yourself, and put the legs and the carcass in the freezer? Then you've got a couple of legs for another dinner one evening and bones for a nice stock or soup.

Bread is always best fresh, but it keeps pretty well in the freezer. Buy an extra loaf, slice it and bag it up two slices at a time. You can cook it straight from frozen in the toaster.

How to freeze safely

Freezing doesn't stop food aging completely, it just slows things down a lot, so if you freeze stuff it's a good idea to slap a sticker on it telling you what it is and when you froze it. Check through it every now and then, use stuff within a couple of months of it being frozen and toss anything that's older than that.

Stock your freezer as you would a fridge, with raw things on the bottom and cooked foods, ice cream and ice cubes on top. Things don't drip in the freezer after they're frozen, but they do while they're freezing.

If you're cooking something from the freezer, make sure it's been completely defrosted first or cooking times won't be valid and you'll serve stuff that's not properly cooked. Be especially careful with things like frozen chickens or turkeys at Christmas.

And last but not least, if you defrost something and then don't end up cooking it, don't refreeze it unless you've cooked it first.

Freezing cooked food and leftovers

Most leftovers freeze brilliantly. Sometimes if I'm cooking dinner, I deliberately make loads extra for the freezer so that if some family or mates pop round unannounced, I've got something up my sleeve. If you've got things like leftover lasagne or shepherd's pie, chop them up when they're cold into portion-sized squares, pop them into freezer bags, squeeze the air out before sealing them and freeze them. (Even if there's a lot left, if you freeze the portions individually they'll defrost and warm up quicker.) Stews, soups, sauces and chilli freeze well – divide leftovers into 9oz portions, bag them up and freeze them.

Here are some chopping techniques that should come in handy. They're not meant to cover everything, but will help you get to grips with some of the recipes in this book.

Zucchini matchsticks
Cut slices about ¼ inch thick with the tip of your knife. Stack your zucchini slices on top of each other and chop them across into thin strips.

Cabbage chiffonade
Cut out the thick stalky part of each leaf with the tip of a chopping knife. Stack your trimmed leaves on top of each other. Roll them up tightly like a big fat cigar and chop them across into ribbons.

Beetroot matchsticks

Slice the peeled beetroot ¼ inch thick. Stack the slices on top of each other and chop them into thin strips.

Beetroot slices

Slice the peeled beetroot on a vegetable slicer or mandolin using the heel of your hand to push it down. Keep your fingers out of the way.

Potato matchsticks

Top and tail your peeled potato so the ends are flat. Sit the potato upright and cut into slices about ¼ inch thick with a knife. Stack the potato slices on top of each other and chop them across into thin strips.

Herbs

Woody herbs are generally too powerful to be eaten raw. They're usually cooked alongside whatever they're intended to flavor and are often removed before serving. Woody herbs dry well, and although they don't have quite the same flavor as fresh herbs, dried woody herbs are worth using as a substitute.

Bay is a small tree with thick shiny green leaves. Bay leaves give a real meatiness and depth of flavor to stocks and stews and they're great in stuffings and threaded between pieces of meat on barbecue skewers.

Marjoram is oregano's little brother. Look at their leaves to tell them apart: marjoram has thinner, more delicate leaves which are rounded rather than pointed. It's used a lot in northern European cuisine and is great friends with beetroot, carrots, pork and baked fish. Although it's a strong herb, marjoram is just mild enough to be eaten raw.

Oregano is a small plant with thick furry leaves that grows all over southern Europe. It's used widely in Italian, Greek and southern French cuisine, goes well with lamb, tomatoes, peppers and grilled fish, and is great with pizzas and pasta.

Rosemary is a tall bush with long woody branches and thin leaves like pine needles. It's widely used in European cuisines and goes brilliantly with lamb, beef, bread and strong Mediterranean flavors like garlic, anchovies and olives.

Sage is a small bush with long oval furry leaves. It's very good friends with pork and in Britain we've been putting sage in sausages and stuffings for centuries. The Italians like it with veal and with pumpkin, and it also goes well with pasta when cooked in butter till crisp, then spooned over ravioli or tortellini.

Thyme is a short sturdy bush with long thin branches and tiny perfumed leaves. Like bay, it's a very popular ingredient in stews and stocks and goes well with all sorts of vegetables like carrots, artichokes, mushrooms, turnips and leeks.

Soft herbs aren't quite as strong as woody ones – they can be eaten raw in salads, scattered over or stirred into cooked food. Dried soft herbs have very little flavor, so always try to use fresh ones.

Basil is an incredibly aromatic herb which smells and tastes somewhere between aniseed, cinnamon, lemon and pepper. It's used all over southern Europe and the Far East, where Thai basil is a key ingredient in many dishes. It's great in salads, wonderful with salmon, it's the basis of pesto, which we all know and love, but it's absolute best friends with tomatoes.

Chervil is similar to tarragon but its flavor isn't quite as strong. It has very delicate leaves and is good in salads and lightly flavored creamy soups. Chefs love to use chervil leaves for garnishing food because they make just about anything look beautiful!

Chives are part of the onion family and have a sharp oniony flavor. They're most often chopped and sprinkled over the top of cooked dishes like soups and salads for presentation and extra flavor. They get on well with eggs and also with boiled new potatoes.

Cilantro is a fragrant herb with a flavor that people either love or hate. It's used right across Asia in Thai salads, Vietnamese soups, Indian curries and Middle Eastern meatballs. When crushed in a pestle and mortar, the stalks have even more flavor than the leaves and are a key ingredient in curry pastes. It's also used widely in Latin America in salads and sauces like guacamole. It's great friends with chilli, lime and cumin seeds.

Dill looks similar to fennel but has a slightly different flavor. It's used all over eastern Europe, from Scandinavia down to Greece, and most famously in gravalax – Swedish cured salmon. It goes really well with all kinds of fish, pickles, mustard and root vegetables like beetroot.

Fennel is a tall thin plant with feathery leaves very similar to the green tops you get on a bulb of fennel. It too is aniseedy in taste and goes very well with fish and shellfish. Fennel stalks have a strong flavor, especially when they're dried, and are great tucked under a whole fish or a loin of pork and roasted.

Mint is very often used with sweet flavors instead of savory. It goes well with fruit like peaches, figs and melons, and pastry chefs always use sprigs of it to garnish their desserts. The two savory flavors it works best with are roast lamb (everyone has tried lamb and mint sauce!) and chillies, where its fresh flavor balances the heat very well.

Parsley is a strong-flavored aromatic herb that comes in two varieties: flat-leaf and curly. Chefs prize parsley stalks and use them to flavor stocks, and the leaves are great chopped and sprinkled over vegetables, soups, pasta dishes and even salads. Parsley is best friends with garlic, lemon, ham and mushrooms.

Tarragon is a delicate plant with long floppy green leaves. It has a flavor quite like aniseed and goes really well with chicken, eggs, tomatoes and potatoes.

Spices

Black pepper is the dried unripe berry of the pepper plant. Whole or ground, it is used as a seasoning all over the world, and is an important ingredient in curry and spice mixes. One of my favorite Indian restaurants, Rasa in London, makes an amazing crab dish with tons of black pepper – screaming hot and absolutely delicious.

Cardamom pods are small green husks with little black seeds inside. They have a strong citrussy eucalyptus flavor you either love or hate – I love it! Use them whole to perfume rice dishes, or ground up in a curry. In India, cardamom's also used in sweets and desserts, much like we use vanilla in the west.

Chilli is one of my favorite spices. I love fresh chillies, but dried chillies have a deeper heat and a more intense flavor that I can't do without in hot curries, arrabiata sauce, crunchy pangrattato and on roast pumpkin. Both fresh and dried chillies are very strong, so wash your hands after cutting or crumbling them!

Cinnamon sticks give a wonderful rich, musky flavor to meat curries and stews; Sicilians use them to flavor their beautiful tomato ragù. Ground cinnamon is great in cakes and biscuits, and essential in apple pie.

Cloves are small and dark brown with a very strong, pungent perfume and flavor. In Africa, the Middle East and southern Asia, cloves are used in stews, curries and rice dishes. In the UK, cloves are most often used in desserts and cakes. They go very well with apples and citrus fruit like oranges and clementines.

Coriander seeds are small, round and light brown in color. When crushed in a pestle and mortar they have a fantastically sweet, orangey, nutty smell that goes well in curry mixes, pickles and stews. Like cumin seeds, they love to be toasted in a pan first before they're crushed. A great way of spicing up carrot soup!

Cumin seeds are small and brown with a mild, sweet, aromatic flavor that people often associate with curries. Their flavor can be perked up a notch or two by toasting them lightly in a dry frying pan before grinding. I love to stir cumin into a chilli at the last minute, and it's the business in guacamole.

Fennel seeds are small and green with a sweet aniseed flavor. They are very good friends with roast pork – try crushing them with some salt and rubbing the mixture into the scores in the skin for the

best crackling ever. They are great in tomato sauces, and can even be used in cookies and pastries. In India people eat them after dinner as a mouth freshener and a stomach settler.

Five-spice is a blend of fennel, star anise, cloves, cinnamon and pepper that the Chinese use to season dishes like Peking duck and barbecued spare ribs. Its smell is unmistakable – one sniff and you'll know exactly what I'm talking about. Try some on your pork chops next time you have a barbecue.

Mustard seeds are small and round, and come in black, brown and yellow. They're often dropped into hot oil at the beginning of making a curry to give it a pungent, nutty flavor. They're great as a seasoning for pickles and spicy chutneys.

Nutmeg is a really elegant spice, fantastic with cheese, cream, dauphinois potatoes and spinach. Just a grating of it makes your bolognese sauce better than anyone else's! Old English cookery used a lot of nutmeg in sweet dishes too, especially in cakes, biscuits and Christmas puddings.

Saffron is made from the dried stamens of crocus flowers – don't ask me how people came up with the idea of using it in cooking! Its bright yellow color and aromatic flavor are strong, so you don't need much at all when you use it – which is just as well, as it's very expensive. It's used a lot in Middle Eastern cooking and is the most important ingredient in the famous risotto Milanese.

Smoked paprika is made from dried smoked sweet chilli peppers that are ground to a rich red powder. It gives a brilliant sweet,

smoky flavor to anything you use it with. Buy a little tin to experiment with next time you see it and I promise your barbecued chicken will never be the same again!

Star anise is a large star-shaped seed pod with a strong aniseed flavor. It's one of the key ingredients in five-spice and is used on its own in stocks and slow-cooked meat stews in the Far East. In the West it's used a lot in desserts and puddings and I love it in pickles and chutneys.

Vanilla is one of my very favorite spices. Real vanilla comes as a long black waxy bean full of tiny black seeds and gives ice cream, custard and loads of other desserts an amazingly luxurious flavor. It isn't cheap because it is only found in a few places around the world and there's not a lot of it about, but if you ever try the real thing there's no going back to vanilla extract.

THANKS

First and foremost, this book has been an incredibly time-consuming and involving book to write, so I want to thank my dear food team who are Peter Begg, Ginny Rolfe, Bobby Sebire, Anna Jones and Tommy Parsons, and my editors Lindsey Evans and Suzanna de Jong. Thanks, guys, I couldn't have done it without you.

I especially want to thank two fantastic friends and brilliant photographers – David Loftus (www.davidloftus.com) for the incredible food pictures and Chris Terry (www.christopherterry .com) who shot the great portrait on the front cover. Thanks also to Rosie Scott and Rat Boy, and Garry Chapman at Scruffs for sorting my barnet out – nice one.

As you can imagine, we rely on good friends and suppliers with all that we do at Fifteen. The following people were a great help on this book as well, so I'd like to thank Sheila Keating, Gennaro Contaldo, Jekka McVicar at Jekka's Herb Farm, Gary and Richard at Moen's butchers, Kevin and everyone at Allen & Co. butchers, Tony Booth at Borough Market, Patricia at La Fromagerie, Mitch Tonks at FishWorks, the team at Kensington Place fish shop, the gang at Secretts Farm, Jon and the gang at The Flour Station, Joe Junior and Joe Senior at The Gazzano's, and Gretchen, Agnes, Ewan and Merly at the Lacquer Chest.

There's a whole team of people at Penguin who work incredibly hard year in, year out, to make my books amazing, and they've done it again this time. A massive thank you to John Hamilton, Tom Weldon, Keith Taylor, Chris Callard, Tiina Wastie, Sophie Brewer, Jessica Jefferys, Rob Williams, Tora Orde-Powlett, Naomi Fidler and her wicked sales team, Clare Pollock, Annie Lee, Charlie Hartley, Eugenie Boyd and the rest of the editorial team.

To my Sweet as Candy gang – Louise Holland, Claire Postans, Danny McCubbin, Paul Rutherford, Tara Donovan, Tessa Graham and Frosty. Thank you, guys.

My profits from this book will go to Fifteen Foundation to help train future generations of chefs. This unusual but amazingly effective charity has a whole team and board of trustees behind it, who give incredibly generous amounts of their time and experience for free: Steve Angel, John Dewar, Mike Trace, Nick Jones, Bill Eyres and Baroness Glenys Thornton. Thank you for making my dream come true and caring for it as much as I do.

A big thanks to all those who help to look after our young people at Fifteen London, and run the business that supports them: Liam Black, Tony Elvin, Ali Noor, Sharon Wright, Claire O'Neill and Vanya Barwell. In the kitchen, thanks to Andrew Parkinson, the executive head chef of Fifteen London, Frenchy, Trevor, Steve K, Steve P, Matt and all the other chefs. Special thanks to Aaron and Lloyd – two of our Fifteen graduates who helped on the photo shoots for this book. Also, respect to Paula Dupuy, head of restaurant operations, sommelier Matt Skinner and all the managers, waiters and pot washers – thank you for constantly working on standards and service and creating an incredibly supportive place for our students to work in.

Thank you to all the guys at Fifteen Amsterdam, Fifteen Cornwall and Fifteen Melbourne.

To the team-building people at HCE Adventure (01443 228 565) – if you're ever going to do it, these are the guys to use – and to Ruth Silver and the gang at Lewisham College. Thanks for looking after all our students year after year.

I'd also like to thank Luc, Florence and everyone at Tefal for getting pots and pans to our shoot locations, Simon Kinder at Magimix, the William Levene gang, Royal Worcester and KitchenAid. Thanks also to Beautiful World Tents Ltd (01403 734 833) – if you ever need incredible teepees and marquees, try them.

And last but certainly not least, a very special thank you to my beautiful wife, Jools, and daughters, Poppy and Daisy, and to my Mum and Dad.

INDEX

page references in bold denote an illustration

v indicates a vegetarian recipe

a

agro dolce: pot-roasted poussins *agro dolce* **188**, 189

all day breakfast salad 52, **53**

v almonds: roasted cauliflower with cumin, coriander and almonds 342, **343**

v amaretti: squash, sage and amaretti risotto 132, **133**

amazing potato and horseradish salad with fine herbs and bresaola 30, **31**

anchovies

    baked potatoes stuffed with bacon, anchovies and sage 304, **305**

    pan-roasted salmon with purple sprouting broccoli and anchovy-rosemary sauce 212, **213**

apples

v   apple and walnut risotto with gorgonzola 136, **137**

    must-try red cabbage braised with apple, bacon and balsamic vinegar 358, **359**

    old-school pork chops with apples and sage **178**, 179

    schnitzel with watercress and spiced apple sauce 182, **183**

v April's rosemary straw potatoes with lemon salt 306, **307**

arugula

    the best stew with potato and arugula pasta cushions **104**, 105

v   herby gnocchi with arugula and butter sauce 116, **116**

asparagus

v   asparagus, mint and lemon risotto 124, **125**

    delicious roasted white fish wrapped in smoked bacon with lemon mayonnaise and asparagus 222, **223**

    grilled spatchcocked chicken with new potatoes, roast asparagus and herby yogurt 190, **191**

    roasted chicken breast with cherry tomatoes and asparagus **186**, 187

v avocados: Greek salad 40, **41**

b

bacon

    all day breakfast salad 52, **53**

    baked potatoes stuffed with bacon, anchovies and sage 304, **305**

    braised white cabbage with bacon and thyme **360**, 361

    buttered peas with crunchy bacon 320, **321**

    delicious roasted white fish wrapped in smoked bacon with lemon mayonnaise and asparagus 222, **223**

    must-try red cabbage braised with apple, bacon and balsamic vinegar 358, **359**

    slow-cooked leek soldiers with bacon 328, **329**

    warm salad of crispy smoked bacon and Jerusalem artichokes **48**, 49

    see also pancetta

v baked and dressed courgettes **366**, 367

baked John Dory in the bag with tomatoes and balsamic vinegar **240**, 241

baked potatoes stuffed with bacon, anchovies and sage 304, **305**

balsamic vinegar 22

    baked John Dory in the bag with tomatoes and balsamic vinegar **240**, 241

v   dressing 24

    must-try red cabbage braised with apple, bacon and balsamic vinegar 358, **359**

v bananas: coconut, banana and passion fruit pavlova **396**, 397

barbecued pork: blackened barbecued pork fillets **180**, 181

basil 432

v   lovely easy caramelle with ricotta, basil and black olives 100, **101**

    real quick mussels spaghetti in a white wine and basil oil broth 62, **63**

    shell-roasted scallops with sweet tomato and basil sauce **246**, 249

v   tomato, basil and ricotta risotto 126, **127**

bay 432

beans

    chargrilled tuna with oregano oil and beautifully dressed peas and fava beans 214, **215**

    grilled fillet steak with the creamiest white beans and leeks **156**, 157

beef 148–9

    grilled fillet steak with the creamiest white beans and leeks **156**, 157

    melt-in-your-mouth shin stew **150**, 151

    pan-fried sirloin steak with simple Chianti butter sauce and olive oil mash 158, **159**

    pappardelle with a ragù of tiny meatballs 92, **93**

    roast fore rib of beef with beetroot and horseradish 154, **155**

    ultimate rib of beef with rosemary and garlic roast potatoes 152, **153**

beetroot

v   crunchy raw beetroot salad with feta and pear 36, **37**

    matchsticks 431

    roast fore rib of beef with beetroot and horseradish 154, **155**

    slices 431

v the best onion gratin **332**, 333

the best roast turkey – Christmas or any time 194, **195**

v the best shortbread in the world 412, **413**

the best stew with potato and arugula pasta cushions **104**, 105

v   the best whole-baked carrots 312, **313**

v   beurre blanc: steamed broccoli with beurre blanc
340, 341

black angel tagliarini **94**, 95

black pepper 434

black pudding: squid with black pudding stuffing and
sticky tomato sauce **290**, 291

blackened barbecued pork fillets **180**, 181

v   bloomin' easy vanilla cheesecake **410**, 411

v   braised peas with spring onions and lettuce 318,
319

braised white cabbage with bacon and thyme **360**, 361

v   bread and butter pudding with a marmalade glaze and
cinnamon and orange butter **416**, 417

breadcrumbs
  pan-fried red mullet with crispy breadcrumbs and a
herby tomato salad **210**, 211
  see also pangrattato

breakfast salad, all day 52, **53**

bream 231
  pan-roasted bream with a quick crispy fennel salad
216, 217

bresaola: amazing potato and horseradish salad with
fine herbs and bresaola 30, **31**

broccoli 295, 334
v   Indian-style broccoli with spiced yogurt 338, **339**
  pan-roasted salmon with purple sprouting broccoli
and anchovy-rosemary sauce 212, **213**
v   steamed broccoli with beurre blanc **340**, 341
v   steamed broccoli with soy and ginger **336**, 337

v   brownies: Fifteen chocolate brownies 384, **385**

butter sauce
v   herby gnocchi with arugula and butter sauce 116, **116**
  pan-fried sirloin steak with simple Chianti butter sauce
and olive oil mash 158, **159**
v   steamed broccoli with beurre blanc **340**, 341

buttered peas with crunchy bacon 320, **321**

butternut squash 346
v   creamy 350, **351**
v   incredible boiled butternut squash with squash seed
and Parmesan pangrattato **348**, 349
v   open stained-glass lasagne with roasted squash **98**, 99
  roasted chicken breast with creamy butternut squash
and chilli **186**, 187
v   squash, sage and amaretti risotto 132, **133**
v   superb sweet and sour squash 352, **353**

c

cabbage 354
  braised white cabbage with bacon and thyme **360**, 361
  chiffonade 430
  must-try red cabbage braised with apple, bacon and
balsamic vinegar 358, **359**
  Savoy cabbage with Worcestershire sauce 356, **357**

cakes 374–5
v   1980s-style Black Forest Swiss roll **380**, 381
v   classic Victoria sponge with all the trimmings 376, **377**
v   Fifteen chocolate brownies 384, **385**
v   my nan's lemon drizzle cake **382**, 383
v   a rather pleasing carrot cake with lime mascarpone
icing **386**, 387
v   tea-party cupcakes 378, **379**

cannelloni: honeycomb cannelloni 76, **77**

caramel
  making safely 424
v   the ultimate fruit meringue with vanilla cream,
hazelnuts and caramel 394, **395**

caramelle
v   lovely easy caramelle with ricotta, basil and
black olives 100, **101**
  shaping 88

cardamom pods 434

carrots 308
v   the best whole-baked carrots 312, **313**
v   dinner-lady carrots **314**, 315
v   a rather pleasing carrot cake with lime mascarpone
icing **386**, 387
v   sticky saucepan carrots 310, **311**

cauliflower 334
  roast rack of lamb with potato and cauliflower
dauphinois 164, **165**
v   roasted cauliflower with cumin, coriander
and almonds 342, **343**
  whole baked cauliflower with tomato and
olive sauce **344**, 345

v   celeriac: raviolini of celeriac and thyme **110**, 111

chargrilled tuna with oregano oil and beautifully
dressed peas and fava beans 214, **215**

v   cheese: macaroni cheese **66**, 67

v   cheesecake: bloomin' easy vanilla cheesecake
410, 411

v   cheesy peas 324, **325**

chervil 432

chicken 184–5
  grilled spatchcocked chicken with new potatoes, roast
asparagus and herby yogurt 190, **191**
  pot-roasted poussins *agro dolce* **188**, 189
  roasted chicken breast with cherry tomatoes and
asparagus **186**, 187
  roasted chicken breast with creamy butternut squash
and chilli **186**, 187
  roasted chicken breast with lemony Bombay potatoes
186, 187
  roasted chicken breast wrapped in pancetta with
leeks and thyme **186**, 187
  tortellini of chicken and gorgonzola in a fragrant
thyme broth 108, **109**

chilli(es) 434
v   grilled chilli dressing 25

chilli(es) – *cont.*
    my favorite crunchy squid with lime and chilli
        mayonnaise 288, **289**
    roasted chicken breast with creamy butternut squash
        and chilli **186**, 187
v   simple sautéed zucchini with chilli and lemon 364, **365**
chives 432
chocolate
v   Fifteen chocolate brownies 384, **385**
v   Fifteen chocolate tart 420, **421**
chopping techniques 430–31
chowder: the nicest clam chowder, Essex girl style
    256, 257
cinnamon 434
v   good old bread and butter pudding with a marmalade
        glaze and cinnamon and orange butter **416**, 417
clams 252
    the nicest clam chowder, Essex girl style **256**, 257
v   classic Victoria sponge with all the trimmings 376, **377**
cloves 434
v   coconut, banana and passion fruit pavlova **396**, 397
cod: my black cod with steamed pak choi and
    cucumber 226, **227**
v   coleslaw: my favorite coleslaw 38, **39**
cilantro 432
    shell-roasted scallops with ginger, soy and cilantro
        246, 249
coriander seeds 434
v   roasted cauliflower with cumin, coriander
        and almonds 342, **343**
crab 266
    delicious crab crostini **272**, 273
    how to pick cooked crabmeat 268
    how to prepare and boil 268
    lovely crab linguine 74, **75**
    old-fashioned potted crab 270, **271**
    Southern Indian crab curry 274, **275**
v   creamy butternut squash 350, **351**
v   creamy French dressing 24
crème fraîche
    mussels steamed with fennel and crème fraîche
        254, **255**
    pan-fried scallops with lentils, crispy pancetta
        and lemon crème fraîche 250, **251**
crispy fragrant jumbo shrimp 262, **263**
crispy grilled trout with parsley and lemon 242, **243**
cross-contamination 427
crostini: delicious crab crostini **272**, 273
v   crunchy raw beetroot salad with feta and pear 36, **37**
cucumber: my black cod with steamed pak choi and
    cucumber 226, **227**
cumin seeds 434
v   roasted cauliflower with cumin, coriander and
    almonds 342, **343**

cupcakes: tea-party cupcakes 378, **379**
curry: Southern Indian crab curry 274, **275**
cushions
    the best stew with potato and arugula pasta cushions
        104, 105
    shaping 88
custard 400
v   floating islands 398, **399**
v   homemade ice cream **406**, 407
v   proper 402, **403**
v   rhubarb and 404, **405**

d

delicious crab crostini **272**, 273
delicious roasted white fish wrapped in smoked bacon
    with lemon mayonnaise and asparagus 222, **223**
desserts 372–3
v   the best shortbread in the world 412, **413**
v   bloomin' easy vanilla cheesecake **410**, 411
v   doughnuts with Old English spiced sugar **418**, 419
v   Fifteen chocolate tart 420, **421**
v   good old bread and butter pudding with a marmalade
        glaze and cinnamon and orange butter **416**, 417
v   pear tarte tatin 422, **423**
v   ultimate gingerbread 414, **415**
    see also cakes; custard; meringues
dill 432
v   dinner-lady carrots **314**, 315
v   doughnuts with Old English spiced sugar **418**, 419
dressings 22–3
v   balsamic vinegar dressing 24
v   basic 23
v   creamy French dressing 24
v   grilled chilli dressing 25
v   Japanese dressing 25
v   lemon oil dressing 24
v   mayonnaise 26, **27**
v   Sicilian dressing 24
v   spiced vinegar dressing 24
duck 192
    gorgeous slow-cooked duck pasta **80**, 81
    Middle Eastern duck salad 54, **55**
    perfectly cooked crispy duck with spiced
        plum chutney 198, **199**
dumplings: tender-as-you-like rabbit stew with the
    best dumplings ever **196**, 197

e

eggplant: roast leg of lamb with eggplant
    and onions **168**, 169
eggs
    all day breakfast salad 52, **53**

v   return of the egg salad **34**, 35
v   oozy egg ravioli 106, **107**
v Eton mess 392, **393**

f

fabulous fish stew 260, **261**
fava beans: chargrilled tuna with oregano oil and
    beautifully dressed peas and broad beans 214, **215**
fantastic fish lasagne 78, **79**
fennel 432
    mussels steamed with fennel and crème fraîche
        254, **255**
    pan-roasted bream with a quick crispy fennel salad
        216, 217
    roast salmon with fennel, parsley and tomato 232, **233**
    slow-roasted pork belly with the sweetest braised
        fennel 176, **177**
fennel seeds 434–5
v feta: crunchy raw beetroot salad with feta and pear
    36, **37**
v Fifteen chocolate brownies 384, **385**
v Fifteen chocolate tart 420, **421**
Fifteen Christmas salad 44, **45**
fish 202–3
    cooking filleted fish 208
    cooking whole fish 230–31
    delicious roasted white fish wrapped in smoked
        bacon with lemon mayonnaise and asparagus
        222, **223**
    fabulous fish stew 260, **261**
    fantastic fish lasagne 78, **79**
    freezing 428
    how to be a better fish shopper 206
    whole fish baked in a salt crust 238, **239**
five-spice 435
v floating islands 398, **399**
food handling 426–7
freezing 428–9
v French dressing, creamy 24
v frisée lettuce: warm grilled peach and frisée salad
    with goat's cheese dressing **50**, 51
v fritters: zucchini fritters 368, **369**
v fruit: the ultimate fruit meringue with vanilla cream,
    hazelnuts and caramel 394, **395**
fusilli: proper blokes' sausage fusilli 72, **73**

g

ginger
    shell-roasted scallops with ginger, soy and cilantro
        246, 249
v   steamed broccoli with soy and ginger 336, **337**
v gingerbread, ultimate 414, **415**

gnocchi 112
v   basic lightest potato gnocchi 112, **113**
v   herby gnocchi with arugula and butter sauce 116, **116**
    with braised oxtail 117, **117**
v   with gorgonzola dolce 114, **115**
v   with mushrooms and sage 114, **115**
goat's cheese
v   spinach and goat's cheese risotto **128**, 129
v   warm grilled peach and frisée salad with goat's
        cheese dressing **50**, 51
v good old bread and butter pudding with a
    marmalade glaze and cinnamon and orange
    butter **416**, 417
gorgeous slow-cooked duck pasta **80**, 81
gorgonzola
v   apple and walnut risotto with gorgonzola 136,
        137
v   gnocchi with gorgonzola dolce 114, **115**
    tortellini of chicken and gorgonzola in a fragrant
        thyme broth 108, **109**
Granddad Ken's crispy grilled trout with parsley and
    lemon 242, **243**
v Greek salad 40, **41**
grilled and roasted red mullet with pancetta and
    thyme **236**, 237
v grilled chilli dressing 25
grilled fillet steak with the creamiest white beans and
    leeks **156**, 157
grilled or roasted monkfish with black olive sauce and
    lemon mash **224**, 225
grilled spatchcocked chicken with new potatocs,
    roast asparagus and herby yogurt 190, **191**

h

v hazelnuts: the ultimate fruit meringue with vanilla
    cream, hazelnuts and caramel 394, **395**
herbs 21, 432–3
    grilled spatchcocked chicken with new potatoes, roast
        asparagus and herby yogurt 190, **191**
    pan-fried red mullet with crispy breadcrumbs and a
        herby tomato salad **210**, 211
v herby gnocchi with arugula and butter sauce 116, **116**
homemade ice cream **406**, 407
honeycomb cannelloni 76, **77**
horseradish
    amazing potato and horseradish salad with fine herbs
        and bresaola 30, **31**
    roast fore rib of beef with beetroot and horseradish
        154, **155**

i

v ice cream: homemade ice cream **406**, 407
incredible baked lamb shanks 162, **163**

v   incredible boiled butternut squash with squash seed
        and Parmesan pangrattato **348**, 349
v   Indian-style broccoli with spiced yogurt 338, **339**

j

v   Japanese dressing 25
    Jerusalem artichokes: warm salad of crispy smoked
        bacon and Jerusalem artichokes **48**, 49
    John Dory 231
        baked John Dory in the bag with tomatoes and
            balsamic vinegar **240**, 241
    Jools' favorite Saturday afternoon pasta 64, **65**

k

    knives
        safety 424–5
        sharpening 425–6

l

    lamb 160–61
        incredible baked lamb shanks 162, **163**
        lovely lamb shank pie 166, **167**
        mad Moroccan lamb 170, **171**
        roast leg of lamb with eggplant and onions **168**, 169
        roast rack of lamb with potato and cauliflower
            dauphinois 164, **165**
    lasagne
        fantastic fish lasagne 78, **79**
v   open stained-glass lasagne with roasted squash **98**, 99
        shaping stained-glass 90
    leeks 294–5, 326–7
        grilled fillet steak with the creamiest white beans
            and leeks **156**, 157
v   roasted baby leeks with thyme 330, **331**
        roasted chicken breast wrapped in pancetta with
            leeks and thyme **186**, 187
        slow-cooked leek soldiers with bacon 328, **329**
    leftover stew risotto 134, **135**
    lemon sole: pan-fried lemon sole fillets with
        salsa verde 218, **219**
    lemons
v   April's rosemary straw potatoes with lemon salt
            306, **307**
v   asparagus, mint and lemon risotto 124, **125**
        delicious roasted white fish wrapped in smoked bacon
            with lemon mayonnaise and asparagus 222, **223**
        Granddad Ken's crispy grilled trout with parsley
            and lemon 242, **243**
        grilled or roasted monkfish with black olive sauce and
            lemon mash **224**, 225
v   lemon oil dressing 24
v   my nan's lemon drizzle cake **382**, 383

        pan-fried scallops with lentils, crispy pancetta and
            lemon crème fraîche 250, **251**
        roasted chicken breast with lemony Bombay potatoes
            186, 187
v   simple sautéed zucchini with chilli and lemon 364, **365**
    lentils: pan-fried scallops with lentils, crispy pancetta
        and lemon crème fraîche 250, **251**
v   lettuce: braised peas with spring onions and lettuce
        318, **319**
    lime
        my favorite crunchy squid with lime and chilli
            mayonnaise 288, **289**
v   a rather pleasing carrot cake with lime mascarpone
            icing **386**, 387
    linguine
        lovely crab linguine 74, **75**
        super squid linguine **70**, 71
    lobsters 276–7
        how to pan-grill 281
        how to prepare a live lobster 278
        how to steam 280
        sticky fingers lobster 282, **283**
    lovely crab linguine 74, **75**
v   lovely easy caramelle with ricotta, basil and black
        olives 100, **101**
    lovely lamb shank pie 166, **167**

m

v   macaroni cheese **66**, 67
    mad Moroccan lamb 170, **171**
    Marie Rose sauce: shrimp cocktail 264, **265**
    marjoram 432
        pappardelle with wild rabbit, olives and marjoram
            96, **97**
v   marmalade: good old bread and butter pudding with a
        marmalade glaze and cinnamon and orange butter
        416, 417
v   mascarpone: a rather pleasing carrot cake with lime
        mascarpone icing **386**, 387
v   mayonnaise 26, **27**
        delicious roasted white fish wrapped in smoked
            bacon with lemon mayonnaise and asparagus
            222, **223**
        my favorite crunchy squid with lime and chilli
            mayonnaise 288, **289**
    meat 140–41, 144
        freezing 428
        how to be a better meat shopper 145
        how to cook 146–7
    meatballs: pappardelle with a ragù of tiny meatballs
        92, **93**
    melt-in-your-mouth shin stew **150**, 151
    meringues 388–9
v   basic 390, **391**

v   coconut, banana and passion fruit pavlova **396**, 397
v   Eton mess 392, **393**
v   floating islands 398, **399**
v   the ultimate fruit meringue with vanilla cream,
        hazelnuts and caramel 394, **395**
Middle Eastern duck salad 54, **55**
mint 433
v   asparagus, mint and lemon risotto 124, **125**
v   minted peas under oil **322**, 323
v   ravioli of pecorino, potato and mint 102, **103**
monkfish: grilled or roasted monkfish with black olive
    sauce and lemon mash **224**, 225
mushrooms
v   gnocchi with mushrooms and sage 114, **115**
v   mushroom risotto **130**, 131
mussels 252
    real quick mussels spaghetti in a white wine and basil
        oil broth 62, **63**
    steamed with fennel and crème fraîche 254, **255**
must-try red cabbage braised with apple, bacon and
    balsamic vinegar 358, **359**
mustard seeds 435
my black cod with steamed pak choi and cucumber
    226, **227**
v   my favorite coleslaw 38, **39**
my favorite crunchy squid with lime and chilli
    mayonnaise 288, **289**
v   my nan's lemon drizzle cake **382**, 383

n

the nicest clam chowder, Essex girl style **256**, 257
v   1980s-style Black Forest Swiss roll **380**, 381
nutmeg 435

o

oil 22
old-fashioned potted crab 270, **271**
old-school pork chops with apples and sage
    178, 179
olive oil
v   minted peas under oil **322**, 323
    pan-fried sirloin steak with simple Chianti butter sauce
        and olive oil mash 158, **159**
olives
v   Greek salad 40, **41**
    grilled or roasted monkfish with black olive sauce and
        lemon mash **224**, 225
v   lovely easy caramelle with ricotta, basil and black
        olives 100, **101**
    pappardelle with wild rabbit, olives and marjoram
        96, **97**
    whole baked cauliflower with tomato and olive sauce
        344, 345

onions 326–7
v   the best onion gratin **332**, 333
    roast leg of lamb with eggplant and onions **168**, 169
v   oozy egg ravioli 106, **107**
v   open stained-glass lasagne with roasted squash 98, 99
v   oranges: good old bread and butter pudding with a
        marmalade glaze and cinnamon and orange butter
        416, 417
oregano 432
    chargrilled tuna with oregano oil and beautifully
        dressed peas and fava beans 214, **215**
overnight slow-roasted pork 174, **175**
oxtail: gnocchi with braised oxtail 117, **117**

p

pak choi: my black cod with steamed pak choi
    and cucumber 226, **227**
pan-fried lemon sole fillets with salsa verde
    218, **219**
pan-fried red mullet with crispy breadcrumbs and a
    herby tomato salad **210**, 211
pan-fried scallops with lentils, crispy pancetta and
    lemon crème fraîche 250, **251**
pan-fried sirloin steak with simple Chianti butter sauce
    and olive oil mash 158, **159**
pan-roasted bream with a quick crispy fennel salad
    216, 217
pan-roasted salmon with purple sprouting broccoli
    and anchovy-rosemary sauce 212, **213**
pancetta
    grilled and roasted red mullet with pancetta and
        thyme **236**, 237
    pan-fried scallops with lentils, crispy pancetta and
        lemon crème fraîche 250, **251**
    roasted chicken breast wrapped in pancetta with
        leeks and thyme **186**, 187
pangrattato
v   incredible boiled butternut squash with squash seed
        and Parmesan pangrattato **348**, 349
    shrimp cocktail 264, **265**
    spicy pangrattato risotto **122**, 123
pappardelle
    with a ragù of tiny meatballs 92, **93**
    shaping 88
    with wild rabbit, olives and marjoram 96, **97**
Parmesan
v   cheesy peas 324, **325**
v   incredible boiled butternut squash with squash seed
        and Parmesan pangrattato **348**, 349
parsley 433
    Granddad Ken's crispy grilled trout with parsley
        and lemon 242, **243**
    roast salmon with fennel, parsley and tomato
        232, **233**

v passion fruit: coconut, banana and passion
      fruit pavlova **396**, 397
   pasta 58–9
      basic fresh egg pasta dough 84, **85**
      the best stew with potato and arugula pasta cushions
         104, 105
      black angel tagliarini **94**, 95
      dried 60
      fantastic fish lasagne 78, **79**
      freezing dough 428
      fresh 82–3
      gorgeous slow-cooked duck pasta **80**, 81
      honeycomb cannelloni 76, **77**
      Jools' favorite Saturday afternoon pasta 64, **65**
      lovely crab linguine 74, **75**
v   lovely easy caramelle with ricotta, basil and black
         olives 100, **101**
v   macaroni cheese **66**, 67
v   oozy egg ravioli 106, **107**
v   open stained-glass lasagne with roasted squash **98**, 99
      pappardelle with a ragù of tiny meatballs 92, **93**
      pappardelle with wild rabbit, olives and marjoram 96, **97**
      proper blokes' sausage fusilli 72, **73**
v   ravioli of pecorino, potato and mint 102, **103**
v   raviolini of celeriac and thyme **110**, 111
      real quick mussels spaghetti in a white wine and basil
         oil broth 62, **63**
      rolling and shaping fresh pasta 86–91
v   summertime tagliarini 68, **69**
      super squid linguine **70**, 71
      tortellini of chicken and gorgonzola in a fragrant thyme
         broth 108, **109**
   pastry
v   Fifteen chocolate tart 420, **421**
      freezing 428
v   pear tarte tatin 422, **423**
v pavlova: coconut, banana and passion fruit pavlova
      396, 397
v peaches: warm grilled peach and frisée salad with
      goat's cheese dressing **50**, 51
   pears
v   crunchy raw beetroot salad with feta and pear 36, **37**
v   pear tarte tatin 422, **423**
   peas 316
v   braised peas with spring onions and lettuce 318, **319**
      buttered peas with crunchy bacon 320, **321**
      chargrilled tuna with oregano oil and beautifully
         dressed peas and fava beans 214, **215**
v   cheesy peas 324, **325**
v   minted peas under oil **322**, 323
v pecorino: ravioli of pecorino, potato and mint 102, **103**
   perfectly cooked crispy duck with spiced plum
      chutney 198, **199**
   plums: perfectly cooked crispy duck with spiced plum
      chutney 198, **199**

   poached salmon steak 220, **221**
   pork 172–3
      blackened barbecued pork fillets **180**, 181
      old-school pork chops with apples and sage **178**, 179
      overnight slow-roasted pork 174, **175**
      schnitzel with watercress and spiced apple sauce
         182, **183**
      slow-roasted pork belly with the sweetest braised
         fennel 176, **177**
   pot-roasted poussins *agro dolce* **188**, 189
   potato(es) 296–7
      amazing potato and horseradish salad with fine herbs
         and bresaola 30, **31**
v   April's rosemary straw potatoes with lemon salt
         306, **307**
      baked potatoes stuffed with bacon, anchovies and
         sage 304, **305**
v   basic lightest potato gnocchi 112, **113**
      the best stew with potato and arugula pasta cushions
         104, 105
      gnocchi with braised oxtail 117, **117**
v   gnocchi with gorgonzola dolce 114, **115**
v   gnocchi with mushrooms and sage 114, **115**
v   gnocchi with arugula and butter sauce
         116, **116**
      grilled or roasted monkfish with black olive sauce and
         lemon mash **224**, 225
      grilled spatchcocked chicken with new potatoes, roast
         asparagus and herby yogurt 190, **191**
      matchsticks 431
      pan-fried sirloin steak with simple Chianti butter sauce
         and olive oil mash 158, **159**
v   potato rösti 302, **303**
v   ravioli of pecorino, potato and mint 102, **103**
      roast rack of lamb with potato and cauliflower
         dauphinois 164, **165**
      roasted chicken breast with lemony Bombay potatoes
         186, 187
v   rosemary-roasted cubed 298, **299**
v   Scotch stovies **300**, 301
   potted crab, old-fashioned 270, **271**
   poussins: pot-roasted poussins *agro dolce* **188**, 189
   proper blokes' sausage fusilli 72, **73**
   proper custard 402, **403**
v proper tomato salad **32**, 33
   purple sprouting broccoli: pan-roasted salmon with
      purple sprouting broccoli and anchovy-rosemary
      sauce 212, **213**

r

   rabbit 192–3
      pappardelle with wild rabbit, olives and marjoram 96, **97**
      tender-as-you-like rabbit stew with the best
         dumplings ever **196**, 197

v   a rather pleasing carrot cake with lime mascarpone
icing **386**, 387

ravioli

    the best stew with potato and arugula pasta cushions
104, 105

v   oozy egg ravioli 106, **107**

v   of pecorino, potato and mint 102, **103**

    shaping 90

    shaping cushion ravioli 88

raviolini

v   of celeriac and thyme **110**, 111

    shaping 90

real quick mussels spaghetti in a white wine and basil
oil broth 62, **63**

red cabbage braised with apple, bacon and balsamic
vinegar 358, **359**

red mullet 231

    grilled and roasted red mullet with pancetta and
thyme **236**, 237

    pan-fried red mullet with crispy breadcrumbs and a
herby tomato salad **210**, 211

v   return of the egg salad **34**, 35

v   rhubarb and custard 404, **405**

rice: steamed Thai-style sea bass and rice **228**, 229

v   ricotta

    lovely easy caramelle with ricotta, basil and
black olives 100, **101**

v   tomato, basil and ricotta risotto 126, **127**

risotto 119

v   apple and walnut risotto with gorgonzola 136, **137**

v   asparagus, mint and lemon risotto 124, **125**

v   basic recipe 120, **121**

    leftover stew risotto 134, **135**

    mushroom risotto **130**, 131

    spicy pangrattato risotto **122**, 123

v   spinach and goat's cheese risotto **128**, 129

v   squash, sage and amaretti risotto 132, **133**

v   tomato, basil and ricotta risotto 126, **127**

roast fore rib of beef with beetroot and horseradish
154, **155**

roast leg of lamb with eggplant and onions **168**, 169

roast rack of lamb with potato and cauliflower
dauphinois 164, **165**

roast salmon with fennel, parsley and tomato 232,
233

v   roasted baby leeks with thyme 330, **331**

v   roasted cauliflower with cumin, coriander and
almonds 342, **343**

roasted chicken breast

    with cherry tomatoes and asparagus **186**, 187

    with creamy butternut squash and chilli **186**, 187

    with lemony Bombay potatoes **186**, 187

    wrapped in pancetta with leeks and thyme **186**, 187

roasted white fish wrapped in smoked bacon with
lemon mayonnaise and asparagus 222, **223**

rosemary 432

v   April's rosemary straw potatoes with lemon salt
306, **307**

    pan-roasted salmon with purple sprouting broccoli
and anchovy-rosemary sauce 212, **213**

v   rosemary-roasted cubed potatoes 298, **299**

    ultimate rib of beef with rosemary and garlic roast
potatoes 152, **153**

v   rösti: potato rösti 302, **303**

s

safe cooking 424–5

saffron 435

    fabulous fish stew 260, **261**

sage 432

    baked potatoes stuffed with bacon, anchovies
and sage 304, **305**

v   gnocchi with mushrooms and sage 114, **115**

    old-school pork chops with apples and sage **178**, 179

v   squash, sage and amaretti risotto 132, **133**

salads 18–19

    all day breakfast salad 52, **53**

    amazing potato and horseradish salad with fine herbs
and bresaola 30, **31**

v   crunchy raw beetroot salad with feta and pear
36, **37**

    dressings 22–6, **27**

    Fifteen Christmas salad 44, **45**

v   Greek salad 40, **41**

    herbs 20, 21

    leaves 20–21

    Middle Eastern duck salad 54, **55**

v   my favorite coleslaw 38, **39**

    pan-fried red mullet with crispy breadcrumbs and
a herby tomato salad **210**, 211

    pan-roasted bream with a quick crispy
fennel salad **216**, 217

v   proper tomato salad **32**, 33

v   return of the egg salad **34**, 35

v   simple crunchy side salad 28, **28**

v   simple green side salad 29, **29**

v   unbelievable root vegetable salad **42**, 43

    vegetables 21

    warm 46

v   warm grilled peach and frisée salad with goat's
cheese dressing **50**, 51

    warm salad of crispy smoked bacon and Jerusalem
artichokes **48**, 49

salmon 231

    pan-roasted salmon with purple sprouting broccoli
and anchovy-rosemary sauce 212, **213**

    poached salmon steak 220, **221**

    roast salmon with fennel, parsley and tomato
232, **233**

salsa verde: pan-fried lemon sole fillets with salsa verde 218, **219**

salt: whole fish baked in a salt crust 238, **239**

sausages: proper blokes' sausage fusilli 72, **73**

Savoy cabbage with Worcestershire sauce 356, **357**

scallops 244

    black angel tagliarini **94**, 95

    pan-fried scallops with lentils, crispy pancetta and lemon crème fraîche 250, **251**

    shell-roasted scallops with ginger, soy and cilantro **246**, 249

    shell-roasted scallops the old-school French way **246**, 248

    shell-roasted scallops with sweet tomato and basil sauce **246**, 249

schnitzel with watercress and spiced apple sauce 182, **183**

v Scotch stovies **300**, 301

sea bass 231

    steamed Thai-style sea bass and rice **228**, 229

shell-roasted scallops

    with ginger, soy and cilantro **246**, 249

    the old-school French way **246**, 248

    with sweet tomato and basil sauce **246**, 249

shin stew: melt-in-your-mouth shin stew **150**, 151

shortbread

v   the best shortbread in the world 412, **413**

v   ultimate gingerbread 414, **415**

shrimp 258

    crispy fragrant jumbo shrimp 262, **263**

    fabulous fish stew 260, **261**

    shrimp cocktail 264, **265**

v Sicilian dressing 24

v simple crunchy side salad 28, **28**

v simple green side salad 29, **29**

v simple sautéed zucchini with chilli and lemon 364, **365**

slow-cooked leek soldiers with bacon 328, **329**

slow-roasted pork belly with the sweetest braised fennel 176, **177**

smoked paprika 435

sole see lemon sole

Southern Indian crab curry 274, **275**

soy sauce

    shell-roasted scallops with ginger, soy and cilantro **246**, 249

v   steamed broccoli with soy and ginger 336, **337**

spaghetti: real quick mussels spaghetti in a white wine and basil oil broth 62, **63**

v spiced vinegar dressing 24

spices 434–5

v   doughnuts with Old English spiced sugar **418**, 419

v   Indian-style broccoli with spiced yogurt 338, **339**

    perfectly cooked crispy duck with spiced plum chutney 198, **199**

schnitzel with watercress and spiced apple sauce 182, **183**

spicy pangrattato risotto **122**, 123

v spinach and goat's cheese risotto **128**, 129

sponges 374–5

v   1980s-style Black Forest Swiss roll **380**, 381

v   classic Victoria sponge with all the trimmings 376, **377**

v   tea-party cupcakes 378, **379**

v spring onions: braised peas with spring onions and lettuce 318, **319**

v spun sugar 398, **399**

squash 346

    see also butternut squash

squid 284

    with black pudding stuffing and sticky tomato sauce **290**, 291

    how to prepare 286

    my favorite crunchy squid with lime and chilli mayonnaise 288, **289**

    super squid linguine **70**, 71

stained-glass lasagne

v   with roasted squash **98**, 99

    shaping 90

star anise 435

steamed broccoli

v   with beurre blanc **340**, 341

v   with soy and ginger 336, **337**

steamed Thai-style sea bass and rice **228**, 229

stew

    the best stew with potato and arugula pasta cushions **104**, 105

    fabulous fish stew 260, **261**

    leftover stew risotto 134, **135**

    melt-in-your-mouth shin stew **150**, 151

sticky fingers lobster 282, **283**

v sticky saucepan carrots 310, **311**

sugar

v   spiced **418**, 419

v   spun 398, **399**

v summertime tagliarini 68, **69**

super squid linguine **70**, 71

v superb sweet and sour squash 352, **353**

v Swiss roll: 1980s-style Black Forest Swiss roll **380**, 381

t

tagliarini

    black angel tagliarini **94**, 95

    shaping 88

v   summertime tagliarini 68, **69**

tagliatelle

    shaping 88

tarragon 433

v tarte tatin: pear tarte tatin 422, **423**

v tea-party cupcakes 378, **379**
tender-as-you-like rabbit stew with the best
    dumplings ever **196**, 197
thyme 432
    braised white cabbage with bacon and thyme
        360, 361
    grilled and roasted red mullet with pancetta and
        thyme **236**, 237
v raviolini of celeriac and thyme **110**, 111
v roasted baby leeks with thyme 330, **331**
    roasted chicken breast wrapped in pancetta with
        leeks and thyme **186**, 187
    tortellini of chicken and gorgonzola in a fragrant
        thyme broth 108, **109**
tomato(es)
    baked John Dory in the bag with tomatoes and
        balsamic vinegar **240**, 241
v Greek salad 40, **41**
    pan-fried red mullet with crispy breadcrumbs and a
        herby tomato salad **210**, 211
v proper tomato salad **32**, 33
    roast salmon with fennel, parsley and tomato 232, **233**
    roasted chicken breast with cherry tomatoes and
        asparagus **186**, 187
    shell-roasted scallops with sweet tomato and
        basil sauce **246**, 249
    squid with black pudding stuffing and sticky
        tomato sauce **290**, 291
v tomato, basil and ricotta risotto 126, **127**
    whole baked cauliflower with tomato and olive sauce
        344, 345
tortellini
    of chicken and gorgonzola in a fragrant thyme broth
        108, **109**
    shaping 90
trout 231
    Granddad Ken's crispy grilled trout with parsley
        and lemon 242, **243**
tuna
    chargrilled tuna with oregano oil and
        beautifully dressed peas and fava beans
        214, **215**
    Jools' favorite Saturday afternoon pasta
        64, **65**
turkey 193
    the best roast turkey – Christmas or any time
        194, **195**

u

v the ultimate fruit meringue with vanilla cream,
    hazelnuts and caramel 394, **395**
v ultimate gingerbread 414, **415**
ultimate rib of beef with rosemary and garlic
    roast potatoes 152, **153**
v unbelievable root vegetable salad **42**, 43

v

v vanilla 435
v bloomin' easy vanilla cheesecake **410**, 411
v the ultimate fruit meringue with vanilla cream,
    hazelnuts and caramel 394, **395**
veal: the best stew with potato and arugula pasta
    cushions **104**, 105
vegetables 294–5
    freezing 428
    in salads 21
v unbelievable root vegetable salad **42**, 43
v Victoria sponge: classic Victoria sponge with all
    the trimmings 376, **377**
vinegar
    in salad dressings 22–3
v spiced vinegar dressing 24
    see also balsamic vinegar

w

v walnuts: apple and walnut risotto with gorgonzola
    136, **137**
warm salads 46
    all day breakfast salad 52, **53**
    crispy smoked bacon and Jerusalem artichokes **48**, 49
v warm grilled peach and frisée salad with goat's
        cheese dressing **50**, 51
watercress: schnitzel with watercress and spiced
    apple sauce 182, **183**
white cabbage: braised white cabbage with bacon
    and thyme **360**, 361
whole baked cauliflower with tomato and
    olive sauce **344**, 345
whole fish baked in a salt crust 238, **239**
wine 12
Worcestershire sauce: Savoy cabbage with
    Worcestershire sauce 356, **357**

y

yogurt
    grilled spatchcocked chicken with new potatoes,
        roast asparagus and herby yogurt
        190, **191**
v Indian-style broccoli with spiced yogurt
        338, **339**

z

zucchini 362
v baked and dressed zucchini **366**, 367
v fritters 368, **369**
    matchsticks 430
v simple sautéed zucchini with chilli and lemon
        364, **365**